Natural Law and Political Ideology in the Philosophy of Hegel

TONY BURNS
Department of Economics and Public Administration
Politics Section
Nottingham Trent University

Avebury

Aldershot · Brookfield USA · Hong Kong · Singapore · Sydney

Published by
Avebury
Ashgate Publishing Ltd
Gower House
Croft Road
Aldershot
Hants GU11 3HR
England

Ashgate Publishing Company
Old Post Road
Brookfield
Vermont 05036
USA

K
457
.H442
B87
1996

British Library Cataloguing in Publication Data

Burns, Tony
    Natural Law and Political Ideology
    in the Philosophy of Hegel
    I. Title
    193

Library of Congress Catalog Card Number: 95-83286

ISBN 1 85972 040 4

Reprinted 1997

Printed and bound in Great Britain by
Antony Rowe Ltd, Chippenham, Wiltshire

Contents

Acknowledgements   **vii**

Preface   **viii**

Introduction   **1**

Hegel and natural law theory   3

The ideological location of Hegel's political thought   5

1   Natural law theory   **12**

The question of the priority of justice or law   12

Cicero and the stoic conception of natural law   15

The stoic conception of natural law and modern commentators   21

Legal positivism   24

Criticisms of the conventional view of natural law theory   28

Voluntarism and natural law   31

Formal conceptions of natural law   34

2   Hegel and natural law theory   **42**

The structure of the *Philosophy of Right*   42

Hegel's interpreters and natural law theory   45

Hegel's essay *On the Scientific Ways of Treating Natural Law* 46

The essay on natural law and the *Philosophy of Right* 56

Hegel's natural law theory 59

Natural law and Hegelian metaphysics 66

3 Liberalism and conservatism **75**

Introduction 75

Pre-modern political thought 75

Classical liberalism 86

Conservatism 100

Conclusion 116

4 Hegel and political ideology **117**

Hegel and conservatism 117

The intellectual antecedents of Hegel's political thought 119

Hegel and human nature 123

Hegel's theory of society 127

The public and the private spheres 130

Hegel and economics 134

Hegel's approach to politics 137

Hegel on law and legislation 150

Hegel's views on history 152

Conclusion 158

Conclusion **163**

Bibliography **169**

Index **192**

Acknowledgements

I would like to thank friends and colleagues at the Nottingham Trent University who have assisted me in finally bringing to fruition a project on which I have been engaged for a number of years, especially David and Sue Baker, Christine Bellamy and Larry Wilde (who was kind enough to read and comment on the script at very short notice). Much of the original research for this book was done whilst I was a postgraduate student in the Department of Politics at the University of Sheffield over a decade ago now. I would, therefore, also like to thank ex-colleagues there for their help and encouragement, especially Anthony Arblaster. Readers familiar with the writings of the late Howard Warrender, who was Professor of Politics at the University of Sheffield when I first arrived there, will recognise at least the traces of his influence. My children, James and Kate, have not seen as much of me as I would have liked in the last few months, and I would like to thank them for being so patient with me. I would also like to thank Helen Baggaley for the same reason. Without her encouragement the book would not have been written. It goes without saying, but nevertheless certainly needs to be said, that I owe most of all to my parents. I dedicate the book to the memory of my father.

Preface

The precepts of the Decalogue belong to the natural law. Accordingly the precepts of the decalogue are immutable in so far as they embody justice in its essence; but as applied to particular acts - as, for example, whether they constitute homicide, theft, or adultery, or not, they admit of change. Such change may be effected by divine authority alone, or else by human authority as to what has been entrusted to human jurisdiction. In these matters men act in the place of God.

Aquinas

Whence it follows that no civil law whatsoever can possibly be against the law of nature forbid theft, adultery, etc.; yet if the civil law command us to invade anything, that invasion is not theft, adultery etc.

Hobbes

Natural law is distinct from positive law; but to pervert their difference into an opposition and a contradiction would be a gross misunderstanding.

Hegel

No natural laws can be done away with. What can change, in historically different circumstances, is only the *form* in which these laws operate.

Marx

Tis writ, 'In the beginning was the Word'.
I pause to wonder what is here inferred.
The Word I cannot set supremely high:
A new translation I will try.
I read, if by the spirit I am taught,
This sense: 'In the beginning was the Thought'.
This opening I need to weigh again,
Or sense may suffer from a hasty pen.
Does Thought create, and work, and rule the hour?
Twere best: 'In the beginning was the Power'.
Yet, while the pen is urged with willing fingers,
A sense of doubt and hesitancy lingers.
The spirit comes to guide me in my need,
I write, 'In the beginning was the Deed'.

Goethe

For my mother,
and in memory of my father

Introduction

In what follows we shall be concentrating our attention, directly or indirectly, on three basic themes, and on the relationship which exists between them. The first of these is the political thought of Hegel. The second is natural law theory and the approach to political speculation which is adopted by natural law theorists. The third is the framework of ideas that are associated with the ideologies of liberalism and conservatism, especially conservatism.

The relationship, or rather network of relationships, which exists between these three themes is evidently triangular, and hence relatively complex. To deal fully with the issues which are raised by a consideration of all of them taken together we would have to perform three separate tasks. We would have to examine the relationship which exists between the political thought of Hegel and natural law theory. We would have to consider the relationship which exists between Hegel's political thought and the ideologies of liberalism and conservatism. And, finally, we would have to examine the relationship which exists between natural law theory and these two political ideologies.

It is not, however, our intention to deal directly and fully with all of the issues which are generated by the combination of our three basic themes. In particular, it is not our intention to consider, in any detail, the last of them. There are three reasons for this omission. The first is that our principal focus of interest is the political thought of Hegel and the light which might be shed upon it by a consideration of the second and third of our three themes. Up to a point, therefore, our interest in these other themes is subordinate to this, our primary concern. We are more interested in the relationship which each of these other themes has to Hegel's political thought than we are in the relationship which they have to each other.

The second reason why we shall not be dealing at length with the relationship which exists between natural law theory and the ideologies of classical liberalism and traditional conservatism is that this is actually unnecessary. For this is already a well trodden path. Certainly, the existence of a link between the concept of natural law and the ideology of classical liberalism is well established and has

1

been much discussed. Much the same, however, might also now be said of the link between the notion of natural law and traditional conservatism.

Until recently, it had long been thought that the idea of natural law has no part at all to play in the ideology of traditional conservatism. The notion of natural law, and the correlative notion of natural rights, were thought to be component elements of the ideology of classical liberalism only. They were essentially liberal and not conservative concepts. For one of the basic principles of traditional conservatism, it was assumed, is the rejection of the doctrine of natural rights, and hence also of the notion of natural law.

It could, however, quite plausibly be maintained that this earlier view is actually quite unjustified. For example, the belief that the notion of natural law is of some importance for the political thought of Edmund Burke has received much discussion in recent years and is now quite widely accepted (Canavan, 1960; Freeman, 1980; Stanlis, 1965; Wilkins, 1967). The existence of a link between the notion of natural law and the ideology of conservatism is something which is already well established. This is, therefore, something which we propose to take for granted.

The third reason for this omission is that the final task referred to above will actually be carried out, if only indirectly, in the course of our discussion of the relationship which exists between Hegel's political thought and natural law theory, on the one hand, and the ideologies of liberalism and conservatism on the other. It is one of our contentions that to clarify the relationship which each of these themes has to Hegel's ideas is, to a certain degree anyway, to clarify the relationship which they have to each other.

In what follows, therefore, we shall attempt to carry out only the first two of the three tasks mentioned above. In Part One, we shall focus on the relationship which exists between Hegel's political thought and natural law theory. In Part Two, we shall concentrate on the relationship which exists between Hegel's political thought and the ideologies of liberalism and conservatism. In both cases we shall seek to draw out the reciprocal nature of the relationship involved. The discussion in Part One is based on the belief that a familiarity with natural law theory will help us to better understand the character of Hegel's political thought, just as a proper appreciation of Hegel's political thought will help us to achieve a greater awareness of the character of natural law theory. Similarly, it is assumed throughout Part Two that a grasp of the ideas which are associated with the ideologies of classical liberalism and traditional conservatism will greatly assist us in our efforts to interpret Hegel's political thought, just as a familiarity with Hegel's ideas will help shed new light on the ideas which are associated with these two ideologies.

Hegel and natural law theory

It is quite common for a distinction to be made between those systems of political thought which are natural law theories and those systems of political thought which, in contrast, are examples of the doctrine known as legal positivism. This distinction is, for example, made by A. P. d'Entreves in his well known and influential study of natural law (d'Entreves, 1970, pp.173-84) According to d'Entreves, all systems of political thought can be placed, rather neatly, into one or the other of these two categories.

It follows from this, of course, that it ought to be possible for a history of political thought to be written from the standpoint of such a classification. Such a history would involve the examination of the views of the major figures in the history of political thought in order to establish whether the theorists in question should be classified as natural law theorists, on the one hand, or as legal positivists on the other.

As a matter of fact, though, a history of this sort would be extremely difficult to write. This is so because there are a number of political theorists whose ideas simply cannot be so neatly placed into just one or the other of these two categories as they are conventionally understood. In the case of these particular theorists, the generally accepted distinction between natural law theory and legal positivism is not a very helpful guide to the interpretation and understanding of their respective systems of political thought. On the contrary, it is rather an obstacle which lies in the way of such an understanding. This is especially true in the case of Hegel.

A review of the relevant literature indicates quite clearly that commentators just do not seem able to agree at all on the question of Hegel's attitude towards natural law and natural law theory. Some commentators, for example, are of the opinion that Hegel is a legal positivist and that, therefore, he rejects the notion of natural law altogether. This is, indeed, probably the most common assessment of Hegel and his ideas. Certainly it has been the predominant view in the twentieth century, especially in the decades immediately following the Second World War. Perhaps the most famous, or even notorious, exponent of this particular interpretation is Karl Popper, who takes the view that Hegel's political thought constitutes a form of 'ethical and juridical positivism' (Popper, 1969, p.41).

Popper's work has, of course, been subjected to a great deal of criticism. His interpretation of Plato has been questioned by Levinson and Wild (Levinson, 1953; Wild, 1953). His interpretation of Marx has been questioned by Cornforth (Cornforth, 1968). And finally, his interpretation of Hegel himself has been criticised by Kaufmann (Kaufmann, 1970b). However, Popper is by no means alone in his conviction that Hegel should be classified as a legal positivist. Other commentators, whose pretensions to scholarship in the fields of jurisprudence and political theory are, perhaps, possess a much stronger foundation have nevertheless arrived at precisely the same conclusion. (Acton, 1975, pp.15-16; Carritt, 1935, pp. 107-14; Haines, 1965, pp.69-70; Lloyd, 1972, p.68; Sabine,

1973, pp. 589, 592, 603-4, 608). Thus, for example, d'Entreves has argued that 'it is impossible to reconcile the notion of natural law with' Hegel's 'doctrine of the ethical state' and that 'there can be no doubt that Hegel's conception of history marks the end of natural law thinking altogether' (d'Entreves, 1970, pp.72, 74). And a similar position is adopted by Bob Fine, according to whom Hegel welcomed 'the attack on natural law theory initiated by Hobbes'. In Fine's opinion, Hegel takes the view that all law 'is positive' and thus his thinking prefigures 'later developments in legal positivism' (Fine, 1984, pp.56-60). It does not seem unfair to say that, at least for a time, this particular interpretation of Hegel had the status of a well established orthodoxy.

The popularity and influence of this interpretation of Hegel is, no doubt, not so great as it once was. It would, however, be going too far to suggest, as Allen Wood has recently done, that there is now virtually a consensus amongst 'knowledgeable scholars' that this earlier assessment is 'simply wrong' and has no evidence at all to support it (Wood, 1991, p.ix). On the other hand though, there are undeniably a number of commentators who now completely reject this earlier interpretation of Hegel's political thought. Like Marx, having found that Hegel is currently standing on his head, these commentators are determined to place him firmly on his feet once more. They argue that far from being a legal positivist Hegel is indeed the very opposite. He is in fact a natural law theorist in the conventional sense. The originator of this radical reinterpretation of Hegel's political thought appears to be Z. A. Pelczynski, who arrived at it, at least in the first instance, on the basis of an analysis, not of Hegel's major work of political theory, the *Philosophy of Right*, but of Hegel's more occasional and minor political writings (Pelczynski, 1969; pp.28-31, 35, 37, 40, 45, 49-52, 55, 115, 134). It is, however, an interpretation which has been taken up by other commentators, who claim to find support for it in the *Philosophy of Right* itself. Thus, for example, Dante Germino claims that there Hegel clearly and explicitly 'distinguishes his own position from the vulgar positivism' that 'he is so often accused of representing' (Germino, 1969, p.888). More significantly, perhaps, a similar position has also been taken by Wood, both in a recent work on Hegel's ethical theory and in his editorial introduction to the latest English edition of the *Philosophy of Right* (Wood, 1990, p.105; Wood, 1991, pp.xvi-xvi).

To say that the existence of two such divergent, indeed mutually contradictory, interpretations of Hegel's political thought is something of a paradox would be to put the point somewhat mildly. It would be more accurate to describe it as astonishing. This, of course, immediately raises the question of how the existence of this paradox is to be explained. It also raises the question of how the disagreement associated with it might be resolved. On the issue of explanation, there would seem to be two possibilities. The first (which is not the explanation favoured here) is to suggest that Hegel's political thought is not internally consistent. Hegel contradicts himself, not only between texts but also, perhaps more significantly, within individual texts, especially within the *Philosophy of*

4

Right. Sometimes he says things which support the view that he is a natural law theorist. At other times he says things which support the view that he is a legal positivist. The second possibility is that Hegel does not contradict himself. His ideas constitute a unified body of thought , both between texts and especially within the *Philosophy of Right* itself. The alleged contradiction, therefore, is more apparent than real. It exists, not in Hegel and his ideas, but in the minds of Hegel's interpreters. According to this second explanation the conflict of interpretations referred to above has occurred, not because of anything which Hegel himself says, but because of the inadequacies of the classificatory system which is adopted by his interpreters. Above all it has arisen as a consequence of the erroneous assumptions which commentators on Hegel's political thought have made about natural law and natural law theory.

This suggests, of course, that there is some third interpretation of Hegel which succeeds in reconciling the apparently contradictory statements which Hegel makes in the different parts of the *Philosophy of Right*. There is a third interpretation which succeeds in laying bare the unifying thread which runs throughout the argument of this work, and which therefore offers a better understanding of Hegel's political thought as a whole. It is such a third interpretation which shall be outlined and defended here. According to this third interpretation, Hegel is not a legal positivist. Neither, however, is he a natural law theorist in the sense in which that term is usually understood. Hegel certainly is, in some sense of the term, a natural law theorist. However, the natural law theory which he develops in the *Philosophy of Right* is, by contemporary standards, somewhat unconventional. For, like Burke, Hegel subscribes to what might best be termed a conservative conception of natural law, the ultimate origins of which are to be found in the writings of Aristotle.

We shall discuss these conflicting interpretations of Hegel, the reasons for their occurrence, and the issue of how the apparent contradiction in Hegel's thinking might be resolved, much more fully in Chapter Two. However, the starting point for such a discussion, and indeed for any adequate treatment of the question of Hegel's attitude towards natural law and natural law theory, must necessarily be a preliminary discussion of what it is that commentators like d'Entreves actually mean when they talk about natural law, natural law theory and legal positivism, and thus what they mean when they refer to someone as being either a legal positivist, on the one hand, or a natural law theorist on the other. It is to these issues that we shall devote Chapter One.

The ideological location of Hegel's political thought

How should Hegel's political thought be classified from the standpoint of the various political ideologies? An examination of the literature indicates that this particular question, also, has been answered in a variety of different ways. One such answer, which is closely associated with the view that Hegel is a legal positivist, is that Hegel's political thought represents a commitment to what, in the twentieth century, has come to be called 'totalitarianism'. It is a forerunner of, and has close intellectual affinities with, the ideology of fascism, and is thus completely hostile, in all important respects, to the ideals and values which are traditionally associated with the ideology of classical liberalism.

This particular interpretation, like the view that Hegel is a positivist, had a certain popularity in the decades immediately following the Second World War. It too is closely associated with the work of Karl Popper. According to Popper, the system presented by Hegel in *The Philosophy of Right*, simply because it represents a form of legal positivism, 'is the theory of modern totalitarianism' (Popper, 1969, p.66). Moreover, once again Popper is not alone in adopting this attitude towards Hegel and his ideas. His views are shared by a number of other commentators. Thus, for example, R. S. Peters has maintained that Hegel's philosophy helped to put 'the stamp of philosophical respectability' on doctrines which were 'necessary for the emergence of a totalitarian state' (Peters, 1990, p.133). Dennis Lloyd has maintained that 'it is not difficult to see' how Hegel's ideas 'could lead naturally to the totalitarianism' which is 'all too familiar in the present century' (Lloyd, 1959, pp.279-80). And Walter Friedmann has claimed that Hegel's philosophy 'has directly inspired modern Fascist ideas on the corporative and totalitarian state' (Friedmann, 1967, pp.167, 170).

Not surprisingly, this interpretation of Hegel has not gone unchallenged. Indeed, those commentators like Z. A. Pelczynski, who have come to reject the view that Hegel is a legal positivist, have also gone on to reject the view that his ideas constitute a form of nascent fascism or totalitarianism. According to this more recent interpretation, Hegel's political thought, precisely because it is a natural law theory and not a form of legal positivism, and because of the historical links which natural law theory has with the ideology of liberalism, is best located, ideologically speaking, against the background of the classical liberal tradition. From this point of view, far from being an enemy of what Popper has called an 'open society', Hegel is in fact the very opposite. He is one of its stoutest defenders.

Thus, for example, Pelczynski maintains that Hegel 'belonged to a constitutionalist or Whig-liberal current of political thought' which is 'the source of modern liberalism' (Pelczynski, 1970, p.82; Pelczynski, 1969, p.55). This is a view which has also been adopted by a number of other commentators (Westphal, 1993, pp. 234-64; Heywood, 1992, p.28; Smith, 1991, pp.xi-xi, 6, 10, 236). Indeed, as A. Wood has pointed out, this particular interpretation now seems to represent a new orthodoxy amongst Hegel scholars (Wood, 1991, p.ix).

This new interpretation is, once again, quite remarkable in that it amounts to a complete reversal of what had been, for a time, a widely accepted assessment of Hegel's political thought. That this is so is something which has already been noted by Sidney Hook. As he puts it, according to this particular interpretation of his ideas, 'far from being a reactionary or totalitarian thinker' Hegel emerges 'washed clean as a constitutional liberal'. As Hook wryly goes on to observe, not 'since the baptism of Aristotle has anything as bold as this transfiguration been attempted' (Hook, 1970a, p. 65; also pp.57, 68; Hook, 1970b, pp. 87-96).

With respect to the issue of its ideological location, there is again, therefore, considerable disagreement as to how Hegel's political thought should be interpreted and classified. And here again there are different possible explanations for the occurrence of this disagreement. One such explanation, as in the case of the question of Hegel's attitude towards natural law, is that Hegel contradicts himself. At times he says things which support the view that he is a forerunner of totalitarianism, whereas at other times he says things which support the view that he is essentially an adherent to the ideals associated with the ideology of liberalism. Again this is not the explanation favoured here. A better explanation is that, just as in the case of the question of Hegel's attitude towards natural law, the source of these radically divergent interpretations of Hegel's political thought does not lie in anything which Hegel himself has to say. It lies rather, once again, in the heads of Hegel's interpreters.

Someone who made this claim might have one or the other of two things in mind. The first is the suggestion that this disagreement has occurred because of the existence of a political or ideological bias on the part of Hegel scholars. According to this explanation, all of Hegel's interpreters have their own ideological beliefs, values and presuppositions, which they bring with them when they engage in the analysis and interpretation of his ideas. It is, therefore, more or less inevitable that they will either approve or disapprove of these ideas. From this point of view, it is this desire to either praise or condemn Hegel which determines the point of view which is actually adopted by a particular commentator. Hence it is the existence of political motivations of this sort which provides the explanation for the different and contradictory ways in which Hegel's political thought has been classified and interpreted.

For example, those interpreters who consider themselves to be either liberal or socialist, and who consequently strongly disapprove of Hegel's ideas, are likely (as we have noted in the case of Karl Popper) to describe them as being either 'conservative', 'reactionary', 'totalitarian' or 'fascist'. On the other hand, those interpreters who are sympathetic to the ideals of liberalism, and who approve of Hegel's ideas, will wish to interpret him as a liberal like themselves. They will hail him as being, at least in some sense, a lost champion of the liberal cause and seek to defend him against the malicious accusations of critics such as Popper. Similarly, those interpreters who consider themselves to be conservative, reactionary, or even fascist will, if they approve of Hegel and his ideas, also seek to enlist him as a supporter of their own particular cause. This attitude is exemplified in the writings of New Right conservative Robert Nisbet. It is also to be found in the works associated with the Neo-Conservatism of Roger Scruton (Nisbet, 1973, pp. 24, 113; Nisbet, 1976, pp. 418-20; Nisbet, 1978, pp. 85, 88,

101; Nisbet, 1986, pp. 2, 35, 38, 49, 79, 111; Scruton, 1988, pp. 135-6, 153). Finally, those of Hegel's interpreters who consider themselves to be conservative, reactionary or fascist and who actually disapprove of Hegel's ideas are quite likely to condemn them for being a variant of the liberalism which they most ardently detest. This is the view which was adopted in Germany in the nineteenth century by the so-called 'revolutionary conservatives', such as Lagarde, Langbehn and Moeller van den Bruck (Stern, 1974, pp. xii, 56, 65, 281-2).

From this point of view, then, it is this wish to either praise or condemn Hegel's ideas, rather than any sincere desire to understand those ideas in their own terms, which influences the final choice of descriptive or classificatory label that is adopted by the commentator. Hence, or so it is alleged, the ideological beliefs of Hegel's interpreters will inevitably constitute a serious obstacle to any adequate understanding of Hegel's political thought as a whole. Some commentators have argued, for this reason, that to examine Hegel's political thought from the standpoint of its ideological location is not a particularly fruitful thing to do. Thus, for example, W. Kaufmann has suggested that any discussion of this question would in fact be 'rather pointless'. One of his reasons for taking this view is precisely because he associates this question with the attempt to classify Hegel and his ideas as being either 'good' or 'bad' (Kaufmann, 1970, p.8). Similarly, Fred Dallmayr also appears to take the view that such 'attempts at political labelling' must inevitably reduce Hegel's philosophy to 'partisan ideology' (Dallmayr, 1993, p.238). And Stephen Smith has suggested that any attempt to identify Hegel 'by appending some kind of 'ism' to his name' is bound to be more or less unsatisfactory. In Smith's opinion, such attempts 'are apt to tell us more about the intellectual or psychological needs of his critics than about Hegel's own views' (Smith, 1991, p.136).

According to all three of these commentators, anyone discussing Hegel's political thought from this point of view is more likely to be interested in evaluating Hegel and his ideas than they are in understanding them. Their concerns are probably more political than they are intellectual. The question of how Hegel's political thought is to be classified, ideologically is, from this point of view, not a question which the scholar may legitimately ask. This, however, is not our view. Whilst being fully aware of the ever present danger of political bias, it is assumed throughout the second part of this book that a consideration of Hegel's political thought from the standpoint of the different ideologies is nevertheless a fruitful intellectual activity. Such a discussion sheds considerable light, not only on our understanding of Hegel's political thought itself, but also on the ideas which are associated with the different political ideologies.

The second thing which someone might have in mind in claiming that the source of these radically conflicting interpretations of Hegel's political thought lies in the heads of Hegel's interpreters, is that the disagreement referred to above has specifically intellectual and not political or ideological causes. It has arisen because of a confusion relating to the use of language and the employment of the

8

relevant descriptive terms. To be more precise, it has occurred because of a lack of clarity on the part of many commentators with respect to the understanding of the circumstances in which it is appropriate to describe someone as being either a 'totalitarian' or a 'liberal'. In short, this disagreement has occurred because of the ambiguities of the classificatory schema which has been adopted by those who have commented on Hegel's political thought. This is something which, again, has already been noted by Kaufmann. In Kaufmann's view, the fact that 'none of the combatants' in the debate over the ideological classification of Hegel's thought 'offers any definitions' of these key descriptive terms is yet another reason for considering the attempt to locate Hegel's views ideologically to be a rather pointless exercise (Kaufmann, 1970, p. 8).

It might be thought that the solution to this problem is to provide the necessary definitions, or at least, failing that, some attempted clarification of the meaning of the descriptive terms in question. Kaufmann, however, rejects such an approach. In his opinion, or so it would seem, any such attempt would be a waste of time. For these terms are 'notoriously ambiguous' and 'have different meanings in different countries and at different times'. As he puts it, all such 'ism' words 'are an impediment to philosophic thought and historical understanding. Philosophy begins beyond 'isms'' (Kaufmann, 1970, pp. 8-9).

Once again, however, the view adopted here is somewhat different. It may be true that the meaning of the relevant descriptive terminology is vague and that the key descriptive concepts cannot be precisely defined. Nevertheless, although this is true, that does not imply that the relevant concepts are meaningless, or that their meaning cannot be clarified. Indeed, there have been a number of works published just recently whose authors have devoted themselves to precisely this task, although none of them have very much to say about Hegel and his ideas (Eatwell and Wright, 1993; Eccleshall et. al., 1994; Heywood, 1992; Vincent, 1993). Nor, therefore, should it be thought that any attempt to engage in the attempted clarification of the relevant conceptual vocabulary would simply be a waste of time. A discussion of these issues will certainly help us to understand better what is involved when we describe someone as a totalitarian, a classical liberal, or a conservative. More to the point, however, it will also help us to better understand the political thought of Hegel.

There are some commentators who do acknowledge the validity and importance of the question of the ideological location of Hegel's political thought. This particular group of commentators, however, cannot quite make up their minds as to how the question should be answered. For Hegel's thought seems to them to have affinities with both the ideology of liberalism and the ideology of conservatism. For these commentators, then, Hegel's ideas appear on the surface to be somewhat incoherent and contradictory (Beiser, 1993, pp. 293-7; Cassirer, 1967, p. 252; Hardimon, 1994, pp. 4, 27; Mehta, 1968, pp. 107-33; O'Sullivan, 1976, pp. 26, 58; de Ruggiero, 1981, pp. 228-9, 240; Wood, 1990, pp. 257-8; Wood, 1991, pp. xi, xxvii-xxviii).

Once more this apparent contradiction presents us with two possibilities. The first of these is simply to argue that Hegel's ideas just *are* basically incoherent and contradictory. The second is to claim, to the contrary, that Hegel's political thought is actually the product of a deliberate attempt to synthesize in a coherent manner the ideas which are usually associated with the ideologies of liberalism and conservatism. From this latter point of view, Hegel's ideas could be said to incorporate the key elements of both liberalism and conservatism into a unified system which is itself quite unique and thus not susceptible of classification in conventional terms. This system of ideas is neither liberal nor conservative, but specifically and uniquely Hegelian (O'Sullivan, 1976, pp. 26, 58; de Ruggiero, 1981, pp. 228-9, 240; Beiser, 1983, pp. 293-7; Hardimon, 1994, pp. 4, 27).

The principal merit of this second approach is the fact that it recognises that Hegel's political thought, especially as we find it in the *Philosophy of Right*, constitutes a synthesis of two opposed theoretical positions. It is an attempt to develop a system of ideas which combines the strengths of both of these positions whilst at the same time suffering from the weaknesses of neither (Colletti, 1975, pp. 31-4; Smith, 1991, pp. 6, 243; Hardimon, 1994, p. 27). Another merit is that this approach recognises that one of the component elements in this Hegelian synthesis is modern political thought, as represented by the ideology of classical liberalism. Hegel does indeed incorporate into his system many of the ideas (suitably modified and interpreted) which are usually associated with the modern, specifically liberal, political thought of the seventeenth and eighteenth centuries. It is, of course, for precisely this reason that some modern commentators have succumbed to the temptation and have gone so far as to take the view that the best way to classify Hegel's political thought is to see it as being essentially nothing more than a form of liberalism. This particular interpretation of Hegel's thought, however, goes too far. It is erroneous precisely because it is partial and one sided.

The principal weakness of this second approach is its assessment of the theoretical position which stands opposed to the principles of classical liberalism within the Hegelian synthesis: the thesis to which modern political thought, as represented by the ideology of liberalism, constitutes an antithesis. It is claimed that this opposed theoretical position is the ideology of conservatism. Later on we shall argue that this claim is based upon an understanding of conservatism which is, in some respects at least, quite inadequate.

Some commentators have maintained that to discuss the ideological location of Hegel's political thought is a waste of time because Hegel's ideas are in fact quite unique. Any attempt to pin Hegel's ideas down in terms of the existing ideological vocabulary will, it is suggested, inevitably lead to an assessment of his thought which is partial and one sided. Thus, for example, Charles Taylor has claimed that the 'attempt to classify' Hegel's ideas 'by picking out liberal or conservative shibboleths' is something which is likely to lead to what are just 'laughable interpretations' of his political thought as a whole. In Taylor's view, these 'ordinary labels', when applied to Hegel's ideas, are likely to 'obscure much more than they clarify' (Taylor, 1989, pp. 374, 449). Against this, however, one might claim that once the task of clarification of the different ideological positions has been carried out, it becomes readily apparent that Hegel's ideas are not at all unique. Nor do they resist classification in conventional terms.

How, then, should Hegel's political thought be classified, from the ideological point of view? As in the case of the question of Hegel's attitude towards natural law, we shall argue that neither of the two approaches to this question which have predominated in the recent literature is satisfactory. They both offer an interpretation of Hegel which is partial and one sided. Thus we shall maintain that Hegel is most certainly not, in any sense, a defender of totalitarianism. On the other hand, however, it would be equally incorrect to locate his political thought against the background of the ideology of liberalism. To claim, as Pelczynski and others do, that Hegel is fundamentally a liberal thinker is to go too far in the opposite direction.

The position which we shall attempt to defend on this question is that, once again, there is a third interpretation which will help us to resolve the apparent contradiction in Hegel's thinking, and which enables us to capture the essential unity of Hegel's political thought as a whole. According to this third interpretation, the ideology with which Hegel's political thought has the greatest affinity is the ideology of conservatism. We shall argue, then that Hegel's ideas are typically conservative. Once the nature of conservatism has been properly understood it becomes readily apparent that to describe or classify Hegel's ideas in this way is to offer an interpretation of his political thought which does not in any way distort its essential character, and which is not at all partial or one sided. On the contrary, to classify Hegel's political thought as a form of conservatism is to capture quite accurately its complex and apparently contradictory nature.

We shall discuss this question of the ideological location of Hegel's views, and the further question of how the disagreement between Hegel's interpreters with respect to it might be resolved, in Chapter Four. However, a necessary preliminary to this, as in the case of the question of Hegel's attitude towards natural law theory, is some discussion of the relevant classificatory system and some attempt to clarify the meaning of the basic concepts which are associated with it. We shall, therefore, devote Chapter Three to a discussion of the ideas and beliefs which it is appropriate to associate with the ideologies of liberalism and conservatism.

11

1 Natural law theory

The question of the priority of justice or law

We may begin by providing what is merely an outline sketch of the ideas which are associated with natural law theory, on the one hand, and the doctrine of legal positivism on the other. We shall elaborate on this preliminary sketch in more detail later on.

The most appropriate starting point here is a discussion of what Lester Crocker has referred to as the question of the priority of justice or law (Crocker, 1962; Crocker, 1963, pp. 189-206). According to Crocker, the criterion which should be used in order to establish whether or not a particular author is a natural law theorist or a legal positivist is the answer which the author gives to this particular question.

Professor Crocker is a student of the moral and political thought of the French Enlightenment. The question of the priority of justice or law was, he informs us, much 'debated throughout the seventeenth and eighteenth centuries' (Crocker, 1962, p.34). In the words of an unknown eighteenth century philosophe, who examines the question in the article on justice which he contributed to the great *Encyclopedie* of Diderot and d'Alembert, and who provides the original inspiration for much of Crocker's own thinking on the subject, this is 'the famous question of whether there is any justice or injustice prior to law' (*Encyclopedie*, 1966, pp.86-7; Thielemann, 1963; Burns, 1986).

According to Crocker, what we are asking when we pose this question is which has logical priority, the idea of justice or the idea of law? Someone who believes that the idea of law has logical priority is someone who accepts the thesis that 'justice is, by definition, what the law orders us to do' (Crocker, 1962, p.34). It is an implication of this thesis that it is logically impossible for any law to be unjust. As against this, on the other hand, someone who believes in the logical priority of the idea of justice over that of law maintains that the notion of justice can be defined independently of that of law. For such a person justice is not simply a

12

matter what the law commands us to do, and for such a person it is, quite definitely, possible for a law to be unjust.

The manner in which Professor Crocker actually formulates this question of the priority of justice or law might, perhaps, be criticised. For example, he does not emphasise sufficiently that when he uses the term 'law' what he really means is 'positive law' or (to be even more precise) what some commentators would refer to as 'human positive law'. Nevertheless, despite this lack of precision, the meaning and significance of the question of the priority of justice or law as interpreted by Crocker are clear enough.

It is, then, at least according to Crocker, to this question of the priority of justice or law that natural law theory and the doctrine of legal positivism are supposed to provide an answer. Natural law theorists are of the opinion that the idea of justice has logical priority over that of law. Legal positivists, on the other hand, maintain that the idea of law has logical priority over that of justice.

In order to clarify Crocker's views, it is necessary for us to say something more about the concept of justice. The term 'justice' is used in a number of different senses (Ginsberg, 1963; Hart, 1961; Kelsen, 1957; Kelsen, 1961; Lloyd, 1972; Perelman, 1963; Ross, 1958). If, therefore, we are to properly understand exactly what is meant by the claim that the notion of justice is either posterior to that of law or, alternatively, prior to it, then we need to clarify which of these different senses Crocker has in mind. More specifically, we need to make a distinction between two particular senses in which the term might be used. We must distinguish between legal justice, on the one hand, and moral justice on the other.

All systems of positive law which constitute a framework of general rules, fairly and impartially applied, may be said to be just in the strictly legal sense of the term. From this point of view, what might be described as the substantive content of such a system of justice is something which is defined by positive law and positive legislation. It is, therefore, a truism to assert that justice in this sense is simply what positive law says that it is. This is so as a matter of definition. Hence the reasons for saying that a system of positive law was actually unjust, in this sense, would necessarily have to be procedural. For example, in a given case, it might be claimed that injustice had occurred because the laws associated with the system were actually administered unfairly, preferential treatment being given to someone who did not, from the point of view of positive law, actually deserve it.

To say that the idea of law has logical priority over that of justice, if we are employing the term 'justice' in this legal sense, is not particularly contentious. This is something on which natural law theorists and legal positivists, conventionally understood, are unlikely to disagree. However, this is not the sense of the term 'justice' which Crocker has in mind when he talks about the question of the priority of justice or law. This question, as he understands it, amounts to asking whether positive law, even though it is and must necessarily be just in the strictly legal sense, might nevertheless legitimately be said to be unjust in the moral sense of that term.

13

If, like Crocker, we interpret the question of the priority of justice or law in this second way, then a natural law theorist is someone who recognises the existence of certain principles of moral justice, usually referred to as the principles of natural justice or natural law, which are logically prior to, and which exist quite independently of, the enactments of any positive law. These principles of moral justice stand alongside the principles of legal justice which are necessarily to be found in all systems of positive law. Morally speaking, these principles constitute what may be termed a standard of justice which is actually higher than that of any positive law. The principles of natural law are, in this moral sense, the ultimate standard of justice. A legal positivist, on the other hand, is someone who refuses to recognise the existence of any such principles of justice or law. From the standpoint of legal positivism, as interpreted by Crocker, the positive law of the state is itself the ultimate standard, not simply of legal justice, but of moral justice also. It is the ultimate standard of right and wrong for all of its citizens, and the source of all of their obligations, both moral as well as legal.

From this point of view, there is for the legal positivist only one kind of law, positive law. As Heinrich Rommen has put it, 'law, according to positivism, is only positive law, that is, statute law and such customary law as is recognised by the state' (Rommen, 1979, p.247). Or alternatively, in the words of d'Entreves, 'positivism is the theory according to which there is no other law except positive law'. Hence it is a doctrine 'which is aimed polemically against natural law, against any law that is not factually existing and empirically verifiable' (d'Entreves, pp.174-75).

The account given so far provides us with a very clear summary outline of the view adopted by Crocker with respect to the character of natural law and natural law theory. According to him, natural law is essentially a critical standard for the evaluation of positive law. Thus a natural law theorist is, by definition, someone who believes in the existence of certain principles of justice or morality, the precepts of natural law, which might be employed by particular individuals to morally evaluate the positive law of the society in which they live.

From this standpoint, a system of political thought which did not incorporate this belief could not, strictly speaking, be said to be a natural law theory at all. This is a point which has also been made by Richard Wollheim. In response to the claim attributed to legal positivists that law has priority over justice, Wollheim points out that this is in effect to insist that 'no law can be unjust' and, he goes on to insist, 'it is obviously a necessary condition of any natural law doctrine that this view should be rejected' (Wollheim, 1967, p.450). D'Entreves, also, has remarked that no assessment of natural law theory would be complete without taking into account 'what may well be said to constitute its most constant feature all through the ages: the assertion of the possibility of testing the validity of all laws by referring them to an ultimate measure, to an ideal law'. Natural law is the 'outcome of man's quest for an absolute standard of justice' (d'Entreves, 1970, p.93).

14

This understanding of what natural law theory involves is not, of course by any means new, or specific to the 'modern' era. The *Encyclopedie* article on justice, for example, claims that this is the attitude which is adopted by the 'scholastic' natural law theorists of the medieval period as well as by 'the majority of ancient philosophers' (*Encyclopedie*, 1966, p.86). It is, in fact, as the article on justice also points out, an approach to natural law theory which can be traced back ultimately to the writings of the stoic philosopher Cicero (Gawlick, 1963; also Carlyle and Carlyle, 1903-36, 1; Sabine and Barney Smith; Watson, 1971). For this reason, and for the sake of convenience, we shall henceforth refer to this particular approach to natural law and natural law theory as the stoic conception of natural law.

Cicero and the stoic conception of natural law

We are now in a position to elaborate in more detail on the view of natural law and natural law theory presented in outline form in the preceding section. We may take as our starting point the following passage from Cicero's *De Republica*, which is of some considerable importance for the history of natural law theory. This passage is almost invariably referred to by commentators writing on the subject of natural law.· It has greatly influenced the modern perception of the ideas that are associated with natural law and natural law theory.

> True law is right reason in agreement with nature. It is of universal application, unchanging and everlasting...it is a sin to try to alter this law, nor is it allowable to attempt to repeal any part of it, and it is impossible to abolish it entirely. We cannot be freed from its obligations by senate or people, and we need not look outside of ourselves for an expounder or interpreter of it. And there will not be different laws at Rome and Athens, or different laws now and in the future, but one eternal and unchangeable law will be valid for all nations and all times (Cicero, 1928a, p.211).

Some commentators would argue that it is difficult to exaggerate the importance that this one passage has had in the history of natural law theory. In the words of Robert Derathe, this influence has been 'prodigious'. There is 'hardly a jurist or a philosopher of the school of natural law who has not referred to it' (Derathe, 1970, p.153). This view is also held by Wolfgang Von Leyden, who refers to Cicero's 'famous definition of natural law' which is 'persistently quoted by writers on natural law throughout the ages' (Von Leyden, 1958, p.35). Similarly, Frederick Pollock, has suggested that this one fragment of the *De Republica* 'probably had more influence than any one passage in the jurists' on later perceptions of natural law and natural law theory (Pollock, 1961, p.129). And David Ritchie has asserted that it is here, in Cicero's *De Republica*, that 'we find the first distinct formulation of the idea of the law of nature, in that very form in which it survives in modern thought' (Ritchie, 1903, p.36).

Thus, for example, this text is both quoted and discussed by nearly all of the major figures in the history of natural law theory both in pre-modern times and in the modern era. In the early seventeenth century the great Spanish jurist and late scholastic natural law theorist, Francisco Suarez, describes it as 'remarkable' (Suarez, 1944, p.22). And later in the seventeenth century, the two major figures of what Ernest Barker has described as 'the continental school of natural law', Hugo Grotius and Samuel Pufendorf, both echo this sentiment. Pufendorf takes pains to refer to it as 'an excellent passage from Cicero' (Barker, 1948; Barker, 1960, pp.xli-l; Grotius, 1925, p.39; Pufendorf, 1934, p.220).

Similarly, approaching closer to the present day, this passage is again cited frequently in the articles dealing with natural law and natural law theory in the great *Encyclopedie* of Diderot and d'Alembert in the eighteenth century. The editors of the *Encyclopedie* clearly considered the views which Cicero expresses in this one passage to be an essential component element in any account of the received wisdom of the day relating to natural law and natural law theory in the sphere of politics (*Encyclopedie*, 1966, 5, pp.131-34; 9, pp.86-87; Vol. 9, pp.665-6; 11, pp.46-7).

So what ideas are associated with the stoic conception of natural law, as represented by Cicero in this important passage? When examined more closely, this stoic conception of natural law may be said to possess seven characteristic features. The first of these is the belief that there are certain principles of natural law or justice which exist quite independently of the positive law of any particular state, such as Rome or Athens. These principles place all people under a moral obligation not to perform certain types of action. Thus, for Cicero, as for Crocker, d'Entreves and Wollheim, justice is not simply a matter of convention. It is not what the positive or civil law of a particular society happens to say that it is. The idea of justice is, indeed, prior to that of law.

The second feature is the belief that knowledge of the precepts of natural law, and hence of right and wrong, is derived by the employment of one's faculty of reason or, more accurately, 'right reason' *(recta ratio)*. From this point of view, whether an action is just or unjust is something that is to be discovered, not decided. The principles of justice are most definitely not created by any act of human volition or will.

The third characteristic feature of the stoic conception of natural law is the belief, which Cicero probably derives from Aristotle, that there are certain actions which are essentially, by their very nature and hence by definition wrong or unjust (Aristotle, 1925, II, 6, 1107a, 10-20). Cicero does not give any examples of such actions in the passage quoted. Indeed, examples of this sort are relatively rare in his works, presumably because he considered it to be self-evident what these actions are. However, in his *De Legibus* at least, he indicates that the acts of robbery, adultery, forgery and rape all fall into this category. As he himself puts it, when discussing the act of rape, 'even if there were no written law against rape' at Rome 'we cannot say on that account that Sextus Tarquinius did not break the eternal law by violating Lucretia'. For nevertheless reason did exist. 'urging men to right conduct and diverting them from wrongdoing', and this reason did not first become law when it was written down. For 'what is right and true is also eternal and does not begin or end with written statutes' (Cicero, 1928b, p.383).

The fourth feature of this stoic conception of natural law is the belief, again probably originating in the writings of Aristotle, that the precepts of natural law are in some sense 'unchangeable' *(immutabile)* (Aristotle, 1925, V, 7, 1134b-1135a). What Cicero means by this is that those actions which are intrinsically wrong must be so always and everywhere, no matter what the circumstances. If the act of rape is necessarily wrong, then it cannot be the case that it wrong for a Roman, but right for an Athenian. Thus, the principles of natural law are, morally speaking, 'valid for all nations and all times'.

It should, however, be noted that Cicero is not entirely consistent on this point. For elsewhere he suggests that there is at least one sense in which justice might be said to be mutable or subject to change. Thus, for example, in his *De Officiis* he acknowledges that the validity of natural law might not always be acknowledged. There may well be certain societies which legally permit the performance of actions which are intrinsically wrong, and which are therefore forbidden by positive law (Cicero, 1960, p.141). And in the *De Republica* he suggests that this is one reason why some people maintain, quite wrongly, that there are no precepts of justice which are universal, and hence no such thing as natural law (Cicero, 1928a, pp.193-201).

In the *De Republica* Cicero does not offer an explanation for this phenomenon, although, in typical stoic fashion, he tends to take the view that injustice, generally, only occurs when reason loses control over the passions. However, in the *De Officiis* he is somewhat more forthcoming. There he attributes it to the 'depravation of manners and the prevalence of evil custom' in certain societies. And in the *De Legibus* he associates it, again, with 'corruption caused by bad habits' (Cicero, 1928a, pp.79, 89-91; Cicero, 1960, pp.141-42; Cicero, 1928b, p.333).

This feature of the stoic conception of natural law is of some considerable importance for the later history of natural law theory. The idea that the precepts of natural law are sometimes not recognised by positive law because of some sort of depravity, but that nevertheless they remain at least morally valid, later becomes a standard response of natural law theorists to the arguments of those who claim that the relative character of moral beliefs is evidence that there is in fact no such thing as natural law. As R. F. Begin has put it, natural law theory 'has always proclaimed that its principles' are 'absolutely immutable'. Thus, they are 'valid for all men of all centuries and nations'. However, this 'does not mean that they will always be recognised' (Begin, 1959, p.88; See also Strauss, 1974, pp.9, 97-8; Maritain, 1958, pp.84-94).

The fifth characteristic feature of stoic natural law theory, as represented Cicero, is its view of the relationship which exists between natural law and positive law. According to this view, the sole function of positive law is to ratify and enforce the principles of natural law by providing them with some coercive sanction. Such sanctions are necessary because of the strength of the passions and the weakness of reason amongst the 'common people' (Cicero, 1960, p.343). A corollary of this view is the belief that positive law is and ought to be an accurate representation or copy of the principles of natural law, down to the smallest detail. If the function of positive law is simply to provide natural law with a coercive sanction then there ought to be no difference at all between the substantive content of positive law and that of natural law. The incorporation of the precepts of natural law into the positive law of a particular society does not in any way involve any process of change, adaptation, or modification of the precepts of natural law.

Thus, for example, in the *De Officiis* Cicero says that 'the laws of the city' are in general 'copied from nature'. And he also suggests that when a society fails to legally proscribe an action which is evidently morally wrong what this shows is that the positive law of this society is not as accurate a copy or representation of the law of nature as it might have been. It is only a 'faint representation' of it. For this reason, the system of positive law in question might be said to be imperfect (Cicero, 1960, p.142).

This idea, again, is of some considerable significance for the later history of natural law and natural law theory. As John Finnis has pointed out, we find it, for example, clearly formulated in the writings of Hooker in the sixteenth century and in those of Blackstone in the eighteenth century. (Finnis, 1980, pp. 28, 281; Hooker, 1836, pp.310-11; Blackstone, 1966, pp.42-3). According to Hans Kelsen, this stoic view that positive law 'merely reproduces' the precepts of natural law is a 'stereotype' for virtually all natural law theorists 'from the Church fathers down to Kant' (Kelsen, 1961, p.416).

It is a logical implication of this view that, just as the positive law of any particular society ought to exactly resemble the precepts of natural law, so also the systems of positive law of all societies ought to exactly resemble one another, down to the smallest detail. There really ought to be no difference at all between the legal systems of different societies, and in practice there would not be if these legal systems were all equally just. Condorcet, writing in the eighteenth century, reflects this stoic position very well when he says that, as truth, reason and justice are the same everywhere, he 'cannot see why all the provinces of a state, or even all states, should not have the same' laws. For a 'good law must be good for all men, just as a true proposition is true for all men' (Condorcet, cited in Waddicor, 1970, pp.126-28).

It has occasionally been suggested that one of the great differences between modern natural law theory and pre-modern natural law theory is that the former is rigid or inflexible whereas the latter is not. Classical and medieval conceptions of natural law, it has been said, do allow for the possibility of a legitimate change in the positive law of a particular society, and for the possibility of a legitimate variation between the systems of positive law of different societies. Thus, E. K. Lewis has suggested that 'the flexibility of medieval natural law theory' contrasts sharply with 'the rigidity of natural law in eighteenth century thought' (Lewis, 1954, p.11; Lewis, 1946, pp.144-63). And J. L. Montrose has claimed that it is 'only the eighteenth century rationalists who thought that detailed rules, valid for all times and all places, could be deduced with certitude from basic principles' (Montrose, 1961, p.214; also Selznick, 1961).

We shall discuss later what is involved in claiming that some natural law theories are flexible, whereas others are not. For the present, it will be sufficient to point out that although this distinction is, in a sense, a valid one, nevertheless the way in which it is presented here is actually quite inaccurate. For this is a distinction which should not be located chronologically, between pre-modern and modern natural law theory, as is suggested by Lewis and Montrose. It is, rather, a distinction between two quite different traditions of natural law theory, each one of which has an intellectual pedigree which can be traced back to classical antiquity.

More specifically, it is the stoic natural law tradition which is rigid and inflexible, whether it is represented in the writings of Cicero or in the writings of the stoic natural law theorists of the eighteenth century. This is not, however, as Lewis and Montrose acknowledge, the only natural law tradition. There are other natural law traditions which differ from the stoic tradition in this particular respect. The existence of these alternative traditions is frequently not recognised, largely because of the tendency of commentators to elevate stoic natural law theory to the status of a paradigm example of natural law theory in general. Such alternative traditions are, most certainly, to be found in pre-modern times. Nevertheless, they are not uniquely pre-modern. They are also to be found in the modern era, in the seventeenth, the eighteenth, and even the nineteenth century.

This is a point which has been hinted at by John Finnis, who takes issue with Kelsen's view that for natural law theorists the function of positive law is merely to 'reproduce' the principles of natural law whilst, at the same time, providing them with a coercive sanction. This view is, he maintains, a 'travesty' of the thinking associated with traditional natural law theory (Finnis, 1980, p.28). There is evidently some substance to this criticism. Kelsen is indeed wrong to suggest that all natural law theory adopts this view of the relationship which exists between natural law and positive law. Nevertheless, it would be equally wrong to suggest, as Finnis himself seems to do, that there is no natural law theory which does so. For, as we have seen, this view is in fact adopted by theorists writing from the standpoint of the stoic natural law tradition.

The sixth feature of the stoic conception of natural law is the belief that the principles of natural law do not require any authoritative or outside interpretation. They are readily intelligible to all people able and willing to employ their faculty of reason. The individual moral agent requires no outside assistance when deciding whether or not a particular action ought to be performed. Cicero is quite clear on this point. In the classic text from the *De Republica* quoted above he strongly emphasises that 'we need not look outside of ourselves for an expounder or interpreter' of the precepts of natural law.

It should be noted that Cicero does not completely deny the need for an interpretation of the principles of natural law in certain cases. If those principles are to be of any practical value as a guide to action for the individual moral agent, then it is necessary that they be applied to a variety of different situations. In practice, therefore, they will always need to be adapted to a specific situation, and to the particular set of circumstances which is presented by a given case. His claim is, rather, that the principles of natural law require no interpretation from a source external to the moral agent. Individuals, according to Cicero, are perfectly capable of applying and interpreting the principles of natural law for themselves in the light of their own faculty of reason.

Thus, for example, according to Cicero, individuals are capable of discerning for themselves that actions such as robbery and rape are wrong or unjust, and hence that they ought not to be performed. In addition, however, they are also capable, on their own, of adapting the moral injunction not to perform an act of robbery or rape, which is a general injunction, to the circumstances of any particular case with which they might be confronted. They are capable of establishing for themselves, in the situation in question, whether some action which they are contemplating performing is or is not an example of robbery or rape, and hence whether or not it is morally permissible to perform it.

The seventh and final characteristic feature of the stoic conception of natural law is its assumption that natural law does constitute a critical standard by means of which the justice of positive law might be assessed. From the standpoint of stoic natural law theory, there are two things which make it possible for natural law to carry out this function. The first is the fact that certain actions are intrinsically wrong or unjust. Evidently, if the positive law of a particular society were to command or permit the performance of such an action then this positive law could itself be said to be unjust. The second is the fact that the principles of natural law do not require any outside, authoritative interpretation. It seems evident that if individuals are assumed to be able to discern for themselves that the act of theft, for example, is morally wrong, but are nevertheless considered to be incapable of ascertaining for themselves whether some particular action which has been commanded or permitted by positive law is actually an example of the act of theft, then these individuals would be unable to appeal to the principle of natural law forbidding theft as a justification for claiming that the positive law in question is an unjust law.

This, then, is the stoic conception of natural law as represented by the writings of Cicero. It should now be evident that when Crocker talks about natural law theory, what he actually has in mind is the stoic conception of natural law and stoic natural law theory.

The stoic conception of natural law and modern commentators

There are two basic assumptions which are made by virtually all of the modern commentators whose views have been referred to so far. The first of these is that the ultimate source for our understanding of natural law and natural law theory is the stoic conception of natural law as it is to be found in the writings of Cicero. This is assumed to be a paradigm example of everything thing which a genuine natural law theory is and ought to be.

The tendency to identify the stoic conception of natural law with natural law theory as such is in fact almost universal amongst modern commentators. When the majority of them refer to natural law and to natural law theory it is actually the stoic conception of natural law which they have in mind. There is, therefore, a broad consensus amongst commentators today with respect to the character of natural law theory. The features which we have associated with the stoic conception of natural law are features which most commentators today associate with natural law theory in general. For most commentators there is only one genuine type of natural law theory, stoic natural law theory, and there is only one authentic natural law tradition, the stoic natural law tradition.

An excellent illustration of this tendency is provided by Robert Derathe's otherwise excellent work on Rousseau and his relationship to the natural law tradition. Here Derathe presents a sketch of the features which, in his view, are to be associated with all natural law theories from the time of Cicero to the eighteenth century. According to Derathe, the 'entire theory of natural law' is based on the belief that 'there exists, independently of all civil laws, and anterior to all human conventions, a universal moral order, an immutable rule of justice', namely natural law. This law 'applies equally to all men'. Moreover, it is this which 'distinguishes it from all positive laws, and which makes it superior to them'. Positive laws are 'neither immutable nor universal'. They are, moreover, 'subordinate to natural law'. For men 'are only subject to civil laws on the tacit condition that those laws should prescribe nothing which might run counter to the law of nature' (Derathe, 1970, pp.151-2).

The account of natural law theory presented here is evidently, in effect, an account of the stoic natural law theory of Cicero. Indeed, Derathe acknowledges this, taking pains to cite the original texts. However, what is particularly noteworthy, from our point of view, is the fact that this sketch is presented as a characterisation, not simply of the stoic conception of natural law, but of natural law theory in general. Derathe finds it difficult to imagine the possibility of there being a type of natural law theory which does not conform to the basic outline presented here.

Another illustration of this tendency is provided by A. G. Chloros in an article appropriately entitled 'What is natural law?' According to Chloros, the traditional view of natural law is that it is 'a body of immutable rules superior to positive law'. Natural law is ideal law, consisting of 'the highest principles of morality towards which humanity is striving'. It is also 'absolute law' since 'it is not the result of any convention, but is discovered by the exercise of reason' (Chloros, 1958, p.609). The view of natural law presented here is, again, the stoic conception of natural law. The characteristic features of stoic natural law theory are all associated by Chloros with the very idea of natural law. Thus Chloros follows Cicero in suggesting that for natural law theorists there are certain principles of morality which are absolute, immutable, discoverable by reason and, most important from our point of view, superior to positive law.

Much the same attitude is taken by a very well know author on the subject of natural law theory, Leo Strauss. In Strauss's opinion, 'to reject natural right is tantamount to saying that all right is positive right', and this means that 'what is right is determined exclusively by the legislators and the courts of different countries'. It is, however, 'obviously meaningful, and sometimes even necessary, to speak of 'unjust' laws. Moreover, it is evident that when we do this 'we imply that there is a standard of right and wrong' which is 'independent of positive right and higher than positive right'. This standard is the natural law. It is a 'standard with reference to which we are able to judge of positive right' (Strauss, 1974, p.2). For Strauss also, then, to accept the existence of natural law, or natural right, is to accept that there is some critical standard which individuals might use to evaluate the justice of the positive law of the state in which they live. Once again, therefore, what we have here is the identification of the stoic conception of natural law with the notion of natural law *per se*. From Strauss' point of view, it would not make sense to talk about a natural law theory in which the principles of natural law did not perform such an evaluative function. A system of political thought which did not allow for the possibility of individuals critically evaluating positive law could not possibly be a genuine natural law theory. To suggest otherwise would be to demonstrate an ignorance of what a natural law theory actually is. It would be to perpetrate an abuse of language. In effect, to refer to such a theory as a natural law theory would be to contradict oneself.

This is a point which has been very well understood by Hans Kelsen, who is quite happy to refer to himself as being a legal positivist. Commenting on the question of the priority of justice or law, Kelsen acknowledges that the answers given to it by natural law theorists and legal positivists are mutually exclusive of one another and totally irreconcilable. This is so, Kelsen argues, because legal positivists identify justice with positive law. In his view, the 'identification of justice with positive law is incompatible with a genuine doctrine of natural law'. For a genuine natural law theory 'must grant - in principle at least - the possibility of a contrast between the two' (Kelsen, 1973, p.129).Thus, according to Kelsen, given the conventional understanding of natural law and natural law

22

theory, if a particular system of political thought is to be considered as a genuine doctrine of law then it must necessarily allow for the possibility of a contrast to be made between natural law and positive law. In other words, it must allow for the possibility of there being a conflict between natural law and positive law. As Kelsen himself puts it, what differentiates a natural law theorist from a legal positivist is the fact that for a legal positivist 'positive law - and positive law alone, basically - is just'. Hence, for the positivist 'there can simply be no question of that possible conflict' between positive law and justice which is 'essential for a genuine natural law theory' (Kelsen, 1973, p.131).

The second assumption which is made by the majority of modern commentators has to do with the meaning of the concept of natural law or of natural law theory. It is usually taken for granted that this is a meaningful concept. It is also generally assumed that the reason why it is meaningful is because it can be given a definition, in the traditional manner. Thus it is assumed that there is a strict rule which governs its use. This rule refers to what might be termed a closed list of defining characteristics which must be present before we could be said to be justified, logically speaking, in referring to anything as being an example of a natural law theory. In other words, given that the concept of natural law theory is a meaningful one, there must be in principle, and hence there are as a matter of fact, certain characteristic features which all natural law theories hold in common. From this point of view, it is only if a particular doctrine possesses all of these necessary features that we are justified in referring to it as a natural law theory at all, in the strict sense of that term.

This attitude is illustrated very well by Richard Wollheim. Wollheim acknowledges that, throughout its long history, the doctrine of natural law has changed considerably, and has engendered a number of different 'variants and modifications'. Accordingly, he suggests, if we are to speak meaningfully about 'the' doctrine of law it is necessary that we isolate those features which all of these different varieties of natural law theory possess in common. We must offer 'a minimal characterisation of the doctrine of natural law'. Wollheim does not question whether it is actually possible to do this. He simply insists that as a matter of fact it is possible, as the term 'natural law' has 'been used over the centuries to designate a remarkably persistent doctrine' (Wollheim, 1967, p.450).

Wollheim then goes on to present the reader with what he claims is such a 'minimal characterisation' of 'the' doctrine of natural law, and of the features which are associated with each of its particular forms. Not surprisingly, this sketch is in fact actually nothing more than a reformulation of the stoic conception of natural law as we find it in the writings of Cicero. Thus Wollheim evidently considers the belief that natural law is a critical standard for the evaluation of positive law to be an absolutely essential component element in any natural law theory. This belief is one of the things which all natural law theories possess in common, without exception. It is for this reason that he claims, as a matter of fact quite wrongly, that 'it is obviously a necessary condition of any natural law doctrine' that the opposite view 'should be rejected' (Wollheim, 1967, pp.450-1).

A similar view is taken by S. B. Drury. According to her, although the tradition of natural law is by no means homogeneous, 'it is nevertheless united by a resilient core of ideas'. The 'most important of these are (1) the conviction that there exists a universal justice that transcends the particular expressions of justice in any given set of laws; (2) that the universal principles of justice are accessible to reason and independent of human volition' and '(3) that a positive law contrary to these universal principles is not properly speaking a law' (Drury, 1981, pp.533-34). Here again it is assumed that there are certain ideas which may be associated with 'the' natural law tradition, in all of its forms. We are offered an account of the characteristic beliefs which are supposed to be representative of this tradition. And, once more, what we are presented with is actually an account of the stoic conception of natural law, the principles of which are simply assumed to be present in all forms of natural law theory. Drury takes the view that these principles constitute a set of minimal beliefs which, no matter how they might differ in other respects, all natural law theories must hold in common.

This, then, is the conventional view of natural law and natural law theory which is adopted by the vast majority of commentators today. It is this view which commentators usually have in mind when they classify individual political theorists as being either natural law theorists on the one hand or legal positivists on the other.

Legal positivism

We are now in a position to provide a more detailed elaboration of the ideas which are usually associated with the doctrine of legal positivism. Clarifying what is meant by the term 'legal positivism' is, as H. L. A. Hart has pointed out, not an easy task. Although there is a broad consensus as regards the character of natural law theory, there is no such consensus in so far as legal positivism is concerned. Legal positivism as a legal positivist understands it is very often quite different from legal positivism as a natural law theorist understands it (Hart, 1961, pp.253-4; Hart, 1958, p.608; see also Kelsen, 1961, Appendix; and Lloyd, 1970).

Those commentators who refer to themselves as legal positivists tend to make a clear distinction between what they consider to be two quite separate and unrelated spheres, the sphere of law or justice, on the one hand, and the sphere of morality on the other. From this point of view, the term 'justice' is logically associated with that of 'law' rather than that of 'morality'. All justice is, therefore, what we have already referred to as legal justice. Hence there is no such thing as moral justice. To employ the term 'justice' in a moral context or to refer to the notion of moral justice is, strictly speaking, an abuse of language (Hart, 1961, pp.202-7; Hart, 1958).

24

These commentators, then, certainly are committed to the view that justice is posterior and not prior to law and that, strictly speaking, no law can be unjust. They are, however, in words which echo those of the *Encyclopedie* article on justice, careful to point out that this should not be considered to imply that positive law cannot be evaluated by reference to some external standard of morality. As Hart puts it, if positive law cannot be unjust, it can certainly be 'iniquitous' (Hart, 1961, pp.202-7).

On the other hand, though, the issue of whether, and if so under what circumstances, positive law might be critically evaluated from the standpoint of its morality, as opposed to its justice, is not considered by legal positivists to be of any interest to the lawyer as such. This is a question which lies outside of what Austin refers to as 'the province of jurisprudence', and which is of concern only to students of ethics, politics or, in Hart's words, 'some other discipline' (Austin, 1995; Hart, 1961, p.205; Finnis, 1980, pp.354-8).

This approach is evidently quite different from that adopted by most of the commentators to whom we have referred so far, who do not make such a clear distinction between justice and morality and who indeed, to the contrary, have a tendency to identify the two.

It follows from this that one and the same person could be a legal positivist in Hart's sense and yet nevertheless, at the same time, if not to the letter then at least in spirit, be a natural law theorist in the sense in which this term is employed by commentators like Crocker and d'Entreves. The paradoxical nature of this situation has been well captured by Lloyd. Legal positivism, he suggests, is usually associated with the rejection of the idea that there is some sort of 'absolute standard by which the validity of a rule may be tested'. However, this does not necessarily imply that a legal positivist must necessarily be a 'relativist' in so far as questions of morality are concerned. 'For a positivist may still insist that the validity of law is distinct from the question of its moral rightness even while adhering to some system of absolute moral values' (Lloyd, 1972, p.111).

The fact that there is such a disagreement as to how the term 'legal positivism' is to be employed clearly complicates matters somewhat. It should therefore be clearly understood that the more detailed account of the doctrine of legal positivism which is to follow is an account of the doctrine as it is understood, not by legal positivists themselves, but by their opponents. It is an account of the doctrine as natural law theory (interpreted in the conventional sense) understands it.

From this point of view, then, the doctrine of legal positivism is, as it were, the inverted mirror image of the doctrine of natural law or, to speak more accurately, of the stoic conception of natural law. All of the central beliefs which, as we have seen, are associated with the stoic conception of natural law are beliefs which are rejected by legal positivists.

Bearing this in mind, we may say that the doctrine of legal positivism possesses four characteristic features. The first of these is the belief that there is, in fact, no

25

such thing as natural law or natural justice. All justice, both moral as well as legal, is arbitrary and conventional. The standard of justice in any particular society is indeed the positive law of that society. From this point of view, as we have already noted, justice is posterior and not prior to law.

The second feature of legal positivism is a belief that there are no principles of moral justice, apart from those encapsulated in positive law, which can be discovered or intellectually apprehended by the faculty of reason, either of the individual moral agent or indeed of the legislator. Principles of justice are not discovered. They are, rather, created by a specific act of volition or legislative will. As Kelsen puts it, from the standpoint of positivism, 'law is always positive law', and its positivity lies in the fact that 'it is created and annulled by acts of human beings'. Thus, the 'particular norms of a legal order cannot be deduced logically'.They are, rather, 'created by a special act of will' (Kelsen, 1961, pp. 113-14).

This assessment is shared by other commentators. According to Franz Neumann, the central thesis of the doctrine of legal positivism is the doctrine that 'law is nothing but the sovereign's will' (Neumann, 1957, p.69). In Rommen's view, the positivist 'is concerned solely with the formal origin of law' and 'not with its content'. For the positivist, therefore, 'law is will' (Rommen, 1979, pp.247-8). And according to d'Entreves, legal positivism is 'that line of thought which rejects any quest after the reason or justification of law' and which, in the old debate as to whether the essence of law is reason or will, 'would have sided in favour of the second part of the alternative' (d'Entreves, 1970, pp.74, 122).

A third feature of legal positivism is the belief that there are no actions which are intrinsically wrong or unjust. Considered quite independently of the dictates of positive law all actions are morally arbitrary or indifferent. This point has been put very well by Rommen. In his view, because the positivist 'is concerned solely with the formal origin of law' and not 'with its content', the question 'whether something can be wrong in itself is meaningless for him'. For right and wrong 'merely denote the presence or absence of agreement with the factual will of the lawmaker' (Rommen, 1979, pp.247-8). A corollary of this is the belief, also held by legal positivists, that the reason why certain actions are forbidden, commanded, or permitted by positive law has to do with the question of their utility or expediency rather than their justice or injustice.

A fourth feature of legal positivism is the denial that there are any principles of justice which are universal, unchangeable or immutable. All justice is relative and conventional. This claim has two component elements. The first is that there are no principles of justice which are, as a matter of fact, to be found in all societies, at all times and in all places. What is recognised and accepted as being just or unjust varies from society to society, from place to place, and from time to time. Thus a legal positivist, as here interpreted, would wholeheartedly endorse Pascal's judgement that 'there is nothing just or unjust but changes colour as it changes climate. Three degrees of latitude upset the whole of jurisprudence'

(Pascal, 1972, p.46). The second element is the belief that there is no reason, morally speaking, why all societies ought to recognise the same principles of justice. The variation which exists between different societies with respect to their understanding of what is just and unjust is something which is entirely legitimate, considered from the moral point of view. Thus the legal positivist rejects the idea that there are certain principles of justice which have a universal validity, morally speaking, and which therefore ought to be recognised in those societies which do not, at present, happen to recognise them. From this point of view, the fact that two societies have different moral values is, most emphatically, not a sign that one is morally superior to the other, or that one of these societies should be considered to be suffering from moral depravity whereas the other is not.

The fifth and final characteristic feature of the doctrine of legal positivism, as it is understood here, is in effect a reformulation of the first. It is the belief that there is no independent standard of justice which might be employed by individual citizens in order to critically evaluate the positive law of the particular society in which they live. It is the belief, clearly formulated by Wollheim, that 'no positive law can be unjust'. This aspect of the doctrine of legal positivism is central to the perception which most commentators have of it. It has been well noted by Neumann, according to whom legal positivism, 'with its thesis that law is nothing but the sovereign's will', has finally 'exterminated all attempts to measure the system of positive law on some normative standard' (Neumann, 1957, p.69).

As in the case of natural law theory, the ideas which we have associated with the legal positivism have a very long history. Thus, for example, these ideas are alluded to by Plato in his dialogues in the course of a discussion of the question of whether justice is natural or conventional (Plato, 1968, pp.89-90; Plato, 1975, pp.77-8; Plato, 1972, pp.172-4, 416-18; also Morrow, 1948). They are also referred to by Cicero in his writings. In the *De Republica* Cicero attributes to the Greek philosopher Carneades the view that there is no such thing as natural justice, that in the evaluation of laws the notion of utility or expediency is more important than that of justice, that all justice is relative, varying from society to society, and that the fact that this is so is not in the slightest disturbing when considered from the moral point of view. Unfortunately, Cicero's own account of the views of Carneades has not been preserved. We do, however, have a paraphrase of that account provided by Lactantius, writing three centuries later. According to Lactantius, Cicero attributed the following beliefs to Carneades, 'that men enacted laws for themselves, with a view to their own advantage, differing indeed according to their characters' and 'often changed according to times', and that, therefore, 'there was no natural law ' (Lactantius, 1886, p.328; Cicero, 1928a, pp.191-203) .

Cicero's account of the views of Carneades was preserved during the medieval period, partly through the work of Lactantius and partly through that of Augustine (Augustine,1945, pp.61-4). In modern times, the views of Carneades are discussed once again in the works of the great natural law theorists of the continental school of natural law in the seventeenth century, whose works were so influential in the period of the Enlightenment. Locke, for example, refers to Carneades in his *Essays on the Law of Nature* (Locke, 1958, p. 205). So also does Grotius in the prolegomena to the *De Jure Belli et Pacis*. One could, indeed, consider this work to be a sustained attempt to refute the doctrine of Carneades as represented in the writings of Cicero (Grotius, 1925, pp.10-11).

More recently, it might well also be argued that it is the spirit of Carneades which underpins the utilitarian philosophy of the eighteenth and nineteenth centuries. Bentham's assault on natural law theory in his examination of Blackstone's *Commentaries on the Laws of England* simply repeats, more or less, the views which Cicero attributes to Carneades (Bentham, 1977). In his *Commentaries,* Blackstone makes a distinction, which is quite typical of stoic natural law theory, between actions which are 'wrong in themselves', or *'mala in se'*, and actions which are not so, and which are, therefore, merely *'mala prohibitiva'.* The latter are matters of 'indifference' from the moral point of view, and are only wrong at all because they have been forbidden by positive law. The reason why actions falling into this latter category are forbidden, says Blackstone, has to do not with justice or injustice but, rather, with utility or expediency. Bentham has little sympathy for the theoretical distinction between these two different kinds of action. As far as he is concerned, there are no actions which might be said to be *'mala in se'.* All of the actions which are forbidden by positive law are forbidden on grounds of utility. Like Carneades, Bentham takes the view that every right and every wrong is 'merely created by law, for the purposes of civil society' (Bentham, 1977, pp.64-6). There is good reason to believe that it is the doctrine of Benthamite utilitarianism which is the principal vehicle by means of which the age old doctrines of Carneades have been transmitted to the twentieth century and have become incorporated into the doctrine of legal positivism as it is known today.

This, then, is the doctrine of legal positivism as it is understood by many modern commentators. It is by referring to this doctrine, taken together with what is, as we have seen, fundamentally a stoic conception of natural law, that the majority of commentators classify individual political theorists as being either natural law theorists on the one hand, or legal positivists on the other.

Criticisms of the conventional view of natural law theory

The assumption that the concept of natural law or of natural law theory can be defined in the traditional manner has not gone unchallenged. Paul. Foriers and Chaim Perelman, for example, have argued that any attempt to 'define' the concept of natural law is 'an undertaking doomed to failure from the start'. In their view it is necessary, if we wish to avoid confusion, 'always to qualify the expression'. Thus we must only speak of 'classical natural law', 'stoic natural

28

law', 'protestant natural law', and so on (Foriers and Perelman, 1973, p.14). In other words, we must only ever refer to the various, different natural law traditions, and we must abandon any attempt to comment on something which is alleged to be 'the' natural law tradition, or to make generalisations which are supposed to be applicable to all forms of natural law theory and all natural law traditions.

The position adopted by Foriers and Perelman is certainly a step in the right direction. Contrary to what Wollheim and Drury might think, there is in fact no hard core of ideas which unites all of the different types of natural law theory in the manner suggested above. However, although Foriers and Perelman certainly do take a step in the right direction when they emphasise the need for us to take account of the existence of different natural law traditions, they do not actually go very far down the path that they have chosen. For example, they do not really explain adequately what the difference between stoic natural law theory and the other alternative natural law traditions which they mention actually is. And to some extent they also undermine their own position by going on to claim, quite inconsistently, after having just taken what is quite the contrary view, that there are nevertheless 'certain essential features' of natural law and natural law theory which 'can be formulated' after all (Foriers and Perelman, 1967, p.14). The attempt by Foriers and Perelman to distance themselves from the general consensus concerning natural law theory is, therefore, in the final analysis, somewhat half hearted.

In addition to Foriers and Perelman, there are also other commentators who, although with a certain degree of hesitation, do seem to recognise not only the theoretical possibility but also the actual existence of 'genuine' natural law theories which nevertheless do not conform strictly to the pattern laid down by Cicero and the stoic conception of natural law. The views of Howard Warrender, who is well known for his work on the political philosophy of Hobbes and its relationship to the natural law tradition, provide a good illustration of such a view. The sketch of natural law theory which Warrender presents is actually quite conventional, and recognisably derived from the stoic tradition. Thus he describes natural law as 'a body of prescriptive rules' capable of being discovered by all men and 'superior to the positive law of individual states'. Nevertheless, Warrender is extremely cautious about making sweeping generalisations which are supposed to apply to all types of natural law theory. theory. For this has 'varied considerably both in its character and its content' throughout the ages. He is, therefore, careful to acknowledge that there are certain 'exceptions' to this general pattern and that it is not the case that all natural law doctrines possess these particular characteristic features (Warrender, 1979, p.933; Warrender, 1962a, p.352).

Similar caution is expressed by Paul Sigmund. As with so many other commentators, Sigmund acknowledges that natural law theory has taken on 'a variety of forms and content' throughout its history, and that this has 'resulted in considerable confusion about its meaning'. Nevertheless, there does seem to be 'a central assertion' which these different forms of natural law theory possess in common. The account which Sigmund offers of this central assertion is, again, based essentially on the ideas of Cicero and the stoic conception of natural law. It amounts, he says, to the belief that there is "a rational order which can provide intelligible value statements independently of human will, unchangeable in their ultimate content, and morally obligatory on all mankind'. These statements are 'expressed in laws or moral imperatives which provide a basis for the evaluation of legal and political structures' (Sigmund, 1971, p.viii). Like Warrender, however, Sigmund is extremely cautious . He takes care to point out that these ideas are only to be found in 'most theories of natural law'. They are not, by any means, to be found in all of them (Sigmund, 1971, p.viii).

Unfortunately, though, neither Warrender nor Sigmund tells us who these exceptional figures in the history of political thought actually are. Nor do they discuss the respects in which the ideas of these exceptional figures differ from those of Cicero and the stoic conception of natural law. It would seem that, according to Warrender and Sigmund, although such exceptional figures do undoubtedly exist, they are nevertheless of no great importance. Our understanding of the history of natural law theory, and indeed of the history of political thought, would not be greatly hindered if we were to assume, as most other commentators do, that Cicero's ideas are quite typical of natural law theory in general.

Warrender and Sigmund are, in fact, perfectly correct to point out that the history of natural law theory contains examples of doctrines which do not conform to the stereotype laid down by the stoic conception of natural law. There are, undoubtedly, or so we shall argue, certain theorists who may be regarded as genuine natural law theorists, but who nevertheless do not write from the standpoint of the stoic tradition. They are wrong, however, when they imply that the existence of such exceptional figures is of no great significance either for our understanding of the history of natural law theory or of the history of political thought generally. They are wrong to suggest, in effect, that no great harm would be done if these exceptional figures were to be ignored. On the contrary, the identification of the stoic conception of natural law with the very idea of natural law as such, the belief that this conception represents the only genuine form of natural law theory, and the corresponding failure by many commentators to recognise the existence and historical importance of alternative natural law traditions, have in fact been something of a disaster. They have led to a considerable degree of confusion and misunderstanding, not just in relation to the character of natural law and natural law theory, but also with respect to the understanding and interpretation of the ideas of a number of major figures in the history of political thought. In particular, these erroneous assumptions have led to a misunderstanding of the attitude which these figures adopt towards natural law and natural law theory, they have led to a misunderstanding of how these figures should be located in relation to the natural law tradition, and finally they have, as a result, led to a misunderstanding of their respective systems of political thought as a whole.

Voluntarism and natural law

For example, a major criticism that might be made of the present academic consensus with respect to the character of natural law theory is that it fails completely to recognise the existence of, or even allow for the possibility, of voluntarist conceptions of natural law or of a voluntarist natural law tradition.

The question of the priority of justice or law can be, and actually has been, interpreted in different ways, depending on which particular type of law one has in mind. Traditionally, there are two main possibilities here. One may, like Lester Crocker, have in mind what is usually referred to as 'human positive law'. Alternatively, however, one might be thinking of 'divine positive law'. If one focuses on the latter, then the question amounts to asking which of the following two possibilities is correct. Are actions like murder and theft wrong simply because they have been forbidden by some command of God, and for no other reason? Or, alternatively, is the reason why God forbids the performance of these actions because they are wrong in and of themselves, quite independently of any divine command? Formulated in this way, the question of the priority of justice or law was the focal point for a debate which was fiercely contested throughout the medieval period.This is the debate between the doctrines of voluntarism and rationalism, respectively (see Gierke, 1958, pp.172-4).

The voluntarist position in this debate, as is well known, is that there are no actions which are wrong in themselves. Those actions, like murder and theft, which are wrong are only wrong because they have been forbidden by God. The medieval voluntarists would have disagreed completely with the famous claim made by Grotius that the precepts of natural law would retain their validity even if God did not exist (Grotius, 1925, p.11). A good illustration of this voluntarist position is provided by William of Ockham, writing in the fourteenth century. According to Francis Oakley, Ockham took the view that adultery, robbery and 'all such vices' could be 'stripped of their evil and rendered meritorious' if their performance were to be commanded by the command of God, 'just as now, *de facto*, their opposites agree with the divine precept' (Oakley, 1964, p.171; also Oakley, 1963).The medieval voluntarists, then, took the view that justice is posterior to law, provided one is talking about the law of God, or divine positive law. In their view, no such law could be said to be unjust. Insofar as human beings are concerned, the law of God is the ultimate standard of justice and of right and wrong.

On the other hand, though, voluntarists take a different position in so far as human positive law is concerned. In this case, justice is prior to law and not posterior to it. It is certainly possible, from this point of view, for a human law, to be unjust. This occurs in those circumstances when human law comes into conflict with the law of God by commanding or permitting the performance of an action which the divine law has forbidden.

What is particularly striking about the voluntarist approach to this issue is that voluntarist thinkers do actually employ the concept of natural law in their writings. They identify the natural law with the law of God, or with divine positive law. And they frequently suggest that natural law, understood in this particular sense, is higher than, or superior to, human positive law, which should not be allowed to contradict or come into conflict with it. As T. G. Callahan has pointed out, in Ockham's writings, 'there is a repeated insistence that natural law is superior to any human positive law'. Thus, according to Callahan, it is Ockham's view that 'if there is any conflict with natural law engendered through the enactment of some human positive law, it is the positive law which must give way or an unjust law will have been created' (Callahan, 1975, p.118).

How, then, should these medieval voluntarist thinkers be classified? Are they natural law theorists or are they legal positivists? This is not the place to offer a detailed analysis of this medieval debate. It will be sufficient to point out that the understanding which most commentators have of natural law and natural law theory makes it very difficult for them to grasp adequately the significance of the notion of natural law for the ethical and political thought of the medieval voluntarists (see Clark, 1971; McDonnell, 1974; Oakley, 1963; Shepherd, 1932; Shepherd, 1933). It also makes it difficult for them to understand the significance which the notion of natural law has for figures like Luther and Calvin, in the period of the Reformation, both of whom employ the notion of natural law, and both of whom are voluntarists (Baum, 1961; Cochrane, 1966; Lang, 1909; McNeill, 1946; McNeill, 1941).

Because they identify stoic natural law theory with natural law theory as such, and hence assume that the belief that there are certain actions which are intrinsically wrong is an essential component element to be found in all forms of natural law theory, the majority of commentators are necessarily committed to the position that voluntarism and natural law theory are incompatible. One could not possibly be a voluntarist and a natural law theorist at the same time. At least one could not be a 'genuine' natural law theorist. The idea of a voluntarist conception of natural law is a contradiction in terms.

It follows from this that, from the standpoint of the existing consensus, voluntarists like Ockham and d'Ailly, or Luther and Calvin, must by default be considered to be legal positivists. Thus, according to Rommen the voluntarism of the medieval period constituted 'the heaviest assault' made from inside scholasticism on 'the idea of natural law'. This is so because 'natural law is the consequence of the doctrine of the priority of the intellect over the will (law is reason) in both God and man'. Positivism, on the other hand, 'is the consequence of the doctrine of the primacy of the will with respect to the intellect' (Rommen, 1979, pp.40, 4).

A similar position is also adopted by M. B. Crowe. In his view, the essence of the rationalist position in this medieval debate is the belief that 'some actions are evil' and that their malice 'is not dependent upon judgement or will, even those of God'. This, however, is also the essence of any genuine doctrine of natural law. Thus the rejection of this belief by the medieval voluntarists is 'the touchstone of the nominalism (and the denial of the natural law) of the fourteenth century'. According to Crowe, voluntarists take the view that 'nothing is good or evil in itself', and this 'positivism', therefore, effectively 'sweeps away the natural law' (Crowe, 1977, pp.194, 202, 212-14).

A good illustration of the problems associated with this approach to the voluntarist position is provided by the cases of Samuel Pufendorf and John Locke. Pufendorf, together with Grotius, was one of the dominant figures in the continental school of natural law of the seventeenth century (Derathe, 1970; Barker, 1948; Barker, 1960). According to d'Entreves he was 'the most celebrated and influential of all seventeenth century writers on natural law'. He was 'the greatest academic expounder of the theory in the seventeenth century' and the first holder of a chair of natural law in a German university (d'Entreves, 1970, pp. 15, 53).

Pufendorf, however, is a voluntarist. As the *Encyclopedie* article on justice points out, the views of Pufendorf are opposed to those of Grotius on the question of the priority of justice or law, if that question is interpreted in the present theological sense (*Encyclopedie*, 9, p.86). Like his medieval predecessors, he rejects the notion that there are any actions which are wrong in themselves, independently of any command of God. As he puts the point himself, we need not maintain, 'that some things are noble or base of themselves' For since 'moral necessity and turpitude' are the consequences of human actions 'arising from their conformity or non-conformity to some norm or law', and since 'law is the bidding of a superior', it 'does not appear that good repute or turpitude can be conceived to exist before law, and without the imposition of a superior' (Pufendorf, 1934, pp. 27, 90).

The case of Locke is a little more complicated than that of Pufendorf. One reason for this is that Locke actually says very little about natural law in his published work. Locke's *Second Treatise of Civil Government* explicitly discusses the subject in just one short chapter (Soles, 1988). Locke has much more to say about natural law in his unpublished writings. Indeed, he wrote extensively on this topic in his early *Essays on the Law of Nature* (Locke, 1958). However, he deliberately refrained from publishing these essays. Clearly, therefore, their usefulness as a source for anyone seeking to interpret Locke's views on natural law must, to some extent at least, be open to question.

Nevertheless, if we do base our assessment of Locke's views on a reading of these *Essays*, one thing seems readily apparent. The position adopted by Locke, on this occasion at least, is basically that of a voluntarist. As Von Leyden points out, Locke 'regards natural law as a set of commands proceeding from the will of God'. Thus, 'the position he adopts in that deep reaching question of scholastic controversy concerning the essence of law' is that of the 'so called voluntarist theory' (Von Leyden, 1958, pp.51, 43).

The cases of Pufendorf and Locke, then, present us with something of a difficulty. Both of these thinkers are voluntarists. They both reject the idea that justice is prior to law, understood as the command of God. From the standpoint of the existing consensus, therefore, they ought not to be considered as natural law theorists at all. They ought, like Ockham and d'Ailly in the medieval period, to be classified as legal positivists. In the case of Pufendorf and Locke, however, this is clearly entirely unacceptable. The credentials of both of these thinkers as genuine natural law theorists are surely unimpeachable.

The source of this difficulty does not, of course, lie in the writings of either Pufendorf or Locke. Rather, it lies in the assumptions which so many commentators make about natural law and natural law theory. It lies in the identification of the stoic conception of natural law with the idea of natural law per se. In order to resolve this difficulty, all that is necessary is that we revise our understanding of natural law and the assumptions which we make concerning the conditions which need to be satisfied before a theory might legitimately be said to be a genuine natural law theory. We need to loosen our understanding of natural law theory so as to allow for, not only the logical or theoretical possibility, but also the actual existence of voluntarist conceptions of natural law and of a voluntarist natural law tradition.

Formal conceptions of natural law

A second major criticism that might be made of the existing academic consensus is that it does not allow for the existence, or indeed the possibility, of what, following a hint provided by Warrender, we shall refer to as 'formal' conceptions of natural law (Warrender, 1957, pp.174, 243, 329).

The most important, although not the only, difference between this type of natural law theory and the stoic conception of natural law has to do with the relationship which is assumed to exist between natural law and positive law. From this point of view, there are, undeniably, certain actions which are wrong or unjust quite independently of the dictates of human positive law. In this sense, at least, justice is prior to law and not posterior to it. Examples of actions of this sort include lying, murder, theft and adultery. Thus it is assumed that these actions, and actions like them, are not wrong or unjust because they have been forbidden by human positive law. On the contrary, positive law forbids them precisely because they are wrong.

34

According to this approach, the precepts of natural law which forbid the performance of such actions are discoverable by the faculty of reason of the individual moral agent. On the other hand, though, these precepts are considered to be difficult to apply in practice. It is easy to see that one ought not to commit acts of murder and theft. It is, however, not so easy to recognise whether, in a given situation, some particular action that one is contemplating performing actually amounts to an act of murder or theft. In order to resolve this problem, the precepts of natural law need to be applied to the specific circumstances presented by the situation in question. They need to be given a particular interpretation or, in the terminology of scholastic natural law theory, a specific 'determination'.

However, in contrast to that of Cicero and stoic natural law theory, the view adopted here by formal conceptions of natural law is that the source for this interpretation is, most emphatically, not the faculty of reason of the individual moral agent. According to formal conceptions of natural law, the precepts of natural law require an interpretation from the outside. They require what, following Hobbes, we may term an 'authoritative' interpretation. The source for this authoritative interpretation is, from the standpoint of formal conceptions of natural law, not the reason of the individual, but the positive law of the community of which that individual is a member.

It follows from this that, for formal conceptions of natural law, the principal function of positive law is not simply to declare or ratify the precepts of natural law and provide them with a coercive sanction. This is, certainly, one of the functions of positive law, but it is not the only one. A second, and equally important function is that of interpreting and applying the principles of natural law to the particular circumstances and historical conditions that are to be found in different societies and in the same society at different times.

When positive law carries out this function, what in effect it is doing is providing individual moral agents with definitions of the key moral concepts of murder, theft, adultery, and so on. According to this type of natural law theory, morally speaking there could be, and indeed are, different ways in which this process might be carried out. The specific actions which are regarded as constituting an act of murder in one society might well be different from those which are so regarded in another, and legitimately so. There is nothing at all morally reprehensible about this. From the moral point of view, the specific character of the definition which is actually adopted in a particular society is actually a matter of indifference. The guiding principle, here at least, is not reason but utility and expediency or will.

A corollary of this is that within formal conceptions of natural law positive law is not considered to be a copy or simple reproduction of the principles of natural law, down to the smallest detail. Nor, morally speaking, is it necessary for the systems of positive law of different societies to be identical with one another. This is so because the actions which one society considers, from the standpoint of utility or expediency, to be acts of murder, theft, and so on, will usually differ in at least some respects from the actions which another society regards as falling to this category. This is, indeed, exactly what is meant when some types of natural law theory are described as being 'flexible' in comparison with the stoic conception of natural law.

An extremely important implication of this approach to the relationship which exists between natural law and positive law, although it is one which is frequently not recognised, is that from this point of view it is actually a logical impossibility for the principles of natural law to act as a critical standard by means of which individuals might evaluate the positive law of the society in which they live. It is a logical impossibility for positive law to conflict with or contradict the requirements of natural law.

Thus, for example, if we consider murder to be any act of wrongful or unjust killing, and if we allow that it is for positive law to decide which acts of killing are to be considered as falling into this category, then it follows automatically that if positive law were to command or permit the performance of any particular act of killing, such an act would not be, and logically speaking could not be, an act of murder in the strict sense. Clearly, therefore, for anyone who subscribes to a formal conception of natural law, it would be logically contradictory, in such a situation, for individual moral agents to argue that the positive law in question ought not to be obeyed on the grounds that it commanded or permitted the performance of an action which is intrinsically wrong or unjust, namely the act of murder.

From the standpoint of formal conceptions of natural law, therefore, it is actually quite impossible for the principles of natural law to carry out the critical function which, according to the stoic natural law tradition, and to the majority of modern commentators, is absolutely essential to any 'genuine' natural law theory.

This is a point which is well understood, and forcefully expressed, by Bentham in his criticisms of Blackstone's *Commentaries*. In the *Commentaries* Blackstone, in typical stoic fashion, takes the view that the act of murder is forbidden by a precept of natural law. If, therefore, 'any human law should allow or injoin us to commit it, we are bound to transgress that human law' (Blackstone, 1966, pp.42-3). In his criticisms of Blackstone, Bentham claims to be puzzled by this statement. He cannot imagine 'what conceivable law it should be that bid us commit murder'. This is so because murder is 'the killing of a man without any alleviation, excuse or justification'. However, one such justification for an act of killing is precisely that of 'being bid or allowed to do it by the law'. This being the case, Bentham concludes on a somewhat triumphant note, to understand how a human law could possibly enjoin or permit an act of murder is to understand how it is that 'the same law speaking to the same person at the same time can mean a thing should be done and not done' (Bentham, 1977, pp.42-3).

Bentham intends this as a criticism, not simply of Blackstone, but of natural law theory in general. It is evident, however, that the critical force of his argument is not so great as Bentham seems to think. There are two reasons for this. In the first place, as a criticism of stoic natural law theory the argument is actually quite weak. This is so because stoic natural law theorists evidently reject one of the basic assumptions upon which Bentham's argument is based, namely that it is for positive law, rather than the conscience of the individual moral agent, to decide which actions are to counts as murder and which are not. With respect to this crucial issue, Bentham's argument simply begs the question. In so far as this central feature of stoic natural law theory is concerned, Bentham appears to miss completely the point that is made by the theory which he is criticising.

In the second place, Bentham's criticism of natural law theory is weak because it has no application at all to what we have termed formal conceptions of natural law. For natural law theories of this type actually share Bentham's belief that, within a particular community, it is positive law which declares which specific actions fall under the general concept of murder and which do not. This is, perhaps, what Frederick Pollock has in mind when he says that if Bentham had known what natural law theory 'was really like' then 'he would have had to speak of it with more respect' (Pollock, 1961, p. 135).

In modern times the idea that the precepts of natural law require an authoritative interpretation, and that the source of such an interpretation ought to be positive law, is usually associated with the political theory of Hobbes (Hobbes, 1839-45b, pp.261-2). Moreover, it is evident that Hobbes is very well aware that a logical implication of such a view is that it is actually quite impossible for natural law to used as a critical standard for the evaluation of positive law. This is a point which he emphasises strongly in his *Philosophical Rudiments Concerning Government and Society*. There Hobbes expresses the view that 'no civil law whatsoever' can 'possibly be against the law of nature'. For 'though the law of nature forbid theft' and 'adultery' yet 'if the civil law command us to invade anything, that invasion is not theft' or 'adultery' (Hobbes, 1839-45a, pp.190-91).

Warrender has claimed that, in this regard, Hobbes' political thought constitutes an innovation in the history of natural law theory. In his view, when Hobbes makes these claims he is moving away from natural law theory as it has been traditionally understood (Warrender, 1979, p.932; Warrender, 1962a, p.438; Warrender, 1962b, p.352). He is supported in this contention by other commentators. For example, F. A. Olafson has maintained that Hobbes' natural law theory marks a shift away 'from a substantive to a formal interpretation of the norms on which the positive law depends for its validity'. According to Olafson, this distinction between substantive and formal conceptions of natural law 'was never made in the medieval theory of natural law'. Thus, a formal conception of natural law, like that of Hobbes, constitutes a fundamental rejection of 'the Thomistic view that substantive moral guidance is available to human beings' in 'a state of nature' (Olafson, 1966, pp. 15, 18, 20-1).

Similarly, Perez Zagorin has argued that with Hobbes the concept of natural law 'has been absolutely emptied of its traditional meaning'. Zagorin associates 'traditional' natural law theory with the views of certain of the medieval scholastics, especially Aquinas. The essence of this traditional view, he claims, is that 'natural law was thought of as embodying ethical rules which were prior to and above the enactments of earthly communities'. Positive law is accepted as valid only if its commands 'were not thought incompatible with natural law'. Zagorin criticises this traditional natural law theory because if its failure to understand that 'even when we are presented with rules which are described as the dictates of natural law, they turn out to be meaningless without a positive legal order to define their operation'. Thus, for example, according to Zagorin, Aquinas takes the view that 'the prohibition of theft is an express first principle of natural law'. It is however, Zagorin insists, obvious 'that such a prohibition is devoid of sense until a positive legal order has defined property'. According to Zagorin, this is a point which Hobbes very well understood. Hobbesian natural law theory, therefore, is not only a departure from, it is also a considerable improvement on, 'the traditional notion of natural law' (Zagorin, 1954, pp.176-7).

As a matter of fact, however, these claims are entirely without foundation. It is certainly true that Hobbes subscribes to what we have termed a formal conception of natural law. And it is also true that Hobbes natural law theory, and especially his view of the relationship which exists between natural law and positive law, constitutes a departure from the stoic conception of natural law, as we find it in the writings of Cicero and others. Moreover, the claims made by Warrender, Olafson and Zagorin would have some substance to them if they were also justified in claiming that the stoic theory does adequately represent 'the' natural law tradition. Unfortunately, though, this last claim simply cannot be justified. For the stoic theory is simply one natural law tradition amongst others. There are other formal conceptions of natural law which pre-date that of Hobbes. These conceptions of natural law view the relationship between natural law and positive law in much the same way as Hobbes does. And these earlier formal conceptions have just as much right to be described as 'traditional' natural law theory as the stoic conception has (see Finnis, 1980, p.28).

Hobbes' view of the relationship which exists between natural law and positive law is in its central features not at all new. On the contrary, it is quite clearly to be found in the writings of some (perhaps most) of the scholastic natural law theorists of the medieval period. This view might even be said to be perfectly orthodox. It is itself 'traditional'. Indeed, and somewhat ironically, it is a view which is to be found in the writings of the very person from whose political thought Hobbesian natural law theory is alleged to constitute a radical departure, namely Aquinas (Aquinas, 1966, p. 115; Aquinas, 1969, pp. 41, 95, 105-7, 255; Battaglia, 1981, pp. 91-4; Copleston, 1955, p. 231; Finnis, 1980, pp. 284-6; Sabine, 1973, p. 242).

This type of natural law theory, however, does not of course originate in the writings of Aquinas. Nor does it originate in the writings of any of the other medieval scholastics. It has it origins, ultimately, as much of the political thought of Aquinas did, in the works of Aristotle. The view of the relationship which exists between natural law and positive law which we have here associated with formal conceptions of natural law is basically Aristotelian in character. It is an integral component element in the Aristotelian conception of natural law (Aquinas, 1964, p. 443; Barker, 1959, p. 327).

How then should we classify those political theorists who subscribe to such a formal conception of natural law? Are they 'genuine' natural law theorists or are they actually legal positivists? We have seen that, according to Crocker, the answer to this question depends on whether these theorists believe that justice (in the moral sense) is prior to law or, alternatively, that law is prior to justice. The theorists to whom we are referring, however, have a somewhat complex position with respect to this issue. Indeed, they have a position which at first sight seems to be a contradictory one. Thus, for example, it is evident that, in one sense, they do take the view that the concept of justice is logically prior to that of human positive law. Human positive law forbids the performance of certain actions, and the reason for, this is precisely because those actions are morally wrong. Being wrong is a characteristic these actions possess quite independently of any human positive law. They do not become wrong simply because they have been forbidden by such a law. It is for this reason that the theorists in question actually employ the concept of natural law in their writings.

On the other hand, though, no theorist subscribing to a formal conception of natural law considers natural law to be a critical standard by means of which the justice of positive law might be evaluated. As far as they are concerned, in the final analysis it is for positive law to decide whether or not the performance of some particular action in any given situation ought to be permitted (in both the moral as well as the legal sense), and hence whether this particular action is or is not just. In this sense at least, therefore, they take the view that justice is not prior but posterior to law.

These theorists, therefore, as we have seen, reject a principle which is not only central to the stoic conception of natural law but also, in the opinion of most commentators, central to natural law theory in general. They reject a principle which most commentators consider to be absolutely essential to any 'genuine' doctrine of natural law. Not surprisingly, this has led to considerable confusion and disagreement on the issue of how the ideas of these theorists should be classified, and hence interpreted. In particular, it has led many commentators to the conclusion that these theorists are actually not natural law theorists at all, but legal positivists. Thus, for example, Crocker takes the view that Hobbes 'revolted against natural law' and that the 'theorists of natural law' who wrote in the seventeenth and eighteenth centuries opposed his views, 'citing an eternal justice prior to law' (Crocker, 1962, pp. 36, 40). And d'Entreves has claimed that Hobbes 'with all his talk about the law of nature, is really outside the tradition of natural law'. According to d'Entreves, 'Hobbes is in fact the forerunner and founder of that theory of law which has ignored natural law altogether', namely the 'theory of 'legal positivism' (d'Entreves, 1970, p.122).

Given the assumptions which Crocker and 'd'Entreves make about the character of natural law theory, it is almost inevitable that they should arrive at this conclusion. It is, however, a conclusion which is somewhat problematical. This is so precisely because Hobbes' view of the relationship which exists between the principles of natural law and those of positive law is, in its essentials, actually shared by Aquinas and Aristotle. If, therefore, it is appropriate to conclude, on these grounds, that Hobbes is a legal positivist, then it is equally appropriate to arrive at the same conclusion in the case of Aquinas and Aristotle.

Such a conclusion would, of course, have an air of paradox about it for most people. Nevertheless one or two commentators, recognising the logical implications of their own basic assumptions about natural law theory, have in fact toyed with the idea that the views of Aristotle, and even Aquinas, do have affinities with the doctrine of legal positivism. Thus, for example, Kelsen makes this suggestion in the case of Aristotle (Kelsen, 1973a, pp. 127, 131-2; Kelsen, 1957a, p. 126). And Thomas Gilby has even gone so far as to claim that, in some respects, the views of Aquinas represent a disturbing 'trend towards legal positivism' in both church and state 'in the thirteenth century' (Gilby, 1958, pp.110-11).

Any claim to the effect that Aquinas should be classified as a legal positivist, the views of Gilby notwithstanding, would clearly seem to be inappropriate. Indeed, to the contrary, as Finnis as insisted, Aquinas 'is unquestionably a paradigm 'natural law theorist' (Finnis, 1980, p. 28). Despite this, however, the natural law theory of Aquinas is for the most part based on principles which are actually inconsistent with a commitment to the stoic conception of natural law. Like Hobbes, Aquinas subscribes to a formal conception of natural law. It follows from this, of course, that if we are justified in continuing to regard Aquinas as a genuine natural law theorist, then we are justified in considering Hobbes, and indeed any other theorist who subscribes to a formal conception of natural law, as being a genuine natural law theorist also.Generally speaking, therefore, the conclusion that those theorists who subscribe to a formal conception of natural law are not 'really' natural law theorists at all, but are rather legal positivists, must be considered to be untenable.

It should be evident from what has been said that the principal reason for the confusion and disagreement amongst commentators as to how theorists subscribing to a formal conception of natural law should be classified, and hence also interpreted, lies in the assumptions which they make about natural law and natural law theory. It lies in their belief that the stoic conception of natural law is the only possible conception of natural law, and that the stoic natural law tradition is the only authentic natural law tradition. It also lies in the sheer crudity of their employment of a simple classificatory schema which insists, in a procrustean manner, on locating the ideas of all political theorists into either one or the other of just two basic categories, neither of which adequately represents the subtlety of the views which many theorists hold on the question of the priority of justice or law.

In short, the principal reason for this confusion and disagreement lies in the adoption by commentators of a view of natural law which eliminates at the outset, by definitional fiat, even the theoretical possibility of there being such a thing as a formal conception of natural law. The solution to this problem, as in the case of voluntarist conceptions of natural law, is for us to adopt a much looser view of the character of natural law and natural law theory. It is to expand our classificatory schema so as to allow for the possibility of alternative, but no less authentic, natural law traditions alongside the stoic natural law tradition. It is only if we do this that we will be in a position to adequately understand the importance which the concept of natural law actually has for a number of major figures in the history of political thought. In particular, it is only by doing this that we shall be able to appreciate the significance which the notion of natural law has for the political thought of Hegel.

2 Hegel and natural law theory

We have already noted that commentators strongly disagree on the classification and interpretation of Hegel's political thought. Many argue that he is a legal positivist. Others maintain, to the contrary, that he is not. He is a natural law theorist in the conventional sense. To say that the existence of two such divergent, indeed mutually contradictory, interpretations of Hegel's political thought is something of a paradox would be to put the point somewhat mildly. It would be more accurate to describe it as astonishing. This, of course, immediately raises the question of how the existence of this paradox is to be explained. It also raises the question of how the disagreement associated with it might be resolved.

On the issue of explanation, there would seem to be two possibilities. The first is to suggest that Hegel's political thought is not internally consistent. Hegel contradicts himself, not only between texts but also, perhaps more significantly, within individual texts, especially within the *Philosophy of Right*. Sometimes he says things which support the view that he is a natural law theorist. At other times he says things which support the view that he is a legal positivist. The second possibility is that Hegel does not contradict himself. His ideas constitute a unified body of thought, both between texts and especially within the *Philosophy of Right* itself. The alleged contradiction, therefore, is more apparent and not real. It exists, not in Hegel and his ideas, but in the minds of Hegel's interpreters. These two explanations will be discussed in turn.

The structure of the *Philosophy of Right*

At times, notably in the First Part of the *Philosophy of Right*, which deals with what Hegel calls the sphere of 'abstract right', Hegel says things which certainly do support the conclusion that he is some sort of natural law theorist. More precisely, a reading of this part of the work undeniably gives the impression that Hegel's intention is to make a contribution to the tradition of political thought

42

developed by the modern natural law theorists of the seventeenth and eighteenth centuries, notably by John Locke.

From this point of view, Part One of the *Philosophy of Right* could be said to be the Hegelian equivalent of a discussion of what life would be like in some hypothetical 'state of nature'. Hegel considers here the question of whether isolated individuals living in a pre-political condition could be said to have any rights, simply in virtue of the fact that they are human being or 'persons'. Having answered this question in the affirmative, he goes on to consider the character of these abstract rights. Here the analysis focuses on themes which are central to modern natural law theory, especially that of Locke. Thus Hegel discusses the nature of property and property rights and whether there is a natural right to property. He discusses the problems that might be associated with the preservation or enforcement of such rights in a pre-political condition. Finally, he discusses the nature of punishment and of the right to punish individual violations of property rights in the absence of a state and the judicial apparatus associated with a system of positive law.

This affinity between Hegel's treatment of the sphere of abstract right and natural law theory has been noted by a number of commentators (Benhabib, 1984, p.160; Friedmann,1967, p.166; Friedrich, 1963, p.133; Ilting, 1971, p.91; Pelczynski, 1971, p.8; Riedel, 1971, p.143; Riedel, 1984, p.41).For example, according to Manfred Riedel 'the overall position of the *Philosophy of Right* remains in an important respect one of natural law'. The discussion of abstract right 'reproduces the pre-political condition of natural law theory' (Riedel, 1984, p.67). This view is also shared by Pelczynski, who goes even further than Riedel by tracing the intellectual ancestry of Hegel's thought back, not simply to Locke and the modern natural law theory of the seventeenth and eighteenth centuries, but to Roman law. According to Pelczynski by 'abstract right' Hegel means 'certain general principles of law which concern such personal rights as the rights to life and property'. These principles were 'derived from Roman law and developed and rationalised by generations of later jurists and exponents of natural law'. They form, Hegel believes, a body of general moral rules which necessarily underlie 'all positive legal systems of civilised countries in so far as these systems are rational' (Pelczynski, 1971, p.8)

It should, however, be noted that when these commentators refer to natural law theory or the natural law tradition, what they actually have in mind is what we have termed the stoic conception of natural law. It is, therefore, not too surprising to find these commentators arguing that, like Locke, Hegel is a natural law theorist in this particular sense. Thus, according to this interpretation, Hegel believes in the existence of natural law. He believes that natural law might be used as a critical standard for the evaluation of positive law. He accepts the doctrine of natural rights, as understood by Locke. And, again like Locke, he also accepts that one of the major functions of the state is to preserve and protect these natural rights, especially the right not to be enslaved and the right to hold private property (Hegel, 1979, pp. 17, 20, 42, 48, 52-3, 134, 136, 169, 224, 236, 239, 241, 283).

Elsewhere in the *Philosophy of Right*, however, notably in his treatment of the sphere of 'ethical life' in Part Three, Hegel appears to contradict everything that he says earlier in Part One about natural law and natural rights. He says things about the nature and function of the State, and about the nature of the relationship which exists (or ought to exist) between the individual and the state, which support the conclusion that he totally rejects the notions of natural law and natural rights, together with the liberal theory of the state that is usually associated with these notions. This attitude of mind may be illustrated by Hegel's claim that 'if the state is confused with civil society, and if its specific end is laid down as the security and protection of property and personal freedom, then the interests of individuals as such becomes the ultimate end of their association' This, however, is to misunderstand the purpose of the state. For 'the state's relationship to the individual is quite different from this'. The state is 'an absolute unmoved end in itself'. As such, it 'has supreme right against the individual, whose supreme duty is to be a member of the state' (Hegel, 1979, pp.156-7).

Establishing precisely what Hegel means when he says this is, of course, not an easy matter. Nevertheless, a cursory reading of this particular passage certainly does give the impression that Hegel emphatically rejects the view that the purpose of the state is either to preserve the freedom of the individual, or to protect the individual's natural rights. Such a view, he suggests here, is based on a misunderstanding of the role of the state. It actually reverses the relationship of priority which ought to exist between the individual and the state.

It is, therefore, again no surprise to find that some of Hegel's interpreters should have arrived at the conclusion, on the basis of a reading of Part Three of the *Philosophy of Right*, that Hegel completely rejects the notions of natural law and natural rights and that he is in fact a legal positivist (see also Hegel, 1979, pp. 59, 71, 88, 91, 165-6, 209, 215, 217, 242, 259, 266-7, 279, 284-5).

At first sight, then, Hegel does appear to contradict himself. There seems to be no systematic argument which is developed throughout the *Philosophy of Right* as whole. This is something which has been noted by G. H. Sabine, who maintains that the *Philosophy of Right* 'is a book that cannot profitably be summarised'. This so, according to Sabine, because 'it is fundamentally ill-arranged' (Sabine, 1973, p.579).

From this point of view, therefore, the disagreement between commentators as to how Hegel should be classified and interpreted is not difficult to explain. Given the absence of a coherent structure to the *Philosophy of Right*, it is only to be expected that commentators should disagree as to the interpretation of Hegel's political thought as a whole. Those who maintain that Hegel is a natural law theorist tend to focus on what Hegel says in Part One and to ignore altogether what he has to say in Part Three. Alternatively, those who maintain that Hegel is a legal positivist tend to base their interpretation on a reading of Part Three and to ignore Part One. Such an attitude, for example, is adopted by Sabine, who maintains that it was 'the third part, and especially its last two subdivisions on civil society and the state, that contained Hegel's important conclusions' (Sabine, 1973, p.579). A similar position is also taken by Friedmann, who dismisses Hegel's treatment of 'abstract right' as having no significance at all for anyone seeking to provide an assessment of the essence of Hegel's political thought. This is so, Friedmann maintains, because in his discussion of abstract right 'Hegel relapses into natural law theories which are contrary to his whole philosophical system' (Friedmann, 1967, p.166).

Each of these two interpretations, then, tends to focus on just one part of the *Philosophy of Right* and to ignore the others. Neither interpretation makes any real effort to relate the different parts of the book to one another, or to discern any underlying structure or unity, that is to say a definite argument, in the work considered as a whole. In both cases it appears to be assumed that , as a matter of fact, the work does not actually possess such a unified structure.

Hegel's interpreters and natural law theory

According to the second explanation of the disagreement which exists with respect to the classification and interpretation of Hegel's political thought, this disagreement has occurred, not because of anything which Hegel himself says, but because of the inadequacies of the classificatory system which is adopted by Hegel's interpreters. Above all it has arisen as a consequence of the erroneous assumptions which commentators have made about natural law and natural law theory, and especially about the relationship which holds, or is supposed to hold, from the standpoint of natural law theory, between natural law and positive law.

From this point of view, the majority of Hegel's interpreters have misunderstood Hegel's attitude towards natural law. In the case of those who classify Hegel as a legal positivist, this is so because they simply do not appreciate the importance which Hegel attaches to the notion of natural law in the *Philosophy of Right*. In the case of those who consider him to be a natural law theorist, this is because they have assumed that Hegel subscribes to what we have termed the stoic conception of natural law, when in fact he does not.

According to this second explanation, then, Hegel is not a legal positivist. He is undeniably a natural law theorist. However, he is not a natural law theorist in the sense in which this term is conventionally understood. In certain respects, and especially with respect to its attitude towards the relationship which exists between natural law and positive law, Hegel's natural law theory does not conform to the stereotype laid down by the stoic conception of natural law. For Hegel subscribes to a formal conception of natural law.

From this standpoint it is the popular, though unjustified, assumption that the stoic conception of natural law is the only possible conception that is the root cause of all of the problems of interpretation encountered so far. It is because they have made this assumption that the commentators to whom we have referred have come to diametrically opposed, and equally erroneous, conclusions as to how Hegel should be classified. And it is because they make this assumption that they have completely misunderstood the significance which the concept of natural law has for any adequate understanding of Hegel's political thought as a whole.

Moreover, from this standpoint, the alleged contradiction in Hegel's thinking which is supposed to lie at the heart of the *Philosophy of Right* is actually more apparent than real. The erroneous belief in the existence of such a contradiction is in fact, once more, the reflection a complete misunderstanding of Hegel. Although, on this occasion, what is misunderstood is the argument which Hegel presents in the work as a whole and the unity of that argument's underlying structure.

This suggests, of course, that there is some third interpretation of Hegel which makes much better sense of what he has to say about natural law, natural rights, and the relationship which exists between the individual and the state. There is an interpretation which succeeds in reconciling the apparently contradictory statements which Hegel makes on these subjects in the different parts of the *Philosophy of Right*. This is an interpretation which, at the same time, succeeds in laying bare the unifying thread which runs throughout the argument of this work. Thus it is an interpretation which offers a better understanding of Hegel's political thought as a whole, precisely because it places his views on natural law (properly understood) where they belong, at the very centre of the system.

What follows is an exploration of this third interpretation. We shall begin with a discussion, not of the *Philosophy of Right*, but of one of Hegel's earlier works, in which he subjects the ideas associated with natural law and natural law theory to critical examination.

Hegel's essay *On the Scientific Ways of Treating Natural Law*

An important source for anyone seeking to assess Hegel's attitude towards natural law theory is his early essay, *On the Scientific Ways of Treating Natural Law* (Hegel, 1975). This essay is of great interest for both Hegel scholars and for students of natural law theory. It helps us to clarify Hegel's attitude towards natural law and natural law theory. It also helps us to understand the importance which the concept of natural law has for the mature expression of Hegel's political thought which is to be found in the *Philosophy of Right.*

Hegel's argument in this early essay is frequently obscure and difficult to interpret (see Smith, 1991, pp. 65-80; also Avineri, 1972, pp.82-85; Dallmayr, 1993, pp. 45-49; Neumann, 1957, pp.70-72; Riedel, 1984). We shall confine ourselves, therefore, to providing a summary account of what, from our own point of view, are its most important themes.

In essence, the task which Hegel sets himself in this essay is to subject two different types of natural law theory to a critical examination. He attempts to draw out the strengths and weaknesses of each of these approaches and to consider how they might be synthesised into a third type of natural law theory which incorporates the strengths of both and the weaknesses of neither. These two theories are what Hegel calls the empirical and the formal conceptions of natural law respectively. The first he associates with the liberal, individualistic doctrine of the rights orientated social contract theorists of the seventeenth and eighteenth centuries (Hegel, 1975, pp.59-70). It is not entirely clear who Hegel has in mind here. Smith suggests that he is thinking of Hobbes and Locke, whereas Neumann suggests that he is referring to Hobbes and Rousseau (Smith, 1991, p.65; Neumann, 1957, p.70). The second approach Hegel associates, unequivocally, with the names of Kant and Fichte (Hegel, 1975, pp.70-83).

The empirical conception of natural law

Hegel makes two key points in criticism of the empirical conception of natural law. The first of these, essentially, is that the approach adopted by this type of natural law theory is based on a circular argument. Natural law theorists, here, are seeking to establish that individuals living together in society have certain rights which others ought to respect. In order to defend this claim, they present to the reader an account of what life would be like in some hypothetical 'state of nature'. They provide 'a list of the capacities found in man, as the nature and destiny of man' (Hegel, 1975, p.63). In other words, they provide a description of human behaviour, and of certain rights and duties associated with it, which are alleged to be 'natural', and hence also of course morally desirable.

According to Hegel, however, this procedure is a dubious one. It is dubious because empirical natural law theory actually derives these so called 'natural' rights and duties on the basis of the observation of human behaviour as we find it manifested, not in 'nature', but in contemporary society. In a manner of speaking, therefore, this type of natural law theory is guilty of assuming in advance the validity of the conclusion which it sets out to prove. As Hegel puts it, if we 'think away everything' which belongs 'to particular manners, to history, to civilisation' then of course what remains is man in 'the bare state of nature', and 'we have only to look in order to find what is necessary' (Hegel, 1975, pp. 63-4). In this way, 'the desired outcome is presupposed' (Hegel, 1975, p. 65).

The theoretical problem associated with the adoption of this procedure, in Hegel's view, is that empirical natural law theory lacks any criterion for determining 'what in the chaos of the state of nature or in the abstraction of man must remain and what must be discarded'. It is, therefore, forced to operate on the principle that 'as much must remain as is required for the exposition of what is found in the real world' (Hegel, 1975, p.64). Thus empirical natural law theory is actually incapable of distinguishing those patterns of behaviour, rights and duties, which are actually natural, and hence 'necessary', from those which are social, and therefore merely 'accidental' (Hegel, 1975, p.64).

This is a line of reasoning which is not in fact strikingly original. It had already been made by some of the critics of Hobbes, writing in the eighteenth century, notably by Montesquieu in his *The Spirit of the Laws* (Montesquieu, 1952) and later by Rousseau in his *Discourse on the Origins of Inequality* (Rousseau, 1975; Neumann, 1957, pp. 70-71). Thus, according to Montesquieu, Hobbes takes the view that the urge to dominate others is a 'natural impulse or desire'. This, however, is evidently incorrect. For the urge to dominate others is a desire which only occurs to men who are living in society. As Montesquieu puts it, 'is it not obvious' that Hobbes 'attributes to mankind before the establishment of society what can happen but in consequence of this establishment?' (Montesquieu, 1952, p.2) Similarly, according to Rousseau, all of the natural law theorists of the seventeenth and eighteenth centuries who preceded him 'felt the necessity of going back to a state of nature'. Unfortunately, though, in Rousseau's opinion, 'not one of them' has actually 'got there'. Each of them 'has transferred to the state of nature ideas which were acquired in society; so that in speaking of the savage, they described the social man' (Rousseau, 1975, p.45).

However, despite its lack of originality, this is a point to which Hegel attaches some considerable importance. For example, he alludes to it again later on in the *Philosophy of Right,* when (in an implicit criticism of Hobbes) he suggests that it is not a 'state of nature' but rather 'civil society' which 'is the battlefield where everyone's individual private interest' meets that of 'everyone else' (Hegel, 1979, p.189). Thus here also the conflict which exists between individuals in society is not 'natural'. On the contrary, it is a phenomenon which has predominantly social causes. In Hegel's opinion, this conflict is a peculiarly modern phenomenon. It is associated with the 'invasion of ethical corruption' and hence the 'downfall' of the ancient world, in which human behaviour was, allegedly, not motivated by the principle of self-interest (Hegel, 1979, p.123).

It is, moreover, not only Hegel who attaches importance to this argument. For it is an argument which appears to have had a significant impact on other social and political theorists who come after Hegel and who were influenced by Hegel's ideas. This is particularly true in the case of Marx. Marx's response to this argument of Hegel's, in his *Critique of Hegel's Philosophy of Right,* is to observe that the point which Hegel makes here 'is remarkable', and this is so precisely 'because of its definition of civil society as the *bellum omnium contra omnes*' (Marx, 1977, p.101).

More or less the same point has also been made, much more recently, presumably as a consequence of the influence of Marx, by C. B. MacPherson. The notion that in *Leviathan* Hobbes is in fact describing the behaviour, not of man but of 'bourgeois man', lies at the heart of MacPherson's interpretation of Hobbes as a key representative of what he calls the 'political theory of possessive individualism'. For MacPherson, also, it is evident that Hobbes's state of nature 'is not about 'natural' man as opposed to civilised man'. It is, rather, about men 'as they are now, with natures formed by living in civilised society' (MacPherson, 1975, p.18; see also MacPherson, 1965; Berlin, 1964; Gauthier, 1977; Lessnoff, 1986; Ryan, 1971; Viner, 1963).

The second major defect of the empirical conception of natural law, in Hegel's view, and one which is closely associated with the first, is that it is a theory which focuses on the idea of a 'content without form'. It does not seek to derive the rights and duties which it claims are natural, rationally, by showing how they are related to some higher, formal principle of right. Neither, therefore, does it show how these rights and duties are actually related to one another. It does not demonstrate that they all possess one common feature, namely that they can all be said to constitute a part of the substantive, rational content of such a formal principle.

As a result, the approach adopted by this type of natural law theory is, Hegel maintains, basically 'arbitrary'. In this respect also, this approach focuses on the merely 'accidental' and misses that which 'essential'. It fails to establish the unity which underlies the plurality and diversity of these different rights and duties. Empirical natural law theory is only able to present its own principles as having what Hegel calls an 'empirical necessity'. It fails completely to capture the relationship of 'inner necessity' which exists between them (Hegel, 1975, pp. 61, 64-5).

Hegel is not alone in taking this view. J. W. Yolton has maintained that Locke, for example, at least in his *Essays on the Law of Nature,* 'nowhere formulates a general maxim which he calls 'the law of nature'. For Locke, 'there is no such single and general law'. The law of nature in fact turns out 'to be a list of laws' such as, for example, 'Do not kill or steal', or 'Keep your promises' (Yolton, 1958, p.488).

This particular criticism of modern natural law theory is, however, quite unjustified. Contrary to what Hegel and Yolton might think, most of the natural law theorists of the seventeenth and eighteenth centuries, including Locke, do isolate some single, basic principle, which is held to be the most fundamental principle of natural law and hence also morality. This is usually some version or other of what we may term the principle of equity or reciprocity. Thus, for example, to take the case of Locke, in his *Essays* Locke points out that all of the principles which are on Yolton's so called 'list of laws' do in fact share the same characteristic feature. They are all what Locke refers to as 'the common rules of human equity' (Locke, 1958, p.207). In the case of Hobbes, the basic principle of natural law is the so called Golden Rule', 'Do not do unto others that which you would not have done to yourself' (Hobbes, 1839-45a, pp. 40, 44-5, 57, 61-2; Hobbes, 1839-45b, pp. 118, 141-2, 144,153, 258, 279, 494). The importance of the Golden Rule is also emphasised by most of the other members of the continental school of natural law the seventeenth and eighteenth centuries, for example, Samuel Pufendorf, Christian Wolff and Jean-Jacques Burlamaqui

(Pufendorf, 1934, pp. 196-7, 204-5, 330, 332, 336-7, 962; Pufendorf, 1931, pp.240-1; Pufendorf, 1716, pp. 141, 245; Wolff, 1758, pp. 10-11, 48, 50; Wolff, 1772, pp. 141-3; Burlamaqui, 1748, pp. 297-9).

The formal conception of natural law

Hegel's criticism of the second type of modern natural law theory, the formal conception of natural law, is on the other hand that this is an approach which is associated with the idea of a 'form without content'. It focuses exclusively on the basic principle of natural law or right, construed as a purely formal principle. It does not seek to show how this purely formal principle might be related to the specific rights, duties and obligations which constitute its rational or objective content. On the contrary, it takes the view that there is in fact no such rational content, or objective system of duties and rights, such as for example property rights, which are necessarily associated with this formal principle. The substantive content for this formal principle, and hence the subsidiary principles of morality or ethics, are to be provided by individual moral agents themselves, in the light of their own consciences. This approach, therefore, constitutes what Hegel refers to as an empty 'formalism' (Hegel, 1975, pp. 75-6; also Smith, 1991, pp. 73-80).

The point which Hegel is making here is quite straightforward. The fundamental principle of morality in the Kantian philosophy is the so called Categorical Imperative. According to Hegel, this asserts that we should always act in such a way that 'a maxim of thy will shall count at the same time as a principle of universal legislation' (Hegel, 1975, p.76). As Hegel understands it, this principle is in effect an alternative formulation of the Golden Rule. It tells each individual that in order to act morally what is required is that they should only do to others things which they are prepared to have done to themselves. That is to say, they should only be prepared to act consistently on 'maxims' which they sincerely consider to be 'universalisable'.

In Hegel's view, however, this principle is entirely inadequate as a characterisation of the fundamental principle of natural law or morality. His objection to it is similar to that which many commentators have raised when discussing the Golden Rule (Blackstone, 1965; Erikson, 1964; Gould, 1963; Gould, 1980; Gould, 1983a; Gould, 1983b; Gewirth, 1978a; Gewirth, 1978b; Singer, 1963). He objects to it because, from the standpoint of this principle, 'there is nothing whatever' which could not 'be made into a moral law' depending on the circumstances (Hegel, 1975, p.77). For any action at all, including actions which Hegel evidently thinks are intrinsically wrong, such as for example murder and theft, could be morally justified on these grounds, provided the individuals who performed these actions did so with a clear conscience, and were themselves prepared to act consistently and hence accept the consequences of such a policy being generally adopted or universalised.

Hegel's interpretation of Kantian moral philosophy attributes to Kant views which are similar to those adopted, in the twentieth century, by the moral philosopher R. M. Hare (Hare, 1972; Hare, 1981; Singer, 1983, pp. 32-3).The Categorical Imperative, as Hegel understands it, might be said to be the Kantian equivalent of Hare's principle of universalisability. It could be argued that, in effect, Hegel transforms Kant into an eighteenth century precursor of Hare's prescriptivist moral philosophy. Moreover, Hare's moral theory also has been subjected to criticism in much the same way as Hegel criticises Kant, namely because of its lack of substantive content and its inability to rule out as immoral actions which most people would consider to be wrong even though the individuals who wished to perform them are sincerely prepared to universalise them (Bronaugh, 1968; Curtler, 1971; Donagan, 1964-65; Emmett, 1963; Robins, 1974; Silverstein, 1973; Warnock, 1967).

Hegel is very fond of the criticism which he makes of Kant in his essay on natural law. He more or less repeats it, a few years later, in the *Phenomenology of Mind*. And it turns up again in the *Philosophy of Right* (Hegel, 1977, pp. 254-62; Hegel, 1979, pp. 85, 90-1, 97-9, 251, 254; also Houlgate, 1991, pp. 95-7; Knox, 1957-58; O'Hagan, 1987; Walsh, 1969). It is, however, debatable whether the view which Hegel criticises in the essay is one which Kant actually held himself. For example, in his *Groundwork to a Metaphysics of Morals* Kant actually dismisses the claim that the Golden Rule is an adequate formulation of the basic principle of morality as being 'trivial' (Kant, 1972, p.92). He evidently does not consider the Categorical Imperative to be simply an alternative formulation of this principle (Curtler, 1971; Gould, 1983a; Hirst, 1934). More than one commentator has argued that any claim to the effect that Kant's doctrine is nothing but an empty formalism is totally unjustified.

For these commentators, Kant's position is in effect fundamentally the same as that of Hegel himself, and hence quite different from that of someone like Hare. For, like Hegel, Kant also argues that the fundamental principle of morality is not a purely formal principle. It is necessarily associated with certain subsidiary principles of morality, which constitute its substantive content (Murphy, 1970, pp.65-86; Smith, 1991, p.78; Williams, 1968, pp. 68, 104, 106-7, 110-11, 124, 126, 130, 134; Wolff, 1973, pp. 117, 132, 138, 177, 181; Wolff, 1977, pp. 20, 103, 108, 110-11).

Perhaps the best contemporary illustration of someone who adopts this particular approach to the interpretation of Kant is provided by John Rawls. According to Rawls, 'it is a mistake' to over emphasise 'the place of generality and universality in Kant's ethics'. This is so simply because, as Hegel also well understood, it is 'impossible to construct a moral theory on so slender a basis'. Hence, to limit any discussion of Kant's doctrine to these notions 'is to reduce it to triviality'. In Rawls's opinion, therefore, the 'real force' of Kant's doctrine 'lies elsewhere' (Rawls, 1978, p.251). Such a substantive interpretation of Kant's moral philosophy lies at the heart of Rawl's own attempt to revive classical social contract theory in his *A Theory of Justice*. It should be noted, though, that Rawls's interpretation of Kant has itself been subjected to criticism (Baumrin, 1976; Darwall, 1976; Johnson, 1974-75; Johnson, 1976-77; Levine, 1974; Mason, 1976).

Hegel's synthesis of the empirical and formal conceptions of natural law

The line of reasoning associated with Hegel's attempt to offer a synthesis of these two types of natural law theory focuses on the idea of 'form plus content'. Hegel maintains that an adequate natural law theory must do three things. First it must establish what the basic, formal principle of natural law actually is. Second it must show how this formal principle can be related to an objective system of rights and duties which might be said to constitute its rational, substantive content. Third it must show how these various rights and duties, and hence also the subsidiary principles of natural law with which they are associated, are conditioned, historically, by the customs and traditions which are peculiar to the 'ethical life' of a particular people or nation (Hegel, 1975, pp. 96, 100, 106, 112-13; Riedel, 1984, pp. 81-2).

That the subsidiary principles of natural law do manifest themselves in different ways in different societies, and hence are conditioned historically, is something which Hegel takes for granted in the essay. According to Hegel, the specific forms which this conditioning takes in different societies constitutes the subject matter, not of natural law theory, but of a quite separate discipline, namely 'political science'. From this point of view, the subject matter of natural law theory is in one sense quite different from that of political science. For the former deals with that which, in the sphere of morality and politics, is necessary and universal, whereas the latter deals with that which is merely accidental and hence historically specific. In another sense, however, as we shall see, the respective subject matters of these two disciplines are actually quite closely related to one another. It is this distinction that Hegel had in mind, later on, when he decided to give his major work of political theory the title *Natural Law and Political Science in Outline* (Riedel,1984, pp. 35-6, 162-3). An understanding of Hegel's view of the relationship which exists between natural law theory and political science is therefore essential for the understanding, not only of the early essay on natural law, but also of Hegel's mature system of political thought.

In the essay on natural law Hegel clearly associates this third type of natural law theory with the political thought of the ancient Greeks and especially with the Greek idea of the polis considered as an 'ethical community' (Hegel, 1975, pp. 112-13; 96, 100, 106). It is Hegel's view that an adequate natural law theory, and hence an adequate theoretical approach to politics based on the idea of natural law, must incorporate some reference to such an ethical community. The principles of natural law, both the purely formal principle and the subsidiary principles which constitute its substantive content, must be related in some way to

52

the customs, morals and traditions, in short the 'laws' of such an ethical community. They must be related to that community's 'ethical life'.

Hegel singles out two individuals in particular as key sources for anyone seeking to develop such an adequate natural law theory. The first, as Riedel has noted, is the political thought of Aristotle (Hegel, 1975, pp. 96, 100, 196, 112-13; Riedel, 1984, pp. 81-2). The second is the political thought of Montesquieu, which may, like Hegel's own work, be regarded as contributing to a general revival of interest in the political thought of the ancient Greeks in the eighteenth century. In the essay Hegel refers to *The Spirit of the Laws* as Montesquieu's 'immortal work' (Hegel, 1975, pp. 128-9; Smith, 1991, p. 72).

It is of course not strikingly original to suggest that Hegel owes a general debt to the ancient Greeks and especially to Aristotle (Riedel, 1984, pp. 81-2; Ritter, 1982, pp. 144-7, 163-8; Taylor, 1989, p. 378; Taylor, 1979, p. 84). It is, however, important to note to that the line of reasoning which Hegel adopts in his essay on natural law can only really be understood if its is related to a specifically Aristotelian conception of natural law, and to Aristotelian natural law theory. This again is a point which has been emphasised by Riedel. According to Riedel, throughout the essay, in his 'struggle against current systems of natural law', Hegel is compelled 'to revert to an earlier time's natural theory of law and society'. The concept of 'nature' which Hegel employs here 'is the traditional one', which he 'attempts to renew as a fruitful basic principle of natural law'. Thus Hegel employs this concept of nature 'in the sense of Aristotle's doctrine that the polis is according to nature prior to the individual'. And hence, as the foundation of his own doctrine, he 'appeals to Aristotle'. It is to Aristotle's political thought that Hegel turns in his efforts to incorporate 'within natural law theory' the idea of what he refers to as 'ethical nature' (Riedel, 1984, pp. 81-2).

The suggestion here, then, is that in this early essay on natural law Hegel is extremely critical of the modern natural law theory of the seventeenth and eighteenth centuries, in both of its major forms. He rejects modern natural law theory, with its emphasis on the idea of a state of nature and the social contract above all because of what he considers to be its excessive individualism. Modern natural law theory, especially because of its 'cosmopolitanism' and its doctrine of natural rights (which Hegel, echoing Burke, considers to be merely 'abstractions', filled with 'exactly the opposite of ethical vitality') is fundamentally inadequate. And this is so, basically, because its political implications are 'revolutionary' (Hegel, 1975, pp. 132-3).

Hegel does not, however, reject the idea of natural law altogether in the essay. Nor does he abandon the idea that it is necessary to construct a theoretical approach to politics based on the idea of natural law. What is required, Hegel maintains, is the construction of an adequate natural law theory, and for Hegel the intellectual starting point for the development of such a theory is Aristotle and the Aristotelian conception of natural law.

53

So far as we are concerned, then, the most important point to note about Hegel's own conception of natural law in this early essay is that it is a modified version of the Aristotelian conception which differs quite markedly, not only from 'modern' natural law theory, but also (implicitly) from what we have ourselves referred to as the stoic conception of natural law. The principal difference here is that Hegel's own theory does not have any revolutionary political implications. Hegel's doctrine of natural law is not committed to any abstract theory of natural rights in the modern sense. Nor is it committed to the idea that there is some critical standard which individuals might use to evaluate the positive law of the ethical community in which they live.

We may complete this brief examination of Hegel's early essay on natural law by considering the attitude of just two of Hegel's interpreters towards it. We shall see that in both cases the argument of the text, and Hegel's intentions in writing it, have been misunderstood. The reason for this misunderstanding lies in the mistaken assumptions which have been made about the character of natural law and natural law theory. It lies in the assumption that there is only one authentic natural law tradition, the stoic tradition.

Our first example is provided by the editor of the English translation of the essay on natural law, H. B. Acton. In his *Introduction* Acton is puzzled by the fact that Hegel should have written the essay at all, or at least that he should have given the title that he did. As Acton himself puts it, Hegel's employment of the term 'Naturrecht' in the title of the essay 'is paradoxical, since he rejects the whole idea that society is deliberately formed by the association of pre-existing individuals'. Indeed, according to Acton, Hegel goes even further than this and 'in effect holds that the positive law of each state is more rational and fundamental than any supposed law of nature held to be valid always and everywhere' (Acton, 1975, pp. 15-16).

Acton is puzzled by what Hegel has to say precisely because, like so many other, he wrongly assumes that all genuine natural law theories are individualistic; that all natural law theories assume the existence of a pre-political state of nature; and that all natural law theories consider natural law to be a critical standard for the evaluation of positive law. As Acton very well understands, in his essay on natural law Hegel rejects these basic assumptions of stoic natural law theory, in its various modern forms. Thus, from Acton's point of view, Hegel rejects the notion of natural law altogether. And it follows from this (although Acton does not make the point explicitly) that Hegel must be considered to be a legal positivist.

The fact that Acton is puzzled is not at all surprising. For it is evident that if one were to identify stoic natural law theory as being the only genuine form of natural law theory; and if one were to acknowledge that Hegel does indeed reject the basic principles associated with such a theory; one would be quite unable to understand why it should be that Hegel nevertheless insists that his essay is a contribution to the development of a theoretical approach to politics based on the notion of natural law. And of course one would also be quite unable to understand why Hegel chose to give his essay the title that he did. It is interesting to note, as we shall see, that exactly the same confusion has also occurred in connection with Hegel's *Philosophy of Right*. The source of this confusion does not, however, lie in anything which Hegel says, either in his early essay or in the *Philosophy of Right* itself. It lies, rather, in the mistaken assumptions which Hegel's interpreters make about natural law and natural law theory.

Our second example is provided by Shlomo Avineri. According to Avineri, in this early essay of natural law Hegel completely rejects what Avineri himself refers to (somewhat confusingly) as 'classical' natural law theory. Hegel does this, in Avineri's view, because classical natural law theory considers the state to be an instrument for the protection of individual liberty and natural rights, especially property rights. Hegel, however, has no time for such a view of nature and purposes of the state. Hegel's view, Avineri maintains, is that 'under no conditions should the state be conceived as an instrument for the preservation and defence of property'. Thus 'the antimony to classical natural law theories could not be more explicit' (Avineri, 1972, p. 85).

It seems evident that, in Avineri's opinion, because Hegel rejects the principles of so called 'classical natural law theory', it follows that he rejects natural law theory altogether. What he is trying to do in this early essay, therefore, is to move beyond the limitations that are placed upon speculation in the sphere of politics by the assumptions of classical natural law theory. The essay on natural law constitutes 'Hegel's attempt to transcend the limits of natural law theories' in the study of politics (Avineri, 1972, p. 86).

An implication of this analysis is that Avineri is quite unable to understand how the last part of Hegel's essay could possibly be regarded as itself being a contribution to natural law theory, or to a theoretical approach to politics based on the idea of natural law. It is not at all surprising, therefore, that he should take the view that Hegel's essay on natural law lacks a coherent structure and that, despite its title, the essay is much wider in scope than 'a mere treatment of natural law' (Avineri, 1972, p. 82).

As a matter of fact, though, Hegel's essay is not wider in scope than a mere treatment of natural law. It does not include material that is irrelevant to a discussion of natural law theory. And it does not seek to transcend the limitations of a natural law approach to the study of politics. On the contrary, in so far as Hegel is concerned, this early essay is itself a contribution to the development of such a theoretical approach. The essay does, most certainly, constitute a rejection of the stoic conception of natural law in either of its modern forms. And one might say that it is an attempt to transcend the limitations of a theoretical approach to politics based on such a conception of natural law. It is not, however, an attempt to abandon the natural law approach to politics altogether. It would be much more accurate to say that in the essay Hegel is attempting to criticise one particular natural law tradition from the standpoint of another. Hegel rejects stoic

55

natural law theory only in order to embrace that of Aristotle. This is something which Avineri does not seem able to appreciate, presumably because he only recognises the existence of one natural law tradition and one type of natural law theory, the theory which he misleadingly refers to as 'classical' natural law theory.

The essay on natural law and the *Philosophy of Right*

That there is a close relationship between Hegel's early essay on natural law and the *Philosophy of Right* is something which has been noted by a number of commentators (Riedel, 1984, p.76). Thus, for example, the three part structure of the *Philosophy of Right* mirrors more or less exactly the corresponding structure of the earlier essay. The First Part deals with the subject matter of that section of the early essay which focuses on the empirical conception of natural law. The Second Part considers the issues dealt with in the earlier treatment of the formal conception of natural law. And the Third Part corresponds to that section of the earlier essay in which Hegel seeks to transcend the limitations of the empirical and formal conceptions of natural law by constructing a synthesis of them based on a revival and modification of the Aristotelian conception of natural law.

There is, of course, much more in the *Philosophy of Right* than there is in the early essay. Hegel's views do undergo a process of change and development in the intervening period between the publication of these two works. In particular, in the *Philosophy of Right*, Hegel emphasises strongly the value of 'subjective freedom' or individual freedom of conscience. This emphasis is not to be found in the earlier essay. Nor indeed, as Hegel himself is careful to point out, is it to be found in the political thought of the ancient Greeks (Hegel, 1979, pp. 84, 123-4, 267-8, 280). It is a value which Hegel associates with modern political thought, with modern conceptions of natural law, and especially with the philosophy of Kant.

It is important to note that Hegel's attitude towards the value of subjective freedom is not one of unreserved hostility. On the contrary, his attitude is a very positive one. The individual desire for subjective freedom is a desire which ought, in so far as it is possible, to be satisfied (Hegel, 1979, pp. 87, 89, 251, 253, 286). Nevertheless, there are limits regarding the extent to which one may go in this direction. To permit an unrestricted freedom of conscience would be to undermine the existing moral (and hence also social) order.

Hegel therefore seeks to incorporate a commitment to the value of subjective freedom into the system of political thought which he develops in the *Philosophy of Right* (Hegel, 1979, pp. 91, 103-4, 106, 109, 161, 255, 258-9, 280). In so doing he undeniably attempts to transcend some of the limitations of Aristotelian natural law theory. This is a point which has been noted by Joachim Ritter. According to Ritter, the *Philosophy of Right* is an attempt to revive the 'institutional ethics' associated with Aristotelian political thought whilst at the same time incorporating 'the great principle of subjectivity and morality'. Hence, in this respect at least, it must be acknowledged that 'ethical life in Hegel is no longer identical with the 'ethos' of Aristotelian practical philosophy' (Ritter, 1982, p. 168; see also Colletti, 1977, pp.30-1).

It is true, as Riedel has pointed out, that after the publication of the early essay on natural law Hegel came to have certain reservations about the general approach which he adopts within it. And it is also true that one way of recording this change in his thinking would be to suggest that it is associated with a weakening of the influence of Aristotle upon him. Nevertheless, although this must be acknowledged, it remains the case that even in the *Philosophy of Right* the influence of Aristotle upon Hegel remains very strong. It would certainly be going too far to suggest, as Riedel seems to do, that in the later work Hegel more or less abandons Aristotle completely, and hence that there is some sort of Althusserian radical break in the development of Hegel's thinking between the essay on natural law and the *Philosophy of Right* (Riedel, 1982, pp. 88, 96, 100, 103; also Dallmayr, 1993, pp. 88-9). Despite Hegel's own reservations, one of the foundation stones of the theory which Hegel outlines in the *Philosophy of Right* remains the political thought of Aristotle, and hence the Aristotelian conception of natural law.

It is, presumably, precisely because the structure of the two works is so similar that so many commentators have taken the view that the essay on natural law is an early version of the *Philosophy of Right* itself. However, the full significance of this has not always been appreciated. For a logical implication of this view is that if, in the earlier essay, Hegel does not reject the notion of natural law and of natural law theory but is, on the contrary, attempting to construct an adequate theoretical approach to politics based on the Aristotelian conception of natural law; and if, further, it is correct that the essay may be considered to be an early version of the ideas which are developed more fully in the *Philosophy of Right*; then it follows that the *Philosophy of Right* itself is a work which is best understood by locating it against the background of the natural law tradition. The *Philosophy of Right* is Hegel's attempt to develop an adequate theoretical approach to politics, based on the notion of natural law.

This assessment of the significance of the concept of natural law for Hegel's political thought, with its clear implication that Hegel is best interpreted as being some sort of natural law theorist, is considerably reinforced when we remind ourselves of something which seems not to have been sufficiently appreciated, namely the title which Hegel chose to give to his major work of political theory when he first published it.

The book that is commonly referred to as the *Philosophy of Right* has what T. M. Knox has called a 'double title' (Knox, 1970, p.14; Knox, 1979, p.v). It is not immediately obvious what Knox actually means by this. However, an examination of the title pages of the first edition provides us with some assistance. Somewhat unusually Hegel's work actually has not one but two title pages. On the first title page the title of the work is given as *Naturrecht und Staatswissenschaft im Grundrisse*. On the second title page the work is given the quite different, and more well known, title of *Grundlinien der Philosophie des Rechts* (Hegel, 1955).

57

The fact that Hegel's work has not one but two titles is both interesting and important, for two reasons. In the first place it establishes that the title *Naturrecht und Staatswissenschaft im Grundrisse* is most definitely not, as is often assumed, a sub-title of the work. On the contrary, it is the first of the work's two main titles (Dallmayr, 1993, pp. 21, 96; Riedel, 1984, p. 162). In the second place, it establishes that the original title of Hegel's work contains an explicit reference to the notion of natural law. A straightforward reading of this title indicates, quite unequivocally, that Hegel himself is of the opinion that his book is a contribution to natural law theory. Indeed, as Knox also points out, in his papers Hegel actually refers to the work as his 'forthcoming book on Naturrecht' (Knox, 1970, p.16).

It is, as Riedel has pointed out, 'remarkable' that Hegel should have given his work such a 'double title' (Riedel, 1984, p. 162). It is, however, even more remarkable that the fact that Hegel's work actually has two titles, not one, and that a reference to natural law occurs in its main title, seems to have been overlooked by many of Hegel's interpreters. For example, the title page of Glockner's edition of the work presents the main title in large type as being *Grundlinien der Philosophie des Rechts*. Underneath this, in much smaller type, are the words *Oder Naturrecht und Staatswissenschaft im Grundrisse* (Hegel, 1964). This clearly suggests that Hegel's book has just one main title, and that the reference to natural law occurs in what is merely a sub-title, and hence does not relate directly to the main themes of the work as a whole (see also Arthur, 1987, p. 56; Avineri, 1972, p. 81; Brod, 1992, pp. 38, 161; Riedel, 1984, pp. 104, 162-4; Ritter, 1982, p. 144; Smith, 1989, p. 6; Smith, 1991, p. 104).

As a consequence of this oversight, the full significance of the fact that Hegel gives his major work of political thought the title that he does, with the clear implication that it is intended to be a contribution to natural law theory, has also not been appreciated by the majority of Hegel scholars. Indeed, the suspicion is that the significance of this has actually not been at all understood. A good illustration of this is provided by S. B. Smith. According to Smith, Hegel's meaning 'is not so much clarified as complicated by a glance at the sub-title of the work, namely *Natural Right and the Science of the State in Outline*'. This is so because, although the term 'natural right' seems to 'point backward' to 'classical antiquity', the term 'science of the state' appears to 'confirm Hegel's status as a forerunner of legal positivism'. Thus, according to Smith, it is 'scarcely any wonder that an early reviewer found Hegel's work to be marred by great ambiguity, darkness and misunderstanding' (Smith, 1991, p.104). The principal reason for this 'darkness and misunderstanding', however, is yet again, the erroneous understanding which commentators have of natural law theory, and their prejudicial assumption that, whatever else he might be, Hegel could not possibly be a natural law theorist.

If our comparison of the *Philosophy of Right* with the earlier essay *On the Scientific Ways of Treating Natural Law* is well founded then it follows that, from Hegel's point of view, the *Philosophy of Right* as a whole should be considered to be a contribution to the development of a theoretical approach to politics based on the notion of natural law. In particular the third part of the work, which deals with what Hegel calls the sphere of 'ethical life', should be considered to be an Hegelian synthesis of two alternative types of natural law theory, each of which is considered by Hegel to be partial and one sided, and hence in some respects deficient. The first of these, which is discussed in the first part of the work entitled 'abstract right', is the stoic-liberal conception of natural law, which Hegel associates with individualism, the notion of abstract natural rights, the idea of a pre-political state of nature, and a social contract theory of the state. The other approach to natural law theory, which Hegel discusses in the second part of the work on 'morality', is associated with the name of Kant and with Kantian moral and political thought.

It follows from this that the part of the *Philosophy of Right* from which those who interpret Hegel as a legal positivist derive their textual support, namely the third part, is actually that part of the work in which Hegel considers himself to be putting the finishing touches to a system of political thought which is clearly intended to be a type of natural law theory. It also follows that those commentators who interpret Hegel as a natural law theorist, are wrong to do so solely on the basis of what Hegel has to say in the first part of the *Philosophy of Right*. For this is not that part of the work which Hegel himself considers as presenting an adequate approach to politics from the standpoint of natural law. In Hegel's opinion the natural law theory presented here is in certain respects quite inadequate. Any attempt to establish that Hegel is a natural law theorist, and not a legal positivist, which is based exclusively on what Hegel has to say about natural law and natural rights in the first part of the *Philosophy of Right* will almost certainly result in the erroneous conclusion that Hegel subscribes to the stoic, and hence to a liberal conception of natural law.

Hegel's natural law theory

The interpretation of Hegel's political thought presented here is based on two claims. The first of these is that although Hegel's political thought is indeed a type of natural law theory, nevertheless Hegel does not subscribe to the stoic conception of natural law. Hegel's political thought is a modified and modernised version of what is fundamentally the Aristotelian conception of natural law. The second is that, as with all formal conceptions of natural law, the central feature of Hegelian natural law theory is its view of the relationship which exists between natural law and positive law. Unlike stoic natural law theory, Hegel's political thought does not consider natural law to be a critical standard which individuals might use to critically evaluate positive law.

A central feature of Hegel's approach to politics, like that of Aristotle, is the assumption that man is by nature a social and political animal. To live a life of justice and morality (and hence a life which conforms to the requirements of the basic principles of natural law) within a particular ethical community is something which, in Hegel's opinion, is natural to human beings.

Hegel's perception of the relationship between positive law and natural law is also basically the same as that of Aristotle. For Hegel, as for Aristotle (and indeed the scholastic natural law theory of medieval thinkers like Aquinas), the positive law of a particular community is considered to be a concrete manifestation of the more general principles of natural law. From this point of view, precisely how men organise themselves into ethical communities is, in so far as the specific details are concerned, entirely a matter of convention.The more detailed formulations of positive law are, morally speaking, arbitrary, contingent and accidental, and hence unimportant from the standpoint of natural law. They are historically conditioned and hence will, inevitably, vary from society to society, depending upon a particular society's culture, customs and traditions, or upon what Montesquieu refers to as the 'spirit' of its laws.

On this particular issue, then, Hegel takes the Aristotelian view that it is the task of art to supplement or complement nature. This is an attitude which has been well summarised by Ernest Barker. According to Barker, 'Aristotle refuses to make an antithesis between Nature and Art'. Thus 'the law of the state and the law of nature are one'. We certainly must distinguish between 'the naturally and the legally just'. These are not ,however, 'antithetical'. Rather, they are 'supplementary to one another' (Barker, 1959, p. 327). Hegel's own formulation of this Aristotelian notion is to be found at the very beginning of the *Philosophy of Right,* when he says that 'Natural law, or law from the philosophical point of view, is distinct from positive law: but to pervert their difference into an opposition would be a gross misunderstanding' (Hegel, 1979, p. 16).

An understanding of what Hegel means by this is a necessary pre-condition for an appreciation of his attitude towards natural law, and hence also for an understanding of his political thought as a whole. Our next task, therefore, is to comment at greater length on what, exactly, Hegel has in mind when he says that natural law and positive law do not stand in 'opposition' to one another.

What, according to Hegel, are the basic principles of natural law? Like Aristotle before him, together with the scholastic natural law theory of the medieval period, and indeed the natural law theory of Kant, Hegel's natural law theory incorporates a definite hierarchy of moral principles. At the top of this hierarchy there is a primary principle of morality or justice. In the case of Hegel, as in the case of all the other theorists just mentioned, this basic principle is a version of what is probably best described as the principle of equity or reciprocity (del Vecchio, 1952, pp. 84-8, 112; Kant, 1965, pp. 64-5, 72). Hegel himself formulates this basic principle of natural law or right in terms of the Kantian principle of equal liberty or equal freedom (Kant, 1965, pp.33-5; Hegel, 1979, pp.29, 32-3, 231-2).

Hegel is of course, as we have seen, very critical of certain aspects of Kant's philosophy.Usually, though, it is not so much the general principles which Kant isolates that Hegel objects to. Rather, what Hegel criticises is Kant's understanding of the method by means of which a definite substantive content is to be given to these 'formal' principles. Hegel is of the opinion that, according to Kant, the source for this substantive content is the conscience of the individual moral agent. Hegel rejects this position because he considers it to be excessively individualistic. In his view, it amounts to suggesting that, in certain circumstances, the performance of an act which is intrinsically wrong might be morally permissible, provided only that this is done conscientiously (Hegel, 1979, pp. 89-92; 94-103; 256-8; Walsh, 1969). To adopt such a position, Hegel suggests, is to undermine all morality and hence also the existing social order.

Beneath this purely formal principle in the hierarchy stand certain other principles of natural law which could be said to constitute its objective or substantive content. What Hegel has in mind here are the principles of morality forbidding actions such as theft and murder. Hegel follows Aristotle in asserting that actions of this sort are intrinsically wrong. That is why they ought to be, and indeed are, forbidden by positive law, always and everywhere (Aristotle, 1925, II, 6, 1107a, 10-20; Hegel, 1979, pp.90, 97-8, 194, 206, 241, 251-2, 273; Houlgate, 1991, pp. 96-7; Smith, 1991, pp. 75, 110-11). These are principles which the scholastic natural law theory of the medieval period refers to as the secondary precepts of natural law (Aquinas, 1966, pp.87-97; Armstrong, 1966).

Hegel's attitude towards these secondary principles of morality, and the relationship which exists between them and the purely formal principle of equity or reciprocity, is greatly influenced by the views of both Kant and Aristotle, but especially by those of Aristotle. It is quite incorrect to suggest, as S. B. Smith has done, that Aristotle has nothing significant to say on this subject, or that there is 'no Aristotelian equivalent of the Kantian Categorical Imperative or the commandments of the Decalogue' (Smith, 1991, pp. 138-9).

In relation to the primary principle of natural law, which is a purely formal principle, these subsidiary moral principles could be said to be substantive principles of natural law. Nevertheless, in their turn, these principles may also be considered as having, in a sense, a formal or abstract character. Thus, Hegel refers to them as principles of abstract right. These principles are abstract principles because although they place upon individuals a moral injunction to refrain from committing certain types of action, for example an act of theft, they provide no help at all when it comes to deciding whether or not some specific action is actually an example of this general type. They require, therefore, what Hegel refers to, in the terminology of scholastic natural law theory, as a further 'practical application' or 'specific determination' (Hegel, 1956, pp.443-4, 447-8; Hegel, 1979, pp.134-41, 176, 193-4; Aquinas, 1966, pp. 103-07; Finnis, 1980, pp. 281-96; Wood, 1991, p. 104).

Support for the claim that Hegel's political thought assumes the existence of a definite hierarchy of moral principles, and that in this respect it bears a close resemblance to scholastic natural law theory, is provided by some interesting remarks which Hegel makes in one of his minor political writings, the *Proceedings of the Estates Assembly in Wurtemburg* (Hegel, 1969). Here Hegel refers to what he describes as being 'simple organic provisions' which together 'make up the rational basis of constitutionalism'. These 'organic provisions' are all closely related to what we have called the principle of equity or reciprocity. Thus, for example, they include the principle that 'all subjects are equal in the eyes of the law'. From our point of view, however, what is particularly interesting about them is Hegel's acknowledgement that 'because of their generality these principles constitute no more than an outline of legislation that is still to be drafted'. In this respect they are similar to 'the Mosaic law' or to 'the famous *Droits de l'homme et du citoyen* of more recent times' (Hegel, 1969, pp. 270-1).

In connection with these remarks, Z. A. Pelczynski has quite rightly observed that Hegel seems here 'to postulate a kind of hierarchy of rules of increasing concreteness'. This hierarchy has three levels. The first level contains just one principle, which Pelczynski calls 'the fundamental rational principle of justice and equality', or the principle of 'absolute right'. The second level contains 'a number of general principles' which are 'suitable for formulation in a bill or declaration of rights'. These are Hegel's own 'organic constitutional provisions'. The third level contains 'a much larger number of specific legal rules', or 'laws proper', which represent 'the application of general principles to concrete circumstances' (Pelczynski, 1969, p. 52). Although he appears to be unaware of it, what Pelczynski actually offers us here is an excellent account of Hegel's view of the relationship which exists between natural law and positive law. Hegel subscribes to this view, not only in his occasional political writings, but also in the *Philosophy of Right*. Moreover, although again Pelczynski appears to be unaware of it, this is a view which is very similar to that of scholastic natural law theory.

According to Hegel, the abstract principles of natural law establish certain types of rights, which might be termed natural rights, for example the right to property. However, these rights, like the principles of natural law which establish them, are also in a sense merely formal or abstract. Whether or not an individual's natural rights have been infringed is a question which is not easy to answer, and to which the relevant principle of natural law does not itself provide an answer. This again is a matter for determination and interpretation.

As Hegel understands it, modern natural law theory argues that the source for such an interpretation is the conscience of the individual moral agent. This is not, however, the position adopted by Aristotelian or scholastic natural law theory, in which the modern principle of individualism is largely absent. As we have seen, according to that theory the source for this interpretation of the abstract principles of natural law is not the individual citizen. It is, rather, the positive law of the ethical community in which the citizen lives.

On this crucially important issue, and this is the key respect in which his natural law theory differs from the stoic conception of natural law, Hegel adopts a position similar to that of Aristotle, the medieval scholastics, and later by Hobbes. Hegel subscribes to what we have referred to as a formal conception of natural law.

In this connection, what is meant by 'positive law', at least in the first instance, is the customary law associated with the constitution of a particular ethical community. It is not statute law. In this respect, therefore, Hegel's views are much closer to those of Montesquieu or Burke than they are to those of Hobbes (Hegel, 1979, pp. 15-16, 107, 135-6, 138, 146, 178-9, 260, 271-2, 286-7, 291).

We may illustrate Hegel's attitude towards the relationship which exists between natural law and positive law by referring to the principle of natural law which forbids the act of theft. Hegel takes the view that if we wish to conform to the moral obligations placed upon us by the principle of equity or reciprocity, which is the supreme principle of natural law, then it follows that we must recognise an obligation not to commit the act of theft. From this point of view, then, the moral principle forbidding theft is a subsidiary principle of natural law. As such it establishes that we have a natural right to property. According to Hegel, however, this right is a purely formal or 'abstract right'. It establishes that we a right to some property, but it does not establish just how much property we are entitled to, or when we are justified in claiming that our property rights have been violated. This formal or abstract right, therefore, needs defining and interpreting more precisely. To carry out this task is the principal function of the positive law of the ethical community in which we live. It is for precisely this reason that natural law and positive law, in Hegel's view, may be said to perform different though complementary functions (Hegel, 1979, pp. 139, 273-4, 289).

In Hegel's view, the precise way in which these natural rights are defined by the positive law of the community is, morally speaking, quite arbitrary or contingent. As we have seen, different communities will in fact do this in different ways, depending on their different cultures, customs and historical traditions. All that really matters is that it should in fact be done, one way or another (Hegel, 1979, pp.289, 137-8, 146, 272, 276; Hegel, 1971, p. 259; Riedel, 1984, pp. 34-5). In Hegel's words, 'that I should hold property is necessary, but my holding of this particular property is contingent' (Hegel, 1979, p. 289). However, no matter how these rights are defined by positive law, it is Hegel's view that we have a moral obligation to obey the positive law which defines them. Not to do so would be to do wrong. It would be to infringe an imperative, not only of positive law, but also and more importantly of natural law.

It is interesting to compare Hegel's views on this subject with those of Burke, on the one hand, and Kant on the other. The similarity between the position adopted by Hegel and that of Burke is really quite striking. Thus, according to Burke, 'although property itself is not, yet almost everything concerning property, and all of its modifications, is of artificial contrivance' (Burke, 1815-27, XIV, p. 397; cited Canavan, 1960, p. 116). According to Kant, however, 'a civil constitution only provides the juridical condition under which each person's property is secured and guaranteed to him, but it does not actually stipulate and determine what that property shall be' (Kant, 1965, p. 65). Both Hegel and Burke are writing here from the standpoint of Aristotle and the Aristotelian tradition of natural law. Kant, on the other hand, writes from the alternative standpoint of the stoic natural law tradition.

Insofar as Hegel is concerned, therefore, the abstract principles of natural law which establish our rights, on the one hand, and the corresponding principle of positive law in a particular society which defines those rights, on the other, stand in an hierarchical relationship to one another. They are in fact related to one another as a genus is to its various species. These principles operate on entirely different levels and, in so doing, perform what are essentially different, though complementary, functions. It is in this sense that, from the standpoint of Hegel's political thought, art might be said to supplement nature. It is for this reason that Hegel insists at the beginning of the *Philosophy of Right* that the assume that natural law and positive law stand in opposition to one another is based on a 'gross misunderstanding'.

Thus, according to Hegel, for all practical purposes it is positive law which is the standard of justice or morality for the individual citizen in every ethical community. However, the reason for this has nothing to do with the 'positive' character of this law. On the contrary, this is only the case because positive law itself is a specific determination of the abstract principles of natural law, principles which are morally obligatory in and of themselves. The only way in which individual citizens can follow a principle of natural law in practice, in Hegel's opinion, is by obeying the corresponding positive law of the ethical community in which they live.

It follows from this that within Hegel's system although individuals do indeed possess certain natural rights these rights are not rights against the state as such. These rights have an abstract character. They require definition and interpretation, and for Hegel it is positive law which should define them. Positive rights, for Hegel, are natural rights, in so far as the latter have been concretely defined. Hence natural law and natural rights cannot, as a consequence, provide the individual with a means of questioning the moral validity of positive law. This is not their function within Hegel's system of political thought. Hegel emphatically rejects the doctrine of natural rights in the revolutionary sense in which this doctrine is interpreted by natural law theory as it is conventionally understood. On the contrary, paradoxical though it may seem, in Hegel's view it is for positive law to decide when an individual's natural rights have been infringed.

From Hegel's point of view, then, the stoic conception of natural law is completely inadequate. Like Hobbes before him, Hegel understands very well that if the principles of natural law require interpretation, and if this is to be provided by positive law, then it is quite impossible for natural law to carry out the critical function which is attributed to it within stoic natural law theory. The view that natural law is a critical standard for the evaluation of positive law is, in Hegel's opinion, based on a fundamental misunderstanding. It involves a failure to see that the principles of natural law have an abstract or formal character. It involves a failure to appreciate the true nature of the relationship which exists between natural law and positive law. And it involves a failure to see that it is the task of positive law, and not the conscience of the individual, to define and interpret the rights which are established by the principles of natural law.

We are now in a position to compare Hegel's natural law theory with the stoic conception of natural law, on the one hand, and the doctrine of legal positivism on the other. Hegel's views do resemble stoic natural law theory at a number of points. Hegel rejects the basic assumption of contemporary legal positivism that there is no such thing as natural law. Hegel also accepts the view that there are certain actions which are intrinsically wrong. These actions are forbidden by positive law because they are wrong. They are not wrong because positive law forbids them. Hegel acknowledges that it is the faculty of reason which discerns what the principles of natural law are.

And finally, Hegel accepts that these principles have a validity which is timeless and universal. They have an application to all societies, in all times and in all places.

On the other hand, however, Hegel's views also bear a resemblance to the doctrine of legal positivism. In particular, Hegel emphatically rejects the view that natural law constitutes a critical standard for the evaluation of positive law. He insists that, in the final analysis, it is positive law which is the standard of justice for the individual in every ethical community. Indeed, Bruce Haddock has even gone so far as to say that, for Hegel, 'it is will and personality', rather than 'nature', which are 'crucial to Hegel's wider account of politics and the state' (Haddock, 1993, pp. 120-21; also Smith, 1989, p. 8).

Thus, to classify Hegel as being either a natural law theorist or a legal positivist, in the sense in which these two terms are conventionally understood, would most certainly be to distort his thinking. It would, inevitably, lead to a misinterpretation of his political thought as a whole. Fortunately, however, we do not have to make a stark choice between just one or the other of these two alternatives. These two ways of classifying Hegel's political thought do not in fact exhaust all of the available possibilities. There is actually a third way of classifying Hegel's views which is more accurate than either of these two. According to this third alternative, Hegel's political thought is indeed a form of natural law theory. However, this is a natural law theory which, by current standards, is of an unconventional type. Essentially, like the medieval scholastics, Hegel subscribes, not to a liberal, but to what we may term a conservative conception of natural law, which is derived ultimately from the political thought of Aristotle.

According to M. B. Foster, Hegel is committed to two basic principles. The first of these is that 'the state can be philosophically derived by a process of necessary reasoning'. And the second is that 'the subject of an historical state can have access to no supra-temporal standard by which he can stand in judgement over it'. Foster quite rightly claims that 'the conjunction of these two principles' may be called 'the kernel of the whole Hegelian philosophy of the state'. However, Foster also seems to think that 'it is only by' some 'confusion' or 'subterfuge' that Hegel could possibly subscribe to both of these principles at the same time. For in his view they are evidently incompatible (Foster, 1935, pp. 172-3).

Foster appears to associate the first of these principles (the adoption of a 'rationalist' approach to political questions) with a commitment to some form of natural law theory. At the same time, however, he associates the second (the rejection of a 'supra-temporal standard' by which individuals might stand in judgement over the state) with a corresponding rejection of natural law theory. Thus he feels that he has perceived a contradiction which lies at the heart of Hegel's political thought.

The fact is though, as we have seen, that Foster is wrong to assume that all natural law theories (and hence all rationalist approaches to politics) must necessarily be committed to a belief in the existence of a critical standard of justice of this sort. Once we recognise the existence of alternative conceptions of natural law, and once we appreciate the specific character of the Aristotelian conception of natural law, then this alleged contradiction disappears. For Hegel, the principles of natural law, like all universals, are not 'transcendent' but 'immanent' principles. They exist in and through the positive laws of a particular historical community. As A. D. Lindsay has quite rightly put it, 'Hegel's doctrine of natural law' asserts that natural law 'must work within the state' (Lindsay, 1932, p. 65).

The importance of Hegel's debt to Aristotelian natural law theory is something which has not been sufficiently appreciated by the majority of Hegel's interpreters, largely because they do not have an adequate understanding of scholastic natural law theory and its history, and hence do not acknowledge the existence of such a thing as a conservative conception of natural law (Finnis, 1980, pp. 281-90). Most commentators wrongly identify the liberal conception as being the only possible conception of natural law. Any doctrine which does not conform to this conception is not considered to be a 'genuine' natural law theory at all (Kelsen, 1973, pp.129, 131). This attitude makes it very difficult for anyone to understand Hegel's political thought. Once we abandon the assumption that there is only one type of natural law theory this problem disappears. It then becomes possible for us to understand the significance which the notion of natural law has for Hegel's political thought as a whole. It also then becomes possible for us to understand how the views expressed in the first part of the *Philosophy of Right*, in which Hegel acknowledges that individuals do indeed possess certain natural rights, might be reconciled with what Hegel has to say in the third part, in which Hegel appears to reject the doctrine of natural rights.

In short, once we abandon our prejudicial assumptions about the nature of natural law, and as a result embrace a much looser conception of natural law theory, then the problem of locating Hegel's position disappears. To do this makes it possible for us to understand the significance which the notion of natural law has for Hegel's system of political thought as a whole. It enables us to better understand the complex structure of the *Philosophy of Right*. And finally, it enables us to see why it is that Hegel should have chosen to give his major work of political theory the title *Natural Law and Political Science in Outline*.

Natural law and Hegelian metaphysics

There is some disagreement on the question of how Hegel's political thought is related to his general philosophy. In particular there is disagreement regarding the issue of whether Hegel's political thought can be properly understood without relating it to his idealist metaphysics. Some commentators take the view that it can be. Thus, for example, Germino has claimed that Hegel's political thought 'can be understood without constant reference to his total metaphysical system', and John Plamenatz has maintained that although Hegel 'uses and extraordinarily difficult philosophical vocabulary', nevertheless 'it is possible to translate his political and social theory into more ordinary language' (Germino, 1969, p. 885; Plamenatz, 1958, p. 177; also Plamenatz, 1963, pp. 129-32; Cairns, 1949, p. 504; Pelczynski, 1969, p. 37; Pelczysnki, 1971a, pp. 1-2).

There are, however, other commentators who reject this assessment completely. Thus Raymond Plant has insisted that an understanding of Hegel's 'metaphysical doctrines' is 'a necessary condition of making his writings on political philosophy intelligible', and George Armstrong Kelly has maintained that a failure to discuss Hegel's metaphysics in this connection is likely to lead to a 'result which is apt to be impoverished or misleading' (Plant, 1973, p.9; Kelly, 1978, p. 8; also Dallmayr, 1993, p. 28; Riedel, 1984, pp. 31-2; Wood, 1990, p. xiii, 6).

The view adopted here is that although an understanding of Hegelian metaphysics is not strictly necessary for an understanding of Hegel's political thought, nevertheless it does help. For there is a very clear relationship between the two. In particular, the technical vocabulary of Hegel's philosophical system provides an excellent vehicle for expressing the complexity of Hegel's view of the relationship which exists between natural law and positive law. This view is, as we have noted, basically Aristotelian. We shall begin, therefore, with a discussion of Aristotle.

Aristotle

We have already seen that most commentators today make a straightforward distinction between just two types of law. They distinguish between natural law, on the one hand and positive law on the other. Aristotle's approach is more complex and sophisticated than this. He adopts a tripartite rather than a dual classification. In an often cited passage in the *Nichomachean Ethics* Aristotle distinguishes between three types of justice, which he calls 'natural justice', 'legal justice' and 'political justice' (Aristotle, 1925, V, 7, 1134b-1135a). In addition he states that natural justice and legal justice are both a 'part' of political justice. An appreciation of what, exactly, Aristotle means by this is vital for an understanding of his view of the relationship which exists between natural law and positive law.

For Aristotle the principles of political justice are the laws of a particular political community. It is Aristotle's view that at least some of these principles of political justice are composed of two constituent 'parts'. That is to say they have a synthetic character, and hence a complex structure. In the case of these particular principles of political justice one component 'part' is a principle of natural justice and the other is a principle of legal or conventional justice.

We may illustrate this by considering an example, which Aristotle himself mentions in the passage cited above. Aristotle refers there to the principle of political justice which states that 'a prisoner's ransom shall be a mina'. According to Aristotle, this principle has two component 'parts'. The first is a principle of natural justice, which states that all prisoners ought to be ransomed. The second is a principle of legal or conventional justice, which states that the ransom in question ought to be a mina. That the principle of political justice which states that a prisoner's ransom should be a mina is also, at the same time, a particular concrete manifestation of a principle of natural justice, namely the principle that all prisoners should be ransomed, is something which is not always understood by Aristotle's interpreters. Thus, for example, Leo Strauss has mistakenly claimed that Aristotle's discussion of natural justice in the *Ethics* is noteworthy because 'it is not illumined by a single example of what is by nature right' (Strauss, 1974, p. 156; also Strauss, 1968, p. 81). This statement demonstrates a complete misunderstanding of Aristotle's view of the relationship which exists between natural law and positive law. In this respect, the earlier judgement of Aquinas is much closer to the mark. As Aquinas quite rightly puts it, in his commentary on the *Ethics*, it is Aristotle's view that 'it is natural' that 'a prisoner should be ransomed'. However, 'the fixing of the price pertains to legal justice' which 'proceeds from natural justice without error' (Aquinas, 1964, p. 443).

When Aristotle says that the principle that prisoners ought to be ransomed is a principle of natural justice what he means is that this is not a matter of indifference from the moral point of view. In his opinion the systems of political justice of all societies ought to (and do) contain a law to this effect. On the other hand, however, the principle that the ransom in question ought to be a mina, as opposed to something else, does not have the same moral status. The question of what precisely a prisoner's ransom ought to be is, in Aristotle's view, a matter of moral indifference. This may legitimately be decided, quite arbitrarily, by the conventions of a particular society. Hence it may (and does) vary from society to society.

For Aristotle, then, at least some of the principles of political justice of a particular society will contain a 'part' which is necessary, 'unchangeable' and hence universal. An important implication of this is that, from Aristotle's point of view, the notions which we have of the principles of natural justice are in fact what philosophers have traditionally called 'universals'. This brings us to the important question of the ontological status of such universals. We shall make a few general comments about Aristotle's position on this question, before turning to consider their significance for our understanding of Aristotle's view of the relationship which exists between natural law and positive law.

With respect to this problem of the ontological status of universals, it is common to find a distinction being made between two basic positions. Some philosophers adopt the standpoint of 'rationalism', 'realism' and 'idealism', whereas others adopt the standpoint of 'empiricism', 'nominalism' and 'materialism' (Aaron, 1967; Staniland, 1972; Woozley, 1969). One frequently meets the suggestion that the position adopted by Aristotle on this issue is diametrically opposed to that adopted by Plato. Plato is considered to be a 'rationalist', a 'realist' and an 'idealist', whereas Aristotle is often assumed to be an 'empiricist', a 'nominalist' and a 'materialist'. Thus, for example, John Cottingham has pointed out that Aristotle 'is not usually classified as a rationalist'. On the contrary, 'it is often claimed that Aristotle is the founder of empiricism' (Cottingham, 1984, pp. 13, 26). And Hilary Staniland has observed that it is not actually so surprising that people should make this assumption. For 'one could easily get the impression' from reading Aristotle's comments on Plato 'that there was no common ground between the two philosophers at all' (Staniland, 1972, p. 8).

The fact that commentators have a tendency to make these assumptions about Plato and Aristotle has long been appreciated. In particular, this is something which is pointed out quite explicitly by Hegel himself in his *Shorter Logic*. There Hegel notes the existence of what he calls 'a widespread prejudice about the relation of the philosophy of Aristotle to that of Plato'. In Hegel's view, 'popular opinion' has a tendency to consider Aristotle as 'the founder and chief of empiricism', thereby clearly contrasting his philosophy with that of Plato. For Plato, being an idealist, 'recognises the idea and the idea only as the truth', whereas Aristotle does not (Hegel, 1975b, p. 202). In Hegel's view this popular assessment of Aristotle's position on the problem of universals, and of Aristotle's relationship to Plato, is in fact completely mistaken. Hegel, has no time for the opinion which presents Aristotle as a 'materialist' and an 'empiricist'. In his view it is true that Aristotle, unlike Plato, 'keeps to what is actual'. This does not mean, however, that Aristotle abandons the principle of philosophical idealism. For, as Hegel puts it, 'although actuality is the principle of Aristotelian philosophy', this is not the 'vulgar actuality of what is immediately at hand'. It is, rather, 'the *idea* as actuality' (Hegel, 1975b, p. 202).

What Aristotle actually says about universals and particulars in the *Categories* is quite obscure, and clearly open to different interpretations (Aristotle, 1926, I, 1a, 20-25; 2, 1a, 25-30; 2, 1b, 1-10; 5, 2a, 1-20, 30-35; 5, 2b, 1-10; 5, 3a, 5-15). It could, however, quite plausibly be argued that Hegel's judgement on the question of Aristotle's attitude towards universals, is in fact perfectly correct. Certainly it is a judgement which, in the twentieth century, has come to be shared by a number of commentators. Thus, for example, Cottingham has acknowledged that Aristotle is actually not an empiricist, but some sort of rationalist, who shared with Plato the belief that 'reason can provide us with substantive necessary truths about the world' (Cottingham, 1984, p. 28). Antony Flew has noted that 'Aristotle's candidate for what is primarily real' is 'closer to Plato's separate ideal forms' than is usually thought (Flew, 1979, p. 27; also Allan, 1970, p. 84; Guthrie, 1967, pp. 125-30). And Staniland has insisted that, contrary to appearances, 'Plato and Aristotle are both realists in the sense of holding that the world contains universals as well as particulars' (Staniland, 1972, p. 15; also Copleston, 1962, pp. 44-6; Ross, 1964, pp. 157-9; Woozley, 1969, pp. 73-4).

Although there are, undeniably, important differences between the philosophies of Plato and Aristotle with respect to the ontological status of universals, one might therefore nevertheless maintain that these differences are nothing like as great as they are usually considered to be. Like Plato, Aristotle's philosophical position is based on an acceptance of the principles of rationalism, realism and idealism. Aristotle does not reject Plato's metaphysics completely. He merely thinks that it is partial and one sided, and hence in some respects quite inadequate.

Aristotle's attitude towards the problem of universals has been well captured by Staniland. According to Staniland, the difference between Plato and Aristotle is not that Plato is a realist whereas Aristotle is not. Rather, it is that Plato and Aristotle 'differ sharply' on the specific question of how these universals are related to particulars. In Plato's view, universals are 'self-sufficient entities which may or may not have particulars related to them'. Aristotle denies this. For Aristotle, 'universals only exist in virtue of their relation to particulars'. This does not mean, however, that

Aristotle adopts the opposed position that particulars could exist even if there were no universals. As Staniland rightly points out, Aristotle is of the opinion that 'it is no more possible' for 'particulars to exist without universals' than it is for 'universals to exist without particulars' (Staniland, 1972, pp. 8, 12, 15).

Unlike Plato, then, Aristotle takes the view that although universals are undoubtedly real entities, nevertheless they are 'immanent' and not 'transcendent' entities (Copleston, 1962, p. 46; Guthrie, 1967, p. 128). They are entities which are necessarily 'embodied' or 'instantiated' in individual things or 'substances'. From the standpoint of Aristotelian metaphysics, the world is composed of a variety of such individual 'substances' or 'concrete individuals'. Each one of these concrete individuals contains, as one of its component parts, both an element which is 'universal' and an element which is 'particular' (Cottingham, 1984, p. 27; Reyburn, 1967, p. 40).

We are now in a position to relate what we have said about Aristotle's metaphysics and his attitude towards the problem of universals to his political thought, and especially his view of the relationship which exists between natural law and positive law. We have seen that the notions which we have of the principles of natural justice are universals. It might possibly be thought, therefore, that for Aristotle these notions are derived by a process of intellectual abstraction from raw materials which are provided by empirical observation of the systems of political justice of different societies. Moreover, it might also be thought that, in Aristotle's view, the principles of natural justice are themselves, therefore, nothing more than mere intellectual abstractions. They are not real. We can now see that this would be a mistake. Aristotle's view is that these principles of natural justice are certainly real. However, although this is so, it nevertheless remains the case that they can only be said to exist in so far as they are associated with a particular principle of political justice, within the legal system of a particular society at a particular time. These principles have no 'transcendent' existence. Rather, they exist immanently in and through the various principles of political justice. From the standpoint of Aristotelian metaphysics, therefore, these principles of political justice might, be said to be 'substances' or 'concrete individuals' in Cottingham's sense. Each one of these principles, is a synthetic unity of a 'universal' with a 'particular', neither of which can exist without the other. The 'universal' is a principle of natural justice and the 'particular' is a principle of legal or conventional justice.

Hegel

As is well known, Hegel's philosophy is based on an important theoretical distinction between what Hegel calls the 'essence' and the 'appearance' of things (Hegel, 1975b, pp. 162-186; 186-200). It is the essence of things which, for Hegel, constitutes 'reality' (Hegel, 1975b, pp. 27, 33, 34-6, 135, 141). Moreover, because he is an idealist, Hegel takes the view that it is ideas and concepts, rather than material objects, or existent things, which are truly real (Hegel, 1975b, pp. 336, 66-67, 69-70, 73-4, 187-8, 228; Cottingham, 1984, p. 93; Mehta, 1968, pp. 26-8). In Hegel's view, the realm of 'existence' is one and the same as the realm of 'appearance' (Hegel, 1975b, pp. 179-81). The belief that reality and existence are one and the same is an illusion of the understanding. It arises as a consequence of our over reliance on the standpoint of 'common sense', and from our naive belief that the evidence of our senses is a reliable source of genuine knowledge (Hegel, 1975b, pp. 60-5, 99; Hegel, 1979, p. 14).This is how things appear to be. It is not, however, how they really are. This is something which we can only recognise if we abandon the standpoint of the understanding and take up that of reason.

This account presents a picture of Hegel's views which makes them closely resemble those of Plato (Dallmayr, 1993, p. 23). It would, however, be a mistake to exaggerate the similarities between Hegel and Plato. For there are important differences also. Indeed, Hegel's views are actually much closer to those of Aristotle. This is certainly true in the case of Hegel's attitude towards the problem of universals. As Beiser has pointed out, Hegel is firmly committed to 'the Aristotelian dictum that universals exist only *in re*' (Beiser, 1993, p. 290; also 276).

Like Aristotle, Hegel shares with Plato a commitment to the principles of realism, idealism and rationalism. However, also like Aristotle, Hegel rejects Plato's belief that the concepts and ideas which constitute reality are independent and self-subsistent. Moreover, again like Aristotle, Hegel criticises Plato's philosophy for being 'other worldly'. In his opinion, with 'such empty and other worldly stuff philosophy has nothing to do' (Hegel, 1975b, pp. 138, 40, 276; Hegel, 1979, p. 10; Hegel, 1892-96, 2, pp. 92-6; Beiser, 1993, pp. 290-1; Hardimon, 1994, pp. 56-7; Kaufmann, 1970, pp. 152-3; Mehta, 1968, p. 34; Wood, 1991, p. 12).

What Hegel likes about Aristotelian metaphysics is the fact that, for Aristotle, the realm of 'essence' is inseparably connected to the realm of 'appearance'. Neither can subsist without the other, and each is dependent on the other. Just as there can be no appearance without reality, so also there can be no reality without appearance. All appearances have to be appearances of some underlying reality. And all reality must appear. That which does not have any appearance is not real.

In Hegel's view, it is the principal task of philosophy to transcend the limitations placed upon us by over reliance on the faculty of the understanding, which apprehends only the surface appearances of things. In general terms this means that it is the task of reason to penetrate beneath these surface appearances in order to grasp the underlying essence which underpins them (Hegel, 1975, pp. 33-6, 72-3, 113-15, 119-21, 162-5; Mehta, 1968, p. 37).

The process by means of which philosophy is to carry out this task has two stages. In the first instance we must employ the faculty of the understanding and undertake an act of analysis or abstraction. This involves the separation of that which is real and essential within some particular 'thing' from that which is merely an appearance or phenomenal form, and hence superficial (Hegel, 1975b, pp. 62-3, 113-14, 285, 294). Once having done this, we must then go further. We must employ the faculty of Reason and undertake an act of intellectual synthesis. We must seek to re-unite what has been parted and show how the appearances of things and the essence or reality which underpins those appearances are related to one another (Hegel, 1975b, pp. 285-6, 294; Wood, 1991, pp. 10-11).

From Hegel's point of view, when the faculty of Reason apprehends things in this way, as complex entities, or 'unities', then it grasps things 'concretely' (Hegel, 1975b, pp. 60, 113, 119, 196, 200-2, 204, 223, 226, 228-9). That is to say, it considers individual things as constituting, in effect, a synthesis of the 'abstract moments' of appearance and reality (Hegel, 1975b, pp. 113, 227). It is only when we see things in this way that, in Hegel's opinion, we see them at all adequately. To apprehend things in this manner is, for Hegel, to consider them in their 'actuality' (Hegel, 1975b, pp. 8-10, 200-2, 204-6, 227-8; Hardimon, 1994, pp. 26, 53-8). Hegel's debt to Aristotle here is clearly very great. The basic insight and inspiration lying behind this aspect of Hegel's metaphysics is provided, above all, by Aristotle. For Hegel, as for Aristotle, to view things correctly as 'individuals' it is necessary to recognise that they constitute, essentially, a synthesis of the principle of 'universality' with that of 'particularity'. And of course, once one has recognised this, then one has come to appreciate that 'individual and actual are the same thing' (Hegel, 1975b, p. 226).

If we now take these fundamental categories of Hegel's philosophical system and apply them to Hegel's political thought, it is immediately apparent that they do indeed shed light on Hegel's view of the relationship which exists between natural law and positive law. According to Hegel, positive law can be viewed in two different ways, from the standpoint of the understanding and from the standpoint of reason. In the first case it is grasped by means of experience or sense perception. That is to say, it is apprehended intellectually on the basis of the empirical observation of the legal system of a particular society at a particular time. From Hegel's point of view, however, this approach focuses merely on the surface appearances of things. It stops at the level of the arbitrary, the conventional and the historically specific. It concentrates on those aspects of law which vary from society to society, from time to time, and from place to place. It is unable, therefore, to pick out from within the different systems of positive law that which is timeless and universal.

In short, this approach does not provide us with true knowledge of things as they really are. It does not present us with the essential reality which underpins all of these different appearances. This is the principal defect of what today we would call 'positivism', just as it is the principal defect of empiricism generally. As Hegel puts it, 'to consider particular laws as they appear and develop in time is a purely historical task'. This task 'has no relation whatever to the philosophical study of the subject' (Hegel, 1979, p. 16; Foster, 1935, pp. 117-18, 170-1; Kaufmann, 1970, pp. 152-3; Plant, 1973, p. 127; Reyburn, 1967, p. 63). This is so because, as Hegel puts it in the Preface to the *Phenomenology of Mind*, 'philosophy deals essentially with the general, in which the particular is subsumed' (Hegel, 1966, p. 6).

It cannot be emphasised too strongly that for Hegel, it is a mistake in matters of jurisprudence (as always) to rely too heavily on the faculty of the understanding. Philosophical knowledge in relation to matters of law and ethics cannot be derived simply on the basis of observation and experience. To adopt the standpoint of empiricism, or of positivism in this area is, from Hegel's point of view, to fail to penetrate beneath the surface appearances of things and to grasp their underlying reality. In Hegel's view, to rely on 'immediate sense perception' in this way is 'the quintessence of shallow thinking' (Hegel, 1979, p. 6; also Hegel, 1969, pp. 143, 281-2; Avineri, 1972, p. 39, 71-4, 120-3, 182-3, 210; Dallmayr, 1993, p. 85; Foster, 1935, pp. 117-18; Mehta, 1968, p. 35; Pelczynski, 1969, p. 116; Plant, 1973, p. 145; Smith, 1991, p. 148; Suter, 1971, p. 66; Taylor, 1989, p. 424).

It should, however, be emphasised that although Hegel is opposed to the principle of 'positivism', this does not mean that he must necessarily also be critical of all positive law. It is incorrect and misleading to talk in an unqualified way, as Avineri does, about Hegel's 'opposition to positive law' (Avineri, 1972, p. 210). What Hegel is opposed to is not positive law as such. It is, rather, the 'positivist' principle that such law should be obeyed simply because it *is* the law. This is a point which has been noted by Foster, who rightly maintains that 'although Hegel denies that it belongs to the essence of law to be positive' nevertheless 'he insists that it belongs to the essence of law to be posited' (Foster, 1935, p. 119; also Dallmayr, 1993, p. 102). This is something which is also appreciated by Knox, who points out that Hegel actually 'agrees with the historical school of jurists against the rationalists in laying emphasis on the historical or positive element in law'. His criticism of the historical school, according to Knox, is simply that 'they are wrong in ignoring the rational element which is present also' (Knox, 1979, p. 307). Indeed, even Z. A. Pelczynski, who is so keen to establish Hegel's credentials as a liberal thinker, acknowledges that 'Hegel's rejection of the positive principle' or of 'traditionalism' in politics, and hence his 'championing of political rationalism', is in fact 'far less sweeping than appears at first sight'. For what Hegel actually condemns is 'the traditionalist *attitude* to law'. He is 'very far' from condemning all of the 'traditional political *institutions* of contemporary Europe' (Pelczynski, 1969a, p. 35).

It is perfectly true, then, that Hegel is critical of traditionalism. That is to say, he criticises those who claim that positive law should be obeyed automatically simply because it is the long established law of the land (Smith, 1991, p. 57). Clearly, however, it would be a mistake to infer from this that Hegel believes that positive laws ought not to be obeyed at all, or that all positive law should be replaced by a system of rational law, along the lines suggested by the French revolutionaries. Such a view is based on a double misunderstanding. In the first place it misunderstands Hegel's view of the relationship which exists between natural law and positive law. And in the second place it misunderstands the whole point of Hegel's philosophical approach to politics. For one of the principal inspirations which lies behind the *Philosophy of Right* is Hegel's desire, not to persuade his readers to reject positive law but, on the contrary, to provide them with solid 'rational' grounds with which justify their acceptance of positive law (Foster, 1935, pp. 172-3; Riedel, 1984, p. 38).

We said above that, according to Hegel, positive law can be looked at in two ways, from the standpoint of the understanding and from that of reason. It is now time to turn to consider the second of these. It is certainly possible, Hegel suggests, for us to apply our faculty of reason and penetrate beneath the surface appearance of things. It is possible for us to apprehend, intellectually, the essence or reality which underpins these phenomenal appearances. In the case of positive law, this underlying reality, which is timeless and universal, which does not vary, and which has an application in all societies, in all times and in all places, is a principle of natural law, or 'abstract right'. This principle of natural law will elude us if we approach the study of politics from the stand point of the understanding, because it cannot be grasped intellectually solely by means of sense perception or empirical observation. It can only be grasped by the faculty of reason (Mehta, 1968, p. 34).

It is Hegel's opinion that an adequate approach to politics must certainly seek to grasp the rational essence of positive law in this way. However, it must also go further than this. As Hegel puts it, philosophy is the 'apprehension of the present and the actual' (Hegel, 1979, p. 10). A genuinely philosophical approach to politics requires, therefore, that we consider positive law in its 'actuality'. It requires us to see it 'concretely', as a constituent element or 'moment' in a principle of objective right. Such a principle has the same status, within Hegel's political thought, as a principle of political justice has in that of Aristotle. A principle of objective right is, from the standpoint of Hegel's metaphysical system, an 'individual' entity. That is to say, it is a synthetic unity of essence and appearance, or of individual and particular. Thus it has two constituent 'parts', one of which is a principle of natural law or 'abstract right' and the other of which is a principle of purely 'positive' law. The first of these, as we have already noted, relates to some matter of moral necessity, whilst the second relates to a matter which is entirely arbitrary or conventional from the moral point of view.

In the sphere of jurisprudence also, then, if we are to be able to see laws or principles of objective right in their Actuality then we must seek to re-unite that which has been separated. For 'actuality is always the unity of individual and particular' (Hegel, 1979, p. 283). This requires us to consider the principles of objective right in a new light. Instead of seeing them in their merely 'positive' aspect, we must go beyond this point and also see them, at the same time, as being inherently 'rational'. As Hegel puts it, 'the content which is already rational in principle must win the *form* of rationality' (Hegel, 1979, p. 3; also, Avineri, 1972, pp. 125-6; Foster, 1935, p. 117; Knox, 1979b, pp. 306-7, 369; Plant, 1973, p. 76).

The concept of 'actuality', then, is central, not only to Hegel's philosophical system in general, but also to his political thought in particular, and especially to his view of the relationship which exists between natural law and positive law. This is something which has been noted by a number of commentators. Thus, for example, Riedel has maintained that in Hegel's view the basic subject matter of the *Philosophy of Right* 'is the actuality of right' (Riedel, 1984, p. 32; also 33-5). And according to Knox, 'Hegel's philosophy as a whole might be regarded as an attempt to justify his identification of rationality with actuality and *vice versa*' (Knox, 1979b, pp. 302, 305; also Pelczynski, 1969a, pp. 114-15). The concept of 'actuality', however, is evidently not a part of the positivist lexicon. From Hegel's point of view, the doctrine of legal positivism is completely unable to grasp the principles of objective right or concrete right as they should be grasped, in their actuality. That is why Hegel rejects it.

74

3 Liberalism and conservatism

Introduction

The ideologies of classical liberalism and traditional conservatism are, of course, both modern doctrines. Like capitalism and the modern state, they come into being with the demise of feudalism, over a period of time running roughly from the sixteenth century through to the end of the eighteenth century. By the end of the eighteenth century, and perhaps even by the end of the seventeenth, the principles which we now associate with them had become reasonably well established. It is quite impossible to achieve an adequate understanding of these doctrines, however, without first saying at least something about the political thought of pre-modern times. We shall, therefore, begin with a discussion of pre-modern political thought.

The comments we are about to make are an attempt to clarify the meaning of the concepts which we have 'pre-modern political thought', 'classical liberalism' and 'conservatism' by outlining just some of the central ideas that are usually associated with these broad theoretical traditions. It is not, however, our intention to seek to define these concepts precisely, or to provide a list of necessary and sufficient conditions which must be satisfied before any particular individual theorist could be located within one or other of these different traditions. The outline sketches which follow are for heuristic purposes only. They are intended to be 'ideal types', in one of the senses in which Max Weber uses this term (Weber, 1964, pp. 92, 96, 107-12; Weber, 1969, pp. 93,105; Burger, 19, pp. 27-9, 31, 115-16, 120-3, 132).

Pre-modern political thought

It is, of course, extremely difficult to make adequate judgements about the political thought of the medieval period. Any attempt to do so must be considered to be a hazardous enterprise. For we are talking about a period of time which covers several centuries. There are many individual theorists and many different traditions of thought, all of which would need to be considered in any treatment which had aspirations to be at all comprehensive. It is not, however, our intention to offer a comprehensive treatment of medieval thought. All we are seeking to do is present to the reader a selection of ideas which might plausibly (though tentatively) be said to represent some at least of the more important ideas associated with the political theory of pre-modern times. What follows, therefore, is necessarily extremely selective.

Intellectual assumptions

There are two points which are of special interest to us in relation to the basic intellectual approach adopted by pre-modern political thought. The first of these, not surprisingly, is the fact that throughout the medieval period scholars have a tendency to adopt a theological (specifically Christian) approach to intellectual affairs, whether this be the study of nature or the study of society, morals and politics. The starting point for theoretical speculation on all matters is Christianity and the beliefs associated with the Christian religion. As Tawney puts it, 'the first legacy of the Middle Ages' was 'the idea of religion as embracing all aspects of human life (Tawney, 1938, p. 36). Thus pre-modern political thought is constructed, quite typically, upon a definite framework of background assumptions, all of which might be said to have been given an early (and classical) formulation in Saint Augustine's great work, *The City of God* (Augustine, 1972).

A second point to note about the general world-view upon which pre-modern political thought is based is the attitude which it adopts towards the question of whether it is possible for men to achieve genuine knowledge, either of the natural, or of the moral and political world. With respect to this question, there are both similarities and differences between the position adopted in the early medieval period, as represented by the writings of Augustine, and that adopted in the later medieval period, as represented by those of Aquinas. In both cases it is accepted that nothing exists without a purpose. Everything which exists, whether in nature or society, is a necessary component element in the divine or cosmic order, what A. O. Lovejoy has referred to as The Great Chain of Being (Lovejoy, 1960). It is a part of God's 'divine plan' for man and the world.

From the standpoint of Augustinian theology, however, the ways of God are often, it is alleged, inscrutable and not always easy for human beings to comprehend. This is true in the case of both the order of nature and that of morals, society and politics. Moreover, intellectual comprehension is made more difficult by the fact that the faculty of reason in men is weak, imperfect and unreliable. There is, therefore, a strong current of scepticism, anti-rationalism and anti-intellectualism, in the thought of Saint Augustine. The emphasis here is on the importance of religious faith as a source of an intuitive, a spiritual, or mystical understanding of the world. As J. B. Morrall has noted, the general trend in early pre-modern times 'was to depreciate both the material world and unaided human reason' (Morrall, 1963, p. 68). Men should not rely upon their own faculty of reason. They should, rather, defer to the authority of the Catholic Church on all matters of an intellectual nature if they wish to avoid undermining their faith and, thereby, condemning themselves to eternal damnation.

In contrast to this, the later thought of Aquinas, under the influence of Aristotle, is much less spiritual and mystical, and much more intellectualistic and rationalistic, than that of Augustine. It is much less sceptical about the possibility of men achieving genuine (and hence useful) knowledge of the world, especially with respect to questions of morality and politics (Berki, 1984, pp. 106-08; Morrall, 1963, pp. 68-9). As R. N. Berki has put it, the ideas of Aquinas are much more 'cheerful', optimistic and 'this worldly' than those of Augustine (Berki, 1984, p. 107).

Human nature

As regards their respective conceptions of human nature there are, once again, both similarities and differences between the earlier and later medieval periods. These two periods have a similar attitude towards the idea of human equality and inequality. With the notable exception of stoicism and the stoic conception of natural law (Carlyle and Carlyle, 1903-32, 1, pp.8-9; Sabine and Barney Smith, 1929, p. 50; Sabine, 1973, p. 162) pre-modern political thought generally is for the most part based, like that of Plato and Aristotle, upon a fundamental belief in human inequality (Plato, 1968, pp. 102-05, 181; Aristotle, 1947, pp. 151-3, 353-5; Berki, 1984, p.107). Thus pre-modern political thought tends to assume that different people possess different degrees of natural aptitude and hence different levels of ability when it comes to their capacity to perform different social tasks. In addition it tends to assume that, because they are by nature unequal, different human beings also have a different value or worth, both in the order of society and in the order of nature as a whole.

These two periods tend to differ, however, on the Aristotelian question of whether man is, by nature, a social and political animal. The view of Augustine with respect to this question is, as before, much more pessimistic than that of Aquinas. According to Augustine, human nature has been corrupted by sin. Men, therefore, are imperfect beings. They are basically egotistical. They have an instinctive psychological predisposition to pursue their own selfish interests at the expense of others. This is so because their behaviour is dominated and determined by their emotions, appetites and desires and not by their reason. Their behaviour is therefore a reflection, not of God's will, but rather of their own personal or private will (Augustine, 1972, pp. 139, 512-13, 547, 553, 571, 573, 593, 595, 598-9, 762, 883).

Thus, for Augustine, human beings are fundamentally immoral and unjust. They are incapable of ever acting justly on their own. They only ever act in accordance with the principles of justice and morality when compelled to do so by fear of punishment, either by other men or by God. Even then, however, they could not really be said to have acted justly. For the motivation which underpins such behaviour remains self-interested (Augustine, 1972, pp. 868-69; Eccleshall, 1978, p. 47; Morrall, 1962, pp. 19-20).

Aquinas, on the other hand, once again has a much 'more positive outlook on social and political life' than Augustine (Morall, 1963, pp. 68-9). Like Aristotle before him, Aquinas is of the opinion that man *is* a social and political animal (Aquinas, 1966, p. 115). Man is a being who was created by God to live in harmonious fellowship together with others in political society, not simply in Heaven but also here on earth. For Aquinas, unlike Augustine, human beings are, in principle at least, capable of acting rationally, that is to say, altruistically, morally and justly (Berki, 1984, p. 106; Morrall, 1962, p. 72). In the case of Aquinas, however, unlike that of Aristotle, it is only possible for the faculty of reason to perform the important function of restraining the passions if it has been purified in some way by religious faith.

Society

The theory of society associated with pre-modern political thought is largely derived from the ideas of the ancient Greeks, and especially the writings of Plato and Aristotle. Because of its assumption that men are by nature unequal, pre-modern political thought sees society as an hierarchical structure. There is a social inequality which matches or corresponds to the natural inequality which exists between men.Thus society is viewed as an ordered hierarchy of unequals, each of which has a definite place or station. These stations in society are each associated with a particular function, the performance of which is considered to be necessary for the common good, or the well being of society as a whole (Barnes, 1969, pp. 18-19; Bindoff, 1953, pp. 27-32; Eccleshall, 1978, p. 49, 78-9; Nisbet, 1974, pp. 197-8; Stone, 1971, pp. 15-16; Tawney, 1938, pp. 37-9).

According to pre-modern thinking, all of the important cleavages in society are defined in this manner. In feudal times society was composed, essentially, of a variety of social groups, estates or corporations, each one of which was devoted to the carrying out of these various social tasks. Corporatism is an essential component element in pre-modern political thought.

From this point of view, the reason why different people have different stations in society is precisely because, by nature, they are unequal and hence possess different levels of ability when it comes to the performance of society's different functions or tasks. As with Plato, therefore, a well ordered society is one in which everyone does the job which, by nature, they are best fitted to do.

It is, moreover, a basic postulate of pre-modern political thought that each of the different stations in society is associated with a corresponding system of correlative rights and duties (in both the moral and the legal sense). From the standpoint of pre-modern thought, it is the duty of every member of society to carry out to the best of their ability the tasks which are associated with their own particular social position. In so doing, they are behaving altruistically. They are sacrificing the pursuit of their own immediate short term self interest for the good of others and for that of society as a whole.

Pre-modern political though also subscribes to what is usually referred to as an organic theory of society. Here society is seen as a whole which is greater than the sum of its individual parts. It is what Ferdinand Tonnies has called a 'community' or 'gemeinschaft', as opposed to an 'association' or 'gesellschaft' (Tonnies, 1955). An important implication of this theory of society is that, for those who subscribe to it, society ought not to be thought of as existing for the individual. Rather, the individual ought to be thought of as existing for society

This theory of society, especially in so far as its emphasis on the principles of order and hierarchy are concerned, has a strong affinity with the general intellectual assumptions of the medieval period, or with medieval cosmology. It might indeed be said to be a straightforward application to human affairs of the notion of the Great Chain of Being (Eccleshall, 1978, pp. 78-9; Fletcher, 1976, pp. 5-6; Lovejoy, 1960, pp. 64-5; Stone, 1971, pp.15-16, 20-1; Tillyard, 1943, pp. 33-5, 37-8; Wootton, 1986, pp. 28-30).

Economics

The approach of pre-modern thought to economic issues is a corollary of its theory of society. It is also much the same as that of the Catholic Church in the medieval period. Here the attitude of Augustine and Augustinian theology is dominant. The hall mark of this approach to economic matters is, like Augustine's attitude generally, decidedly other worldly. From this point of view, as R. H. Tawney puts it, 'economic motives are suspect'. Economic activity is associated with the psychological characteristics of egotism and greed, and hence with man's sinful or corrupted nature. To become too absorbed in such matters is to put one's material interests before those of others and the common good of the community in which one lives, which is a clear breach of moral duty. It is also to give what are merely material interests precedence over one's higher spiritual needs. Thus, the pursuit of wealth, and even the institution of private property itself, are considered to be distractions which are likely to get in the way of the successful achievement of personal salvation by each individual Christian. For always, economic interests ought to be 'subordinate to the real business of life, which is salvation' (Tawney, 1938, pp. 44-5).

The attitude of the Catholic Church in the medieval period was, therefore, certainly not one of wholehearted enthusiasm or encouragement for unrestrained commercial activity. Rather, such activity was, as Weber puts it, 'at best ethically tolerated' (Weber, 1967, p. 74). This attitude towards economic affairs is very well illustrated by the position adopted by the Church with respect to usury and the so-called 'theory of the just price' (Kitch, 1969, pp.95-144; Laski, 1962, pp. 17-18; Tawney, 1938, pp.30-64).The claim that this approach to economic affairs was to be severely challenged from the sixteenth century onwards by the more individualistic social and economic teachings of the Protestant Reformation is, of course, central to what is usually referred to as the 'Weber thesis' on the relationship between Protestantism and capitalism (Green, 1959; Kitch, 1969; Marshall, 1982; Poggi, 1983; Smith, 1981; Tawney, 1938).

Law

The attitude of pre-modern political thought to the nature and function of law is extremely complex. Individuals in the medieval period were, of course, subject to more than one kind of law, including especially the canon law of the Catholic Church and the customary law of the particular community within which they lived. Moreover, the legal and political thinking of feudal times was also moulded to some degree by the influence of the principles of Roman law, on the one hand, and those of natural law on the other.

In connection with law, the most important point, so far as we are concerned, is the dominance of customary law in pre-modern times, if not in theory then certainly in practice. This dominance takes two forms. In the first place, customary law is dominant in relation to the principles of natural law. An important theoretical question for medieval jurists, as we have already seen, was which is to take precedence over the other, customary law or natural law? The answer that is usually given to this question by the jurists is that it is natural law that has priority (Gierke, 1957, p. 75; Morrall, 1962, pp. 120-1; Ullmann, 1965, p. 180). In practice, however, only lip-service was ever paid to this doctrine of the precedence of natural law in the medieval period. The reality was actually one of the practical domination of the principles of customary law over those of natural law.

One way of responding to this observation would be to claim that there is evidently an inconsistency between the legal theories expounded by medieval lawyers and medieval legal practice (Friedrich, 1963, pp. 77-84; Friedrich, 1972, pp. 16, 26-7). On the other hand, however, as we have already seen from our discussion of the notion of natural law earlier, it could with equal plausibility be maintained that this practical dominance of customary law over natural law in medieval times is not inconsistent with the natural law principles of medieval political thought. Moreover, the belief that it is based on a misunderstanding of the view which medieval jurists had of the relationship between natural law and customary law.

From this standpoint, as we have already noted, the function of customary law is considered to be that of providing a particular interpretation or specific 'determination' of the more general principles of natural law. It is, therefore, only by following the legal customs and traditions of the community in which they live that individuals are able, in any practical sense, to actually obey the commands of the precepts of natural law, which is also God's law (Battaglia, 1981, pp. 91-4; Copleston, 1955, p. 231; Eccleshall, 1978, pp. 54-5, 101-2; Finnis, 1980, pp. 284-6; McIlwain, 1910, pp. vii, 94; Sabine, 1973, p. 242). This attitude of mind is very well illustrated by the views of Sir Edward Coke, the great seventeenth century defender of the principle of the supremacy of the English common law. As Lloyd has pointed out, Coke considered the common law of England to be 'the embodiment of human reason and therefore coterminous with natural law' (Lloyd, 1970, p. 83; also Boorstin, 1973, p. 60; Holdsworth, 1923-32, 2, pp. 602-4; O'Sullivan, 1945; Pollock, 1961, p. 142; Sommerville, 1986, p. 99; Stanlis, 1958, pp. 37-8; Wilkins, 1967, pp. 35-6).

In the second place, custom and tradition are considered to have a superiority in relation to statute law. There is, as is well known, a relative lack of emphasis on the notion of legislation, or of creating new law in the medieval period. This is a situation which, of course, begins to change only from the sixteenth century onwards, with the rise of the modern state and the development of the notion of sovereignty. Before then, the emphasis is on the notion of 'declaration' or 'interpretation' rather than that of legislation. Generally speaking, in pre-modern times, the function of statutes, or of statute law, is considered to be that of providing an officially sanctioned interpretation of the principles of customary law (Berki, 1984, pp. 95-7; Eccleshall, 1978, pp. 100-1, 123-5; Morall, 1962, pp. 10, 15-16, 123-4; Sabine, 1973, pp. 196-7).

A further point to note about the attitude towards law adopted in the medieval period is an acceptance of the principle of inequality before the law. As Sabine as pointed out, the central thrust of the medieval view was not, in any way, a commitment to the principle of equality before the law. It was, rather, an acceptance of the alternative principle that 'every man was entitled to enjoy the law according to his rank and order' (Sabine, 1973, p. 200). This principle is a logical consequence of the medieval acceptance of the principle of natural inequality between men. It is a principle which prevailed in the legal systems of virtually all Western European societies until the seventeenth and eighteenth centuries. Even in the early modern England of the sixteenth century, as S. T. Bindoff has remarked, 'neither liberty nor equality was a Tudor watchword' (Bindoff, 1953, p. 32).

Politics

From the standpoint of pre-modern political thought, just as for Plato, 'ruling' is a job like any other. It is a necessary precondition for the existence and survival of

81

any society that this particular task or function be carried out by somebody. Here also, however, when it comes to the ability to perform this particular task, men are by nature unequal. In matters of ruling some people know better than others. By nature some people are born to rule and others to be ruled. It is, therefore, the duty of this 'natural aristocracy' to carry out this particular task of ruling, just as it is the duty of every other member of society to carry out the tasks associated with their own station in life (Plato, 1968, 102-5, 108-9, 157-9, 181-3, 185-97, 233, 286).

A central feature of pre-modern political thought, therefore, is an acceptance of the principle of paternalism, the belief that individuals are not necessarily the best judges of what is in their own self interest. Paternalists believe in the existence of objective or real interests, and they believe that some people, in this case the natural aristocracy, know better than others what is really in the interests of every member of society.This paternalistic attitude is clearly a corollary of the pre-modern belief in natural inequality.

The principle of paternalism also informs the medieval conception of the monarchy. It is, from this point of view, the duty of the rulers to rule justly. They must have an eye, not to their own selfish private interests, but to the interests of others and the good of the community as a whole. They must seek to promote the general interest or the common good. Here it is the monarch who is thought of as being a wise and benevolent ruler. The ultimate justification for this theory of the role of the monarchy is, of course, provided by theology and the principles of Christianity. The monarch, like everyone else, has a particular place or 'station' within the Great Chain of Being. The principle of monarchical rule is thus conceived of as being a part of God's divine plan for mankind (Augustine, 1972, pp. 870, 874; Berki, 1984, p. 94; Deane, 1963, p.153; Gierke, 1958, p. 30).

It should be emphasised that this medieval conception of kingship is quite different from the 'absolutist' conception of later times (Berki, 1984, pp. 95-7; Bowle, 1961b; Sabine, 1973, p. 199). In the medieval conception the relationship between ruler and ruled is, as Gierke points out, based on a conception of 'reciprocal rights and duties'. The idea that the ruled should have an 'unconditioned duty of obedience' to the ruler was, therefore, 'wholly foreign to the Middle Age'. An implication of this position is that although, generally speaking, disobedience to the monarch was thought of as being 'sinful', nevertheless, under certain circumstances, such disobedience might well be justified. For the monarch is expected to rule wisely and justly. In particular he is expected to rule in accordance with a respect for the principles of natural law, on the one hand, and those of custom and tradition on the other. If he does not do this, and becomes instead a 'tyrant', then his subjects have a 'right of resistance'. Indeed, at the limit, even tyrannicide 'is justifiable or at least excusable' (Gierke, 1957, pp. 34-5).

It is sometimes claimed that pre-modern thought lacks what today we would call a philosophy of history. For this idea is a peculiarly modern one. W. H. Walsh, for example, has suggested that 'for practical purposes' it comes into existence only in the eighteenth century (Walsh, 1967, p. 13). Indeed, the term itself, according to R. G. Collingwood, was actually coined by Voltaire (Collingwood, 1976, p. 1; also Lowith, 1949, p. 1).

There are two closely related reasons why commentators might want to take this view. The first has to do with the extremely slow rate of social change in pre-modern times. It is suggested that, because of this, pre-modern thinkers do not possess what Sidney Pollard has called the 'sense of history' (Pollard, 1971, p. 15). Thus, for example, Kingsley Martin has suggested that 'the structure of society based on social orders with appropriate functions' seemed to those writing in the medieval period to be 'static, divinely ordained and final' (Martin, 1962, p. 279; also Nisbet, 1970, p. 46).

The second reason why a commentator might want to take this view follows on from the first. It is that, precisely because they lack any sense of historical change and development, pre-modern thinkers have no perception that there might be some underlying meaning or purpose which underpins the pattern of historical events and which ties them together. They lack, as Walsh puts it, an appreciation that there might be 'a unity embodying an overall plan' which, if only we could grasp it, would enable us to 'attain an understanding of the course of history as a whole' (Walsh, 1967, p. 13; Lowith, 1949, p. 1). Such an appreciation, according to Walsh, is an essential component element in any genuine philosophy of history.

On the other hand, however, there are also commentators who maintain that this claim is entirely unjustified. For these commentators pre-modern thought certainly does possess an understanding of the notion of change and development. Hence it also possesses a sense of history. Moreover, it has a perception that this change is change in a particular direction. It is change which is in some sense meaningful. Thus, in addition to a sense of history, pre-modern thought also possesses a very clear philosophy of history. For these commentators, the best example of such a philosophy of history in pre-modern times is provided by the writings of Augustine (Nisbet, 1970, pp. 63, 65, 69, 77-8, 80, 82, 91; Keyes, 1966; Mommsen, 1951; Pollard, 1971, p. 18).

The most decisive feature of Augustine's philosophy of history is that, as we have already noted, all historical events, including those associated with human suffering, are considered to be an integral part of the cosmic order. They are a necessary element in God's Divine Plan for the world and for mankind (Bury, 1920, p. 21; Nisbet, 1970, p. 69). From this point of view, as Collingwood has put it, 'the historical process is the working out not of man's purposes but of God's' (Collingwood, 1976, p. 48; also Pollard, 1968, p. 17). An integral element in this approach, then, is an acceptance of the idea that meaningful change and development does in fact occur in history. History, for Augustine, is 'a process with a dynamic purpose' (Pollard, 1968, p. 18).

Despite this, however, the attitude which Augustine adopts towards history and historical change, understood in this sense, remains intensely pessimistic. It is, as J. A. Mazzeo puts it, one of 'gloomy otherworldliness' (Mazzeo, 1969, p. 285). Perhaps the most significant feature of Augustine's philosophy of history, in this regard, is the absence within it of any doctrine of 'progress'. Indeed, as Pollard has argued, the *City of God* appears to have been written in order to decisively '*combat* the doctrine of mundane progress' (Pollard, 1971, p. 18; also Bury, 1920, p. 21). For pre-modern thought generally, although there may well be periods in history in which there are various improvements of one kind or another, invariably such periods are followed by periods of calamity and crisis. The course of history is, in this sense, cyclical and not linear.

Nevertheless, in the later medieval period figures like Aquinas do take a much more optimistic view than that of Augustine. Aquinas accepts the traditional Christian notion of the existence of a meaningful cosmic order. Unlike Augustine, however, he does not consider the ways of God to be inscrutable and inexplicable. Our belief in the existence of such an order is no longer based simply on an article of Christian faith. From the standpoint of the later Middle Ages, as Isaiah Berlin has pointed out, all historical explanation involves the attempt to actually establish a thing's 'proper place in the universal pattern'. It is an attempt to 'make it intelligible' by locating it against the 'one unique plan' which is the 'goal of the universe' (Berlin, 1978, pp. 161-2; Collingwood, 1976, p. 50). This is, of course, to be done by applying the metaphysical principles of Aristotelian philosophy.

Saint Augustine's 'philosophical interpretation of history' has clear implications for the position which he adopts on what Walsh has called 'the general metaphysical problem of evil'. In Walsh's view, to present a philosophy of history is also at the same time, and necessarily, to present a theodicy. From this point of view, a philosophy of history is never simply an attempt to describe or even explain the pattern of historical events. It is also, in addition, always a theoretical attempt to 'justify the ways of God to man' (Walsh, 1967, p. 119).

This general assumption of the existence of a meaningful and purposive cosmic order has important implications for the question of what practical attitude one ought to adopt towards historical change. In particular, it has implications for the question of whether men should seek to actively intervene in the historical process in an attempt to direct the course of historical events, perhaps with the intention of alleviating human suffering. With respect to this particular issue, the attitude of Augustine and of the earlier medieval period is once again one of profound pessimism. Pain and suffering, poverty, disease and death, will always be with us. They, too, are an essential part of the divine plan, a justified punishment for man's original sin. From the standpoint of Augustinian theology a commitment to social progress or social reform is, therefore, as H. E. Barnes has suggested, not merely 'relatively unimportant', it is in fact a threat to one's personal salvation. In Saint Augustine's view, man had much 'better endure serious social inconveniences than jeopardise his salvation by dissipating his energy in attempting to improve earthly conditions' (Barnes, 1969, p.16).

Saint Augustine's views may be considered to be quite typical of the attitude adopted towards the question of social reform in pre-modern times. As Andrew Gamble puts it, 'the idea that human societies might be radically improved, and that human energies should be directed to securing such improvements, was not widely entertained by Christians in classical times or in medieval Europe' (Gamble, 1983, p. 23; also Cobban, 1962, p. 22).

Conclusion

The one dominant value of pre-modern political thought is that of *order*. This particular conception of order, once it has been fully understood, may be seen to encapsulate almost every other aspect of pre-modern political thought. This order is one which is alleged to exist both in nature and in society. It is an order which is associated, as we have seen, with the general principles of medieval cosmology, and especially the idea of the Great Chain of Being. It is an order which exists as a consequence of God's divine plan for the world, and hence one which, ultimately, may be said to have a theological sanction.

In the early medieval period the belief in the existence of such a cosmic order is based on the principle of Christian *faith* and is associated with a general attitude which is at once both *other worldly* and profoundly *pessimistic* with respect to human affairs in general. In the later medieval period the belief in a cosmic order is based as much on *reason* as on faith. It is also associated with an attitude which is much less pessimistic and other worldly than that of earlier times.

In so far as politics and society specifically are concerned, this supreme value of order, more narrowly conceived, is associated with a number of subsidiary values. These include the values of *hierarchy, inequality,* and *deference;* the values of *altruism, duty, community* and the *common good;* and finally the values of *custom* and *tradition.*

These, then, are the key component elements of pre-modern political thought. This was the world view that dominated most of western Europe throughout the medieval period, up until the sixteenth and seventeenth centuries. It is a world view that was, as we shall see, fundamentally challenged at this time by the principles of modern political thought as we find them expressed within the ideology of classical liberalism.

Classical liberalism

Classical liberalism is a decidedly modern doctrine. It comes into existence, approximately, in the seventeenth and eighteenth centuries, and is closely associated, historically, with the English Revolutions of 1642-1649 and 1688-89, the American revolution of 1776, and the French Revolution of 1789. The basic attitude of mind of the classical liberal is that of someone who either rejects, or significantly re-interprets, almost all of the ideals and assumptions of what we have called pre-modern political thought.

Intellectual assumptions

When looking at the broad, intellectual assumptions of classical liberalism, what is most striking in the first place is its secular approach to intellectual matters. As is well known, in both the study of nature and that of society, morals and politics, the modern political thought of the seventeenth and eighteenth centuries, and hence also the ideology of classical liberalism, both abandon the traditional, theological approach which had been adopted by European intellectuals throughout the medieval period (Arblaster, 1984, p. 98). This is the period in which, we see the rise of the modern state, 'whose authority was entirely secular' (Gamble, 1983, p. 7, 47; Laski, 1962, pp. 41, 55).

Broadly speaking, then, the intellectual foundations of classical liberalism are closely associated with the with the philosophical movement known as the Enlightenment, a movement for which, as Harold Laski has put it, the main object of theoretical speculation 'was to disrupt scholastic teleology', thus ensuring that the idea 'of original sin gave way to the doctrine of progress, with its own concomitant idea of perfectibility through reason' (Laski, 1961, p. 186; Laski, 1962, p. 11, 83).

A second point to note about the intellectual assumptions of classical liberalism, therefore, is its attitude towards reason and knowledge. The attitude of mind of classical liberal thinkers in this regard is quite different from that of the theologians of the earlier medieval period. For classical liberalism rejects the principle of scepticism, or the idea that it is impossible for us ever to gain genuine (and useful) knowledge of either the natural or the social world. The classical liberals of the seventeenth and eighteenth centuries are extremely optimistic about such matters (Arblaster, 1984, pp. 61-2).

In so far as the natural world is concerned, this is of course the age of the 'scientific revolution', and of the development of new ways of thinking about the processes of nature by such figures as Galileo and Newton, ways of thinking which frequently brought their individual proponents into conflict with the orthodoxies, and hence also the authority, of the Catholic Church. A number of commentators have emphasised the importance of the links between liberalism and science (Arblaster, 1984, pp. 25-7, 55, 61-2, 82; Gamble, 1983, p. 61; Laski, pp. 49-51). As J. A. Hall has put it, 'a fundamental characteristic of liberalism' has been that it has sought to address all problems of an intellectual nature 'by making use of the cognitive practices of modern science' (Hall, 1988, p. 9).

A third point to note about the intellectual assumptions of classical liberalism, and one which is closely associated with the second, is its emphasis on the ideas that the ultimate source of knowledge, with respect to all matters, is the individual. The reason which is of importance to early liberal thought is, most emphatically, the reason of the individual. The motto of classical liberalism, and indeed for the Enlightenment generally, as Kant forcefully emphasises, is 'Sapere Aude!', 'Dare to Know!', 'Have the Courage to Use Your Own Understanding'(Kant, 1991, p. 54). From this point of view, all individuals are enjoined to accept nothing on trust, or on the basis of faith, or out of deference to any higher authority. Everything is to be subject to critical examination by the light of one's own understanding (Arblaster, 1984, p. 182; Brumfitt, 1972, p. 18).

Human nature

Classical liberalism has a perception of human nature which is diametrically opposed to that of pre-modern political thought in two respects In the first place, classical liberalism is based upon an assumption of human equality (Gamble, 1983, p. 42). In the history of modern political thought, this belief receives its most forceful expression, paradoxically, in the writings of that extremely illiberal thinker, Hobbes. In *Leviathan* Hobbes quite explicitly rejects the view of human nature subscribed to by Plato and Aristotle, and by pre-modern thought generally (Hobbes, 1992, p.107). This belief in human equality was, of course, to become a commonplace of liberal thinking in the eighteenth century.

An extreme formulation of this view would involve the claim that all human beings possessed the same natural capacities with respect to all areas of human activity. Most classical liberals, however, do not go this far (Gamble, 1983, p. 76). Nevertheless, like Hobbes, they believe that this principle does have an application within the sphere of politics. Here, at least, all human beings are thought of (at least in principle) as possessing an equal ability to make informed judgements about issues of common concern. To suggest otherwise is, as Adam Smith puts it, merely 'the vanity of the philosopher' (Smith, 1905, p. 12).

Moreover, from the standpoint of classical liberalism all men are assumed to have an equal value or worth, both in the order of nature and in that of society. Thus, morally speaking, all persons possess equal rights. They have a moral right to be treated in the same way as other persons in similar circumstances (Arblaster, 1984, p. 89; Gamble, 1983, p. 88). This notion of the equal dignity or worth of all human beings or persons is, as is well known, central to the moral and political thought Kant, and to Kant's version of liberalism, towards the end of the eighteenth century (Kant, 1972, pp. 90-7).

The second respect in which the classical liberal view of human nature differs from that of pre-modern thought is that the former, unlike the latter, tends to see human beings as isolated, rational, calculating, self-interested individuals. These individuals are assumed always to pursue their own self-interests as they understand them. Thus, for the ideology of classical liberalism, man is most definitely not a 'social and political animal', at least not in the sense in which the ancient Greeks and medieval scholastics like Aquinas understood this expression. Man is not a communal being. Human beings are not, by nature, destined to live together in harmonious fellowship with others. It is perfectly natural for human beings to seek to pursue their own self interest in everything that they do (Arblaster, 1984, pp. 28-33, 39-43; Bullock and Shock, 1956, p. xxiii; Laski, 1961, p. 186; Laski, 1962, p. 84). Once again, as is well known, this is a principle which is contributed to classical liberalism by the political thought of Hobbes (Hobbes, 1992, pp. 86-90).

It could, of course, be argued that this view of human nature is actually not so very different from that of the early pre-modern thought of a figure like Augustine. For he also sees human behaviour (at least the behaviour associated with the 'corrupted' human nature of the City of Man) as being motivated fundamentally by the pursuit of self-interest. There are, nevertheless, important differences between these two assessments of human nature. Perhaps the most important of these differences is the fact that, because of its secular approach, classical liberalism, and the modern political thought of the seventeenth and eighteenth centuries generally, do not see the pursuit of self-interest by individuals as being wicked or morally wrong. As Hobbes puts it, the 'desires and other passions of man are in themselves no sin' (Hobbes, 1992, p. 89).

Behaviour of this sort is not thought of as occurring as a consequence of sin and is not considered a bad thing. On the contrary, as such behaviour is natural to man it should, be applauded rather than condemned. For it is evident that it can have extremely beneficial social consequences. This is an attitude of mind which is expressed in the writings of a number of Enlightenment thinkers. As Barbara Goodwin has put it, liberal thinkers at this time 'achieved what seemed impossible in the Christian middle ages: they made a virtue of selfishness' (Goodwin, 1987, p. 35). From this point of view, then, there is a definite 'harmony' of interests between man and man, although Enlightenment thinkers tend to disagree on the question of whether this harmony can be relied upon to occur naturally or whether, alternatively, it needs to be artificially created and sustained by political means (Halevy, 1972, pp. 13-20; Bullock and Shock, 1956, p. xxiii; Hampson, 1968, p. 100, 118, 126; Pollard, 1971, p. 63).

Society

Classical liberalism envisages society, not as a community of unequals, but as an association of equals. In the terminology of Tonnies, society is a 'gesellschaft' rather than a 'gemeinschaft'. According to the principles of classical liberalism, the relations which exist between individuals living together in society are based entirely on the pursuit of individual self-interest. All social relationships are, therefore, essentially 'contractual' in nature. Society as a whole is seen as being nothing more than a network of such over-lapping contractual relationships. This attitude of mind is quite typical of the social contract theory of the seventeenth and eighteenth centuries (Arblaster, 1984, pp. 40-1; Gamble, 1983, p. 45; Heywood, 1992, p. 19, 24, 27-8; Laski, 1961, p. 186; Laski, 1962, pp. 20-1)

Classical liberalism, therefore, rejects the organic theory of society. It rejects the notion that society should be considered to be an organism which exists in its own right, independently of the individuals who compose it, and which has a life of its own. For classical liberalism, society understood in this particular sense does not exist. A basic assumption of the classical liberal theory of society is the principle of radical individualism (Bullock and Shock, 1956, p. xxiii; Heywood, 1992, pp. 18-20; Lukes, 1979, pp. 79-85; Vincent, 1992, pp. 32-7).

Associated with this view of society is a particular attitude towards the issue of equality and inequality. We have seen that, in at least two senses, classical liberals are committed to a belief in human equality. One consequence of this commitment is a strong negative reaction to those existing legal, political and social inequalities or privileges which, in their view, cannot be morally justified because they constitute an affront to the natural equality which exists between human beings. Classical liberalism, therefore, most definitely rejects the corporatist, or estatist, attitude of mind of pre-modern thought, together with its emphasis on the desirability of there being a system of differential rights and duties for the individual members of society, depending upon their particular group membership or status.

This is not to say, however, that classical liberalism is opposed to all inequalities. For they are not. In particular, they accept the existence of social or economic inequalities, and feel that in certain circumstances these might be morally justified. Classical liberalism is not opposed to the institution of private property or to an unequal distribution of wealth. Generally speaking, it is quite happy to accept these things, provided they are not associated with the existence of legal and political inequality and privilege. The ideal society of classical liberalism is one which accepts the existence of social and economic inequality, on the understanding that this is associated with a situation in which there is legal and political equality; that is to say, a situation of 'equality of opportunity' in which all may benefit to the full from the exercise of their own natural capacities. In these circumstances, social inequality is acceptable from the moral point of view precisely because it might justifiably be said to be 'natural'. From this point of view, as Anthony Arblaster has pointed out, it is merit and not birth or title that should be rewarded. 'Hereditary inequality is unacceptable. Inequality which reflects merit or desert is not' (Arblaster, 1984, p. 87; also Gamble, 1983, p. 89; Heywood, 1992, p. 16; Vincent, 1992, pp. 41-2).

Finally, an important implication of this classical liberal theory of society, based as it is on an acceptance of the principle of radical individualism, is that society is thought of as existing to benefit the individual and not *vice versa*. The individual is considered to have priority over society, in several different senses: ontologically, historically, morally and politically (Arblaster, 1984, pp. 22-3).

Economics

The approach to economic affairs which is most closely associated with the ideology of classical liberalism is, of course, that espoused by Adam Smith in his *An Inquiry Into The Nature And Causes Of The Wealth Of Nations* (Arblaster, 1984, pp. 237-243; Bullock and Shock, 1956, pp. xxiii-xxiv; Gamble, 1983, pp. 43-4; Heywood, 1992, pp. 36-8; Hobhouse, 1911, pp. 78-101; Laski, 1961, pp. 184-206; Vincent, 1992, pp. 45-8).

In Smith's ideal economic system, as is well known, there is a division of labour and all human needs are satisfied by means of economic exchange through a market. This is an economic system based upon contractual agreements entered into voluntarily by free and equal individuals for reasons of self-interest. Smith's economic theory is based on the assumption that because these arrangements are 'free contracts' then we are justified in claiming that, in all cases, both contractants may be said to benefit equally (Smith, 1905, pp. 1-13).

The principal economic reason why Smith feels that such a system is superior to all possible alternatives is that, in his view, it leads to national prosperity or 'opulence'. It is an economic system in which the productivity of labour is high, and this leads to the maximisation of the total quantity of goods available for consumption by each individual member of society (Smith, 1905, pp. 263-69).There is, therefore, a 'hidden hand' or 'pre-established harmony' which guarantees that although all individuals pursue their own self interest and that alone, nevertheless this leads to a state of affairs from which everyone benefits and no one is harmed (Smith, 1905, p. 345).

From our point of view, there are two points to note about Smith's economic ideas. The first is that they are indeed based on assumptions about human nature and society which are quite typical of classical liberalism generally. The second is that these assumptions are quite different from those of the economic thinking of the medieval period. For, as we have seen, in pre-modern economic thought the pursuit of wealth for its own sake, or for reasons of self-interest, is frowned upon as being incompatible with the pursuit of heavenly salvation. As Laski has put it, the 'whole social morality of the middle ages is built upon this doctrine' which was 'enforced both by the rules of the church and by the civil law' (Laski, 1962, p. 18).

The attitude of classical liberalism towards questions of law and rights is usually thought to be best represented by the writings of John Locke (Locke, 1988). Locke's political thought may be seen as an intellectual response to the doctrines put forward by the defenders of the principle of absolute monarchy in the seventeenth century. In so far as the history of political thought is concerned, the most noteworthy of these is Thomas Hobbes.

The doctrine of absolutism, as we find it expressed in the conventional interpretation of Hobbes, possesses a number of characteristic features. Of these perhaps the most important is the claim that the sovereign can neither do wrong nor act unjustly. From this point of view, law, morality and justice are all thought of as being associated with the commands of the sovereign. For Hobbes, positive law, that is to say statute law (or 'civil law'), has priority over all other kinds of law. It is statute law which is the standard of justice and morality for the individual subject.

Individuals, on this interpretation of Hobbes, certainly do possess rights. They have rights against one another (for example property rights) which are granted and defended by the civil law. In the absence of the sovereign, and of civil law, no such rights would exist. In a hypothetical pure state of nature, therefore, there would be no law, no morality, and no justice. As Hobbes himself expresses it, the notions of right and wrong, justice and injustice have there no place' (Hobbes, 1992, p. 90).

According to this conventional interpretation it is Hobbes's view that although individuals do have rights against one another, they do not and cannot have any rights against the sovereign. There is no standard of morality or justice (whether this be natural law or the common law) which is higher than civil law and which might be employed as a critical standard for the evaluation of civil law. There is, therefore, no standard to which the individual might appeal in order to justify an act of disobedience to the commands of the sovereign. Individuals have an unconditional duty to obey those commands, no matter what the circumstances (Hobbes, 1839-45a, p. 151, 190-1, 271; Hobbes, 1839-45b, p. 29; Hobbes, 1992, p. 239).

Like that of Hobbes, the political thought of John Locke has been interpreted in a variety of different ways. According to the conventional interpretation of Locke's political thought, Locke's work constitutes an attempt to refute the principle of absolutism. Thus, in Locke's view, the sovereign most emphatically can do wrong. It certainly is possible for the sovereign to act unjustly. It is not the case that law is merely the command of the sovereign. Nor is it correct to say that it is positive law (whether this be customary law or statute law) which is the standard of right and wrong, or justice and injustice, for the individual citizen (Locke, 1988a, pp. 270-1, 326-8, 353, 357-63, 367, 370, 398-9, 400-2, 416-7, 419, 426-7).

On this interpretation, it is Locke's view that individuals possess certain rights (for example property rights) which ought to be protected and defended by the sovereign and by civil law. These rights are not created by either the sovereign or civil law. They are natural rights. Hence, according to Locke, not only do individuals have rights against one another, they also have rights against the sovereign. There is a higher law to which individuals might appeal to in order to question the legitimacy of the commands of the sovereign and of the dictates of civil law. There are certain rights which the sovereign is under an obligation to respect (Locke, 1988, pp. 271-2). Indeed, the sole function of the sovereign is act as a guarantor of these rights (Locke, 1988, pp. 350-1).

From this point of view, then, Locke is of the opinion that the duty of the individual to obey the commands of the sovereign is not one which is absolute and unconditional. Under certain circumstances, if the sovereign acts unjustly by infringing the natural rights of the subject, then disobedience and even resistance is most certainly morally justified (Locke, 1988, pp. 370, 401-2, 419; Gamble, 1983, p.79). The conventional interpretation of Locke, therefore, is one which presents Locke as a radical individualist whose beliefs have potentially revolutionary political implications.

It should be clear from this brief account that, like Hobbes, Locke is indeed a modern thinker. The attitude of both Hobbes and Locke to questions of law and rights is, in several important respects, quite different from that of pre-modern political thought. In particular, their views constitute a departure from the typically pre-modern emphasis on the importance of custom and tradition. A commitment to the moral or legal supremacy of English common law has no part to play in the political thought of either Hobbes or Locke.

One final point to note about the attitude towards law which is adopted by classical liberalism is that, as we have already observed, it is strongly committed to the principle of equality before the law (Bellamy, 1993, pp. 26-7). This principle is quite typical of classical liberalism in both the seventeenth and the eighteenth centuries. It is clearly enunciated in both the writings of English liberal thinkers like Locke and those of French liberals, like l'abbe de Sieyes, writing at the end of the eighteenth century (Locke, 1988, pp. 324, 363; Ritchie, 1903, pp. 290-4; Sieyes, 1963, pp. 57-9, 61-4, 161-2). Indeed, this principle might be said to provide a concise summary of what the French Revolution was really all about. As George Lefebvre has put it, the Third Estate 'loudly demanded equality before the law. At this point, strictly speaking, the Revolution of 1789 began' (Lefebvre, 1947, p. 34). This commitment to equality before the law derives from classical liberalism's acceptance of the principle of natural equality. It is a commitment which clearly differentiates classical liberalism, and modern political thought generally, from the pre-modern thinking of the medieval period.

The approach to politics that is adopted by the ideology of classical liberalism possesses four basic features. In the first place, this approach is usually based, as one might expect, on the principles of secularism and rationalism. It is reason, and not theology, which is the source of all of our knowledge of political affairs. In this particular area, knowledge is discoverable not on the basis of empirical observation but rather, as Leslie Stephen has put it, 'either by intuition or by an *a priori* method of reasoning entirely independent of experience' (Stephen, 1962, 2, p. 112; also Cassirer,1961, p. 270).

In the sphere of politics, then, the typical starting for intellectual inquiry by classical liberal thinkers is reflection upon human nature and on what life would be like in some pre-social, natural condition. This is the 'state of nature' which is so important to the modern version of social contract theory which dominated political thought at this time (Barker, 1948; Bellamy, 1993, p. 27; Gough, 1957; Hobhouse, 1911, pp. 54-65; Lessnoff, 1986.)

The most important point to note here is that the conclusions arrived at as a consequence of such speculation, because they are based on a rational examination of human nature, are thought of by liberal thinkers as having a valid application to 'man in general', or to all mankind (Arblaster, 1984, p. 35, 135; Becker, 1979, pp. 102-5; Manning, 1976, p. 24). It was this attitude of mind which, at the end of the eighteenth century, underpinned the efforts of the French revolutionaries to draw up a blueprint for a new French constitution, based on a *Declaration of the Rights of Man*. This constitution would be not only ideally just but also universally valid, because it conformed to the essential requirements of human nature, which is everywhere the same.

A second feature of the classical liberal approach to politics is its view of the proper role of the state in a free society. For classical liberalism freedom or liberty is, of course, the most important political value. There is, however, an ambivalence within classical liberalism regarding the notion of freedom or liberty.

Traditionally, the state is seen by liberal thinkers as being a potential threat to individual freedom in either one or the other of two different ways. In the first place, it may threaten the freedom of the individual because it does not respect the principle of the rule of law. Such a commitment to the rule of law is clearly to be found in Locke's defence of the principles of the English Revolution of 1688-89 (Locke, 1988, pp. 283-4, 305-6, 400). It is also to be found in the French *Declaration of the Rights of Man* a century later (Ritchie, 1903, pp. 290-4). From this point of view, the rule of law and hence law itself is not seen by liberal thinkers as being something which limits the liberty of the individual. On the contrary, it actually enhances it (Arblaster, 1984, p. 166; Bullock and Shock, 1956, p.xx). This is an idea which is usually associated with what is called the 'positive' conception of freedom (Berlin, 1969; Buttle, 1984; Crocker, 1980; Gray and Pelczynski, 1984; MacCallum, 1967; Miller, 1984; Ryan, 1979; Scott, 1956;

Seidentop, 1979). It is, therefore, quite important to note that it is an idea which is to be found, not simply in the later history of political thought, but also within classical liberalism itself. The origins of the 'positive' conception of liberty lie within the political thought of the seventeenth century, and especially in Whig political thought.

In the second place, the state is considered by early liberals to be a threat to the freedom of the individual for quite a different reason. This is so because law itself, even when impartially administered, might in certain circumstances actually serve to undermine rather than enhance the freedom of the individual. From the point of view of this 'negative' conception of liberty, individuals are thought of as being at liberty to the extent that they are unhindered by the laws of the state (Skinner, 1984; White; 1970). Freedom, here, is associated with the absence of law and legal restraint. Individuals are free (primarily) in so far as they are legally able to do those things which they have freely chosen to do with their own person and their own property (Arblaster, 1984, pp. 56-8; Heywood, 1992, pp. 20-1; Vincent, 1992, pp. 37-41). Thus, in this case, liberty and law are considered to be incompatible. The more that individuals are subjected to law, or laws, the less liberty they possess.

On this second view, therefore, a free society is a society in which there is a maximum of individual freedom and hence a minimum amount of law. It is for this reason that many classical liberal thinkers advocate what is usually referred to as a 'laissez faire' or 'minimal' state (Bullock and Shock, 1956, pp. xxv-xxvi; Eccleshall, 1986, pp. 43, 53-4; Gamble, 1983, p.44; Heywood, 1992, p. 16, 36-8; Vincent, 1992, pp. 29-30, 45-6).

In the broadest sense, the task of such a minimal state, according to classical liberals, is to promote the common good, or the general interest, by providing that basic amount of regulation of the private lives of its individual citizens which is necessary for the survival of society. In carrying out this task the minimal state, in the words of Locke, acts as an impartial 'umpire' in cases of dispute or conflict between its individual citizens (Locke, 1988, p. 324; Eccleshall, 1986, p. 46). Conceived more narrowly, there are three particular functions which a minimal state ought to perform. It must make and enforce laws designed to protect individual citizens from personal injury. It must make and enforce laws designed to protect individuals in the possession of their property. It must make and enforce laws designed to enforce contractual agreements and hence facilitate the workings of the free market economy, along the lines indicated by Adam Smith (Smith, 1905, p. 540; Bullock and Shock, 1956, p. xxv; Laski, 1961, pp. 191-3; Vincent, 1992, p. 48).

A third feature of the classical liberal approach to politics is its emphasis on the value of individual privacy and the theoretical distinction which liberal theorists make (either explicitly or implicitly) between the 'public' and the 'private' spheres (Arblaster, 1984, pp. 43-5; Bellamy, 1993, p. 27; Gamble, 1983, p. 56; Goodwill, 1987, pp. 42-3; Mill, 1972, pp. 68-75; Vincent, 1992, p. 48).

Those actions which fall within the public sphere are actions which, according to classical liberals, are matters of legitimate concern for the state. Here it is accepted that the state has the moral right to take away from individual citizens the freedom to decide for themselves whether or not they are going to perform the actions in question. All other actions are not considered to be matters of legitimate concern for the state, and hence fall within the 'private' sphere. In this area the state is under a moral obligation to leave individuals at liberty to decide for themselves whether or not they are going to perform a particular action or engage in a particular type of activity.

Needless to say, from the standpoint of classical liberalism, the public sphere ought to be as small as possible. There is only a very small and narrowly delimited range of actions which are considered to be matters of legitimate concern for the state: actions such as murder, theft and the keeping of contracts. Ideally, in the vast majority of cases, the state will leave individuals free to decide for themselves how they are going to act.

Although the public-private distinction is first explicitly articulated and defended by John Stuart Mill in the nineteenth century (Mill, 1972, pp. 68-75), it is evident that it can be quite clearly discerned, at least implicitly, within the ideology of classical liberalism from its inception. Thus, for example, it could be argued that the whole purpose of the doctrine of natural rights is, precisely, to establish the existence of a protected private sphere of action in which individuals are 'sovereign', with respect to their own persons and their own property. For Locke, at least according to the conventional interpretation of his thought, the freedom of the individual is of supreme importance. In Locke's opinion, as Richard Aaron has put it, 'the state is made for the individual and not the individual for the state' (Aaron, 1965, p. 286). It is because they hold such a view that Locke, the founding fathers of the American Revolution, and the French revolutionaries who drew up the *Declaration of the Rights of Man,* are all considered to be genuinely liberal thinkers.

From this point of view, then, it is this implicit distinction between the public and the private spheres which clearly differentiates the ideas of Locke, and again those of classical liberalism generally, from those of anti-liberal thinkers, such as absolutists, who do not afford to individuals any protection at all against the legal intrusions of an all powerful, state. Within the political thought of absolutism, as conventionally understood, everything is public, or a matter of legitimate concern for the state. There is nothing at all which might be said to be essentially a private matter, and hence no business of the state. The theoretical distinction between the public and the private spheres has, therefore, no part to play within the doctrine of absolutism. It is for precisely this reason that absolutist ideas are considered to be fundamentally 'illiberal' (Arblaster, 1984, p. 136; Held, 1983, p. 5).

Similarly, in the twentieth century, it is the existence of this theoretical distinction between the public and the private spheres which constitutes the decisive point of difference between liberalism and a 'totalitarian' ideology such as fascism; of which the ideology of absolutism might be said, at least in certain key respects, to be a seventeenth and eighteenth century ancestor. For within the ideology of totalitarianism, also, the sphere within which the state is considered to have a legitimate right to regulate the lives of its individual citizens is considered to be, as the name suggests, 'total'. For defenders of totalitarianism, all things are considered to be public and nothing is private. Where classical liberal ideals subordinate the state to the individual, the totalitarian ideal subordinates the individual to the state (Bellamy, 1993, p. 27; Goodwill, 1987, p. 165; Heywood, 1992, pp. 190-2; O'Sullivan, 1983, pp. 35-6, 61-4, 159; Sternhell, 1979, pp. 354-5, 366-7, 379-80; Vincent, 1992, pp. 149-50, 163-4; Wilford, 1986, pp. 245-6).

A fourth feature of the classical liberal approach to politics is its attitude towards democracy. As is well known, this attitude is an ambivalent one. Some classical liberals are clearly in favour of democracy, whereas others are either opposed to it or seek to limit its operation in some way. It could, perhaps, be argued that classical liberals really ought to be democrats, and that if they were consistent with their own self professed principles then they certainly would be democrats. This is so for two reasons. In the first place, following Locke, classical liberalism is based on an acceptance of the principle that all legitimate government rests upon the consent of the governed (Locke, 1988, p. 330, 333, 347-8; Dunn, 1969, pp. 130-47; Dunn, 1971, pp. 129-61; Gough, 1973, pp. 52-79). Most liberal thinkers after Locke, although not Locke himself, tend to associate this principle with the notion of democracy (Parry, 1978, p. 96). The whole point of democracy, many would argue, is to provide a guarantee that the laws of the state do indeed have the consent of those who have to obey them (Arblaster, 1984, p. 75).

The second reason why it could be argued that classical liberals really ought to be democrats has to do with their claim that, to be legitimate, the laws of the state ought to promote the interests of those who have to obey them, that is to say the general interest or the common good (Locke, 1988, pp. 353, 357, 360, 363; Paine, 1976b, pp. 91-4, 193-4, 200; Sieyes, 1963, pp. 156-7, 161-2). With respect to this issue, classical liberalism emphatically rejects the approach adopted by pre-modern political thought. In particular, because of its commitment to a belief in human equality, it rejects the principle of paternalism. According to classical liberals, individuals are most definitely the best judges of their own self-interest (Arblaster, 1984, p. 30; Eccleshall, 1986, pp. 52, 58; Goodwill, 1987, pp. 50-2; Held, 1983, p. 13; Heywood, 1992, p. 35; Jay, 1986, pp. 158-9, 165)

If we take the principle that laws ought to promote the interests of the individuals who have to obey them, and if we combine this principle with the further principle that these individuals are the best judges of what their own interests are, then it follows that each and every individual whose interests are affected by the law ought to have a say in determining what the law is going to be. From this a commitment to some form of democracy follows more or less automatically. This could of course be a direct democracy similar to that advocated by Rousseau (Rousseau, 1975, pp. 182, 191-3). Alternatively it could be a representative democracy, like that advocated at the time of the French Revolution, not only in the *Declaration of Rights,* but also in the writings of liberal theorists such as l'abbe de Sieyes and Tom Paine (Sieyes, 1963, pp. 124, 135-6, 151, 154; Paine, 1976a, pp. 65-8; Paine, 1976b, pp. 199-202). In the latter case, it is the accountability of representatives to those who have elected them which, in theory, provides a guarantee that the laws will indeed promote the interests of every individual.

Some classical liberal thinkers, however, are either opposed to democracy or at least very anxious about it. For these thinkers democracy is, potentially, a threat to the institution of private property and hence to natural rights and the freedom of the individual (Arblaster, 1984, pp. 75-9; Bellamy, 1993, p. 28; Berlin, 1973, p. 148; Eccleshall, 1986, pp. 57-8; Friedman, 1979, p. 172; Hayek, 1973, pp. 9-12; Hayek, 1976, p. 403; Hayek, 1980, p. 56; Vincent, 1992, pp. 44-4). Pure democracy is nothing more than a modern, form of absolutism. There are no limitations or constraints regarding what it might legitimately demand from the individual citizen. J. L. Talmon has claimed that unrestrained democracy of the sort advocated by Rousseau and the French revolutionaries is actually a form of 'totalitarian' democracy (Talmon, 1970, pp. 1-3).

History

We have already noted that for some commentators the difference between the age of the Enlightenment and the medieval period, in so far as their respective attitudes towards history are concerned, is simply that the later period possesses both a sense of history and a philosophy of history, whereas the earlier period possesses neither.We have also noted, however, that this particular way of differentiating between the two periods is not a very satisfactory one. Genuine philosophies of history are to be found in both periods.

It would be more accurate to say that the difference between these two periods is that, as many commentators have indicated, the Enlightenment liberal approach to history is quite typically based on the idea of 'progress', whereas the philosophy of history of pre-modern times is not. Thus, to take just one example, Kingsley Martin has insisted that the Middle Ages 'were almost wholly free from the notion of progress' (Martin, 1962, p. 279; also Brock, 1978, p. 41; Bury, 1920, pp. viii, 7, 20-1; Cobban, 1962, p. 22; Lowith, 1949, p. 60; Nisbet, 1970, p. 46; Plamenatz, 1976, 2, p. 410; Pollard, 1971, p. 15; Schapiro, 1978, p. 234).

A number of liberal philosophies of history were produced during the period of the Enlightenment, especially in France and in Germany. Of these perhaps the most typical is the doctrine developed in 1793 by Condorcet in his *Sketch For a Historical Picture of the Progress of the Human Mind* (Condorcet, 1955; Brumfitt, 1972, p. 87; Collingwood, 1976, p. 80; Hampson, 1968, p. 232; Kumar, 1986, p. 21; Martin, 1962, p. 286-98; Stanley, 1973, p. xix). Condorcet's *Sketch* has been described by F. E. Manuel as 'the canonical eighteenth century French text on the idea of progress'(Manuel, 1965, p. 96), and by Stuart Hampshire as 'one of the few really great monuments of liberal thought'(Hampshire, 1955, pp. ix-x; also Pollard, 1971, p.93; Schapiro, 1978, pp. 78-9, 84, 86, 108, 110-12, 136, 141, 161, 167, 267).

What characteristic features are associated with the liberal idea of progress, as we find it in the writings of Condorcet? There are, perhaps, six in all. The first is a feature that is to be found in all philosophies of history. It is the recognition of the occurrence of change and development over time. The second feature, also, is one that is present in all philosophies of history. It is the belief that there is some direction, meaning, purpose or pattern which underlies the process of historical change. So far, then, there is nothing especially novel about the doctrine of progress, or about the liberal philosophy of history of the Enlightenment. It is the remaining four features which clearly differentiate the attitude of the Enlightenment from that of earlier times.

The third characteristic feature of the liberal doctrine of progress is the belief that because the process of historical change is patterned or law governed, and hence in a sense inevitable and necessary, then it is possible for us to come to understand it. As in the case of the order of nature and the laws which regulate the occurrence of natural events, it is possible for us to develop a genuinely scientific understanding of the laws which regulate the occurrence of social and historical events. Moreover, to the extent that it is possible for us to do this, then to the same extent it is also possible for us to actually influence and control the occurrence of these events. As Kingsley Martin has put it, from this point of view, 'the growth of knowledge is the key to progress' (Martin, 1962, p. 280, 286-7; also Collingwood, 1976, p. 80; Kumar, 1986, pp. 22-3; Manuel, 1965, p. 97; Mazzeo, 1969, p. 278; Plamenatz, 1976, p. 410; Pollard, 1971, p. 46, 88-9; Schapiro, 1978, p. 241, 243).

A fourth characteristic feature of the Enlightenment approach to history is the fact that it is predominantly secular (Kumar, 1986, p. 22). It does not seek to provide a theological, that is to say a Christian, interpretation of the pattern or order which it claims underlies the process of historical events. Unlike medieval Christianity, then, the undoubted evils which exist in the world are not seen as being a punishment for sin. For, as with Enlightenment thinking generally, human nature is considered to be fundamentally good (Brumfitt, 1972, pp. 88-9, 96; Hampson, 1968, pp. 84, 99-100). If men are presently morally corrupt then this is so not because of sin, but because of the nature of the society in which they are living. We can change human behaviour for the better by improving society. In this sense human nature itself is 'perfectible' or susceptible of moral improvement. As Condorcet himself expresses the point, 'nature has set no term to the perfection of the human faculties'. The perfectibility of man 'is truly indefinite' (Condorcet, 1955, p. 4; Hampson, 1968, pp 126, 233; Manuel, 1965, p. 103; Martin, 1962, p. 280).

The fifth feature of the doctrine of progress is a feeling of what J. H. Brumfitt has called 'a naively confident optimism' about the possibility of our being able to use the knowledge that we have gained in order to directly intervene in the process of history and, thereby, ameliorate many of the evils which beset mankind (Brumfitt, 1972, p. 87; Hampson, 1968, pp. 232-3; Manuel, 1965, p. 104; Stanley, 1973, p. xviii, xxi). For the first time in history, it is actually possible for us increase the amount of happiness and decrease the amount of misery that there is in the world (Plamenatz, 1976, p. 410). In particular, it is possible for us to do away with those problems which have (allegedly) continued to exist until now only because of our own ignorance of their underlying social or political causes. For Condorcet, as Sidney Pollard suggests, though progress is based on knowledge and science, nevertheless it is not a purely intellectual matter. It is above all progress 'in morals and in happiness' (Pollard, 1971, p. 90).

Finally, the sixth feature of the typical Enlightenment approach to history is the belief that, henceforth, historical change in the direction of improvement, or increased human happiness and well being, will be constant, indefinite and linear. In the words of Condorcet, such progress 'will doubtless vary in speed, but it will never be reversed' (Condorcet, 1955, p. 4). The liberal philosophy of history of the Enlightenment is, therefore, based on a clear rejection of the earlier cyclical view of history, in which there might well be periods or phases of 'improvement' but these are invariably followed by corresponding periods of gloom, catastrophe and disaster. In the view of John Stanley, 'this linear rather than cyclical concept of history is perhaps the most important single attribute of the contemporary view of progress' (Stanley, 1973, p. xviii; Hampson, 1968, pp. 232; Manuel, 1965, p. 97; Martin, 1962, p. 281; Mazzeo, 1969, pp. 275-6).

Conclusion

The dominant values of the ideology of classical liberalism are, in many respects, diametrically opposed to those which, as we have seen, are associated with pre-modern political thought. Whereas pre-modern thought emphasises the value of *order*, classical liberalism, and indeed modern political thought generally, emphasises pre-eminently that of *liberty* or *freedom*. Whereas pre-modern thought emphasises the value of *hierarchy* and *inequality*, liberalism emphasises the value of *equality*. Whereas pre-modern thought emphasises the values of *altruism* and *duty*, liberalism emphasises those of *egotism* and the pursuit of *self-interest*. Whereas the thought of the early medieval period is profoundly *pessimistic*, the thinking of classical liberalism is intensely *optimistic*. Whereas the political principles of the early medieval period are based on religious *faith*, those of classical liberalism are based on *reason*. Finally, whilst pre-modern thought attaches supreme importance to the value of *community*, modern political thought and liberalism attach supreme importance to the value of the *individual*.

99

Conservatism

The ideology of conservatism comes into being at roughly the same time as classical liberalism, in the seventeenth and eighteenth centuries. Essentially conservatism at this time constitutes a negative response to the ideology of classical liberalism, and to modern political thought generally, which most conservative thinkers of the late eighteenth and early nineteenth centuries associated with the 'excesses' of the French Revolution. The best illustration of the basic principles associated with early conservatism is generally acknowledged to be found in the writings of Edmund Burke.

Generally speaking, this conservative response to classical liberalism is greatly indebted to the principles of pre-modern political thought discussed earlier. This is true to such an extent that some commentators take the view that conservatism is an attempt simply to revive, without modification, the intellectual approach adopted by pre-modern political thought. From this point of view, the conflict between classical liberalism and conservatism is a conflict between 'tradition' and 'modernism'. In the words of Robert Nisbet, conservatism might be said to constitute a wholesale 'assault on modernity'. The principles of conservatism are the 'antithesis' of everything that classical liberalism and modern political thought stand for (Nisbet, 1973, pp. 6-8, 11-16, 51; Nisbet, 1978, p. 90; Nisbet, 1986, pp. 3, 18-20, 35-38, 50-51, 79, 84-85, 88, 90, 92).

To argue in this way, however, is to go much too far. There are, undeniably, many points of similarity between the ideology of conservatism and those of medieval political thought, but there are also important differences, which ought not to be glossed over or ignored. Most certainly, mainstream conservatism, as exemplified by the views of Burke, is not simply and solely a medievalist attempt to return to an idealised or mythical feudal past. Conservatism, despite the fact that it certainly does incorporate central elements of the political thought of pre-modern times, is fundamentally a modern doctrine. To fail to appreciate this is to fundamentally misunderstand the nature of conservatism as an ideology (Cobban, 1962, pp. 94, 197; Freeman, 1980, pp. 32, 78, 98-100; MacPherson, 1980, p. 5; O'Gorman, 1986, p. 17; Vincent, 1993, p. 59).

The specific nature of the conservative response to the ideals of classical liberalism, and to the principles of modern political thought, is not simply one of outright rejection. For conservatism is greatly influenced by these ideals even when it departs from them. In order to deal with the problems of modern politics, theoretically, conservative thinkers are to some considerable extent obliged to draw upon (and reinterpret), not only the conceptual vocabulary, but even some of the ideas of their liberal opponents (Heywood, 1992, p. 77). As O'Sullivan has suggested, there is thus a theoretical 'overlap' between conservatism and classical liberalism, although conservatism rarely takes over liberal values 'in an unmodified form' (O'Sullivan, 1993, p. 60).

There is, therefore an ambivalence or tension between the medieval and the modern which lies at the heart of conservatism. An appreciation of the nature of this tension is vital to any adequate understanding of the nature of conservatism as an ideology. Conservatism is not, as Nisbet suggests, simply the theoretical 'antithesis' of classical liberalism. It would be much more accurate to say that it is, rather, an attempt at an intellectual synthesis of classical liberal ideals with those of pre-modern political thought (Epstein, 1966, p. 17; Willets, pp. 92, 109). As W. H. Greenleaf has quite rightly pointed out conservatism, like most political ideologies, embodies a 'tension or interplay', that is to say a 'dialectic', of two such 'opposing tendencies' (Greenleaf, 1973, p. 183).

Intellectual assumptions

There are two points to note about the intellectual assumptions which underpin the ideology of conservatism in the late eighteenth and early nineteenth centuries. The first of these is that conservative thinkers reject the basic philosophical principles of the Enlightenment (Cobban, 1962, p. 13; Nisbet, 1973, p. 12; Nisbet, 1978, p. 86; Nisbet, 1986, p. 2; Kirk, 1964, p. 27). In particular, they are sceptical about the Enlightenment emphasis on the claims of individual reason as a source of knowledge in the area of morals and politics (Beiser, 1992, p. 283; Canavan, 1960, p. 54; Church, 1964, p. 18; Cobban, 1962, p. 75; Eccleshall, 1986, p. 100; Epstein, 1966, pp. 14, 17; Laski, 1961, p. 156; O'Sullivan, 1993, p. 60; Schuettinger, 1970, pp. 12, 17).

The early conservative thinkers were hostile to the principles of the Enlightenment because of what they perceived to be their radical social and political implications. They take the view that the root cause of the French Revolution was the corrosive influence of the allegedly atheistic doctrines of the Enlightenment on the religious beliefs and hence the morals of the French peasantry (Burke, 1969, pp. 182-3; Church, 1964, p.18; Nisbet, 1973, p. 12; O'Sullivan, 1993, p. 55; Weiss, 1977, p.22).

We should not, however, exaggerate the importance of the sceptical dimension to conservative thought. In particular, it would be a mistake to suggest that conservative thinkers take the view that human beings are actually incapable of acting 'rationally', or that conservatives are completely sceptical about the possibility of our achieving genuine knowledge in the sphere of morals and politics by the application of our faculty of reason.

A qualified acceptance of the importance of reason is most certainly to be found within conservatism. It is, in particular, to be found in the works of Edmund Burke. This does not mean that Burke is less hostile to the principles of the Enlightenment than he is usually thought to be. It means, rather, that there is more than one 'rationalist' approach to questions of morality and politics (Cameron, 1973, pp. 37, 39, 136-8; Canavan, 1960, pp. 5-6, 23-4, 27, 54, 60, 93; Freeman, 1980, pp. 17, 27-9, 39, 46, 84; O'Gorman, 1973, p.107, 114; Parkin,

1956, pp. 94-5, 98, 102, 109, 115-18, 131; Vincent, 1992, p. 63, 70-1, 82). What conservative thinkers reject, then, is not the Enlightenment emphasis on reason *per se*. It is, rather, the Enlightenment emphasis on *individual* reason. What they mistrust is the reason of the isolated individual.

The second point to note about the intellectual assumptions of early conservatism is that, as in the case of pre-modern political thought, conservative thinkers have a tendency to adopt a religious approach to politics. They reject the secular approach adopted by classical liberalism, and modern political thought generally. For conservative thinkers, in the words of Burke, 'man is by his constitution a religious animal' (Burke, 1969, p.187; Freeman, 1980, pp. 17-18; Kirk, 1964, p. 43). This link between conservatism and religion has been noted by a number of commentators (Goodwill, 1987, p. 150; Heywood, 1992, p. 63; Honderich, 1990, pp. 51-3; Nisbet, 1986, p. 68; O'Gorman, 1986, pp.1-2; O'Sullivan, 1976, pp. 9-12, 22; Scruton, 1989, pp. 170-1).The reason for the emphasis on religion on the part of conservative thinkers has largely to do with the relationship which they perceive to exist between religion and morality and hence between religion and order, that is to say, the existing social order. Burke strongly emphasises in the *Reflections* his belief that 'religion is the basis of civil society' (Burke, 1969, pp. 186-7; Freeman, 1980, p. 17; Hogg, 1947, pp. 16-23).

As with pre-modern political thought, this religious approach to politics, is associated with a corresponding belief in the existence of some sort of divine or cosmic order which manifests itself in both nature and society. Early conservative thinkers, then, share with pre-modern thought a commitment to the doctrine of the Great Chain of Being. The classic expression of this view, as a number of commentators have noted, is to be found in Burke's claim that all men are 'born in subjection' to 'one great immutable, pre-existent law' by which they 'are knit and connected in the eternal frame of the Universe' (Burke, 1815-27, 13, p. 166; also Burke, 1968b, p. 163; Burke, 1969, pp. 120, 194-5). In the words of Noel O'Sullivan, this is a view of the world 'as an ordered, hierarchical whole in which everything, including man, has had a place assigned to it by God, who created the universe' (O'Sullivan, 1976, p. 22; also Allison, 1984, pp. 10-11; Canavan, 1960, pp. 19-24; Dickinson, 1977, pp. 25-6; Freeman, 1980, pp. 17-18; MacPherson, 1980, pp. 33-4; Nisbet, 1986, p. 51; O'Gorman, 1986, p. 13; Parkin, 1956, p. 24; Vincent, 1992, p. 74).

Human nature

The perception of human nature that is adopted by the ideology of conservatism is fundamentally the same as that of pre-modern political thought. In the first place, conservative thinkers are firmly committed to the Platonic belief in the natural inequality of men. They emphatically reject the liberal principle that, by nature, all men are equal with respect to their native talents and abilities. According to Burke such a belief in natural equality is a 'monstrous fiction' maintained by

102

those who wish only to 'pervert the natural order of things' (Burke, 1969, pp. 124, 138; Eccleshall, 1986, p. 90; Eccleshall, 1990, pp. 10-11, 14; Heywood, 1992, pp. 65-6; Honderich, 1990, p. 169-71; Nisbet, 1986, pp. 47, 51; O'Gorman, 1973, pp. 120-1; Scruton, 1989, pp. 59, 86-7; Vincent, 1992, p. 69; Willets, 1992, p. 111).

On the other hand, however, conservative thinkers like Burke are quite happy to subscribe to the notion of the moral or spiritual equality of men, understood in the traditional Christian sense, provided that acceptance of this principle does not involve any corresponding commitment to radical social or political reform (Honderich, 1990, p. 173; Kirk, 1964, pp. 8, 31, 51; Stephen, 1962, 2, p. 191).

In the second place, conservative thinkers also reject the Enlightenment belief in the essential goodness and perfectibility of man. For them, as for pre-modern thought generally, man is an imperfect being whose nature is essentially corrupt and selfish (Eccleshall, 1990, p. 1; Heywood, 1992, pp. 59-61; O'Gorman, 1986, p. 1, 13; O'Sullivan, 1976, 11-12, 22-6; O'Sullivan, 1993, p. 55; Vincent, 1992, pp. 69, 75). In the late eighteenth and early nineteenth centuries, this belief in human imperfection is usually associated with an acceptance by conservatives of some version of the religious doctrine of original sin, whether this be the conventional Christian form of the doctrine, as in Burke, or the more unconventional form that we find in the writings of a figure like Coleridge (Coleridge, 1913, pp. 172-95; Cobban, 1962, pp. 83-4; Honderich, 1991, p. 45; Lovejoy, 1948, pp. 268-72, 275-6; O'Gorman, 1986, pp 1-2; Viereck, 1956, pp. 13-4).

Nevertheless, as with the political thought of the later medieval period, it is accepted that that this does not necessarily preclude the possibility of men living together harmoniously in political communities. As Andrew Vincent has observed, conservatives take the view that man is 'naturally, but not exclusively, selfish' (Vincent, 1992, p. 68). Thus they are capable, at least in principle, of sacrificing their own self-interest for the sake of moral duty and for the good of the community of which they are a member. It is, indeed, this 'limited capacity for altruism' which makes it possible for them to live together in society, always provided that there is 'a sufficient restraint upon their passions' (Burke, 1969, p.151). Moreover, as again with pre-modern political thought, for early conservatism one of the principal sources of such restraint is provided by religion. Burke, for example, takes the view that it is 'utterly impossible' for man to rid himself of his own selfish will 'without religion' (Burke, 1969, p.191; Hogg, 1947, p. 18).

Early conservative thinkers, then, might be said to subscribe to a 'christianised' form of the traditional, Aristotelian doctrine that man is a social and political animal (Burke, 1968b, p. 169; Burke, 1969, p. 196; Cameron, 1973, pp. 56, 84; Canavan, 1960, pp. 86-7; Kirk, 1964, p. 58; Stanlis, 1958, pp. 112, 131; Strauss, 1965, p. 296; Wilkins, 1967, pp. 18-19, 32-5).

As is well known, conservative thinkers generally subscribe to an organic theory of society (Eccleshall, 1986, pp. 86-7; Gilmour, 1978, p. 63; Goodwin, 1987, pp. 145-7; Heywood, 1992, pp. 61-2; Honderich, 1990, pp. 148-68; Nisbet, 1986, pp. 79-80; O'Gorman, 1986, p. 2; Parkin, 1990, p. 123; Scruton, 1989, pp. 21, 25; Vincent, 1992, p. 73-4). Like the political theorists of pre-modern times, and unlike classical liberals, early conservative thinkers have a tendency to view society as a whole which is greater than the sum of its individual parts.

This organic theory of society is intimately associated with the notion of inequality. For early conservatism, the social community is an ordered hierarchy of unequals. Early conservatism accepts the existence of a wide range of social inequalities, especially of economic wealth and property, all of which are justified by reference to the principle of natural inequality. Social inequality and hierarchy are perceived to be a part of the natural order of things (Burke, 1969, p. 140; Dickinson, 1977, pp. 292-3; Eccleshall, 1986, p. 87, 90-1; Eccleshall, 1990, pp. 10-15; Freeman, 1980, p. 21; Heywood, 1992, p. 65-6; Nisbet, 1986, p. 51; O'Gorman, 1986, p. 3; Scruton, 1989, pp. 86-7; Vincent, 1992, p. 75; Willets, 1992, pp. 109-19).

Also closely connected with this organic theory is the belief that society is best seen as a 'community' rather than as an 'association' (Nisbet, 1973, pp. 6, 48). There is a marked tendency for conservatives to think that social relationships ought to be based, ultimately, not on the pursuit of self interest, but rather on the recognition of one's moral duties, the duties which are associated with one's station in society (Clarke, 1975, pp. 165-68). Early conservative thinkers, therefore, reject the liberal 'contractual' theory of society (Dickinson, 1977, pp. 294-7; Parkin, 1956, pp. 6-30).

Because they subscribe to such an organic theory of society, conservative thinkers necessarily reject the liberal principle of radical individualism. That is to say, they reject the view that society is composed of isolated, abstract or atomic individuals. Like the political thought of pre-modern times, the conservative theory is of a society composed of a plurality of different corporate groups, each of which has a different social function to perform, each one of which is associated with a framework of clearly defined rights and duties, and each one of which has an ordered, hierarchical structure. A commitment to some form of corporatism, and also to some form of pluralism, is a central feature of the theory of society associated with conservatism at this time (Burke, 1969, pp. 122, 135, 196, 247, 273, 300; Cobban, 1962, pp. 49-50; Freeman, 1980, p. 62; Gilmour, 1978, p. 148; Harris, 1971, p. 110; Nisbet, 1973, pp. 409-16; Nisbet, 1978, pp. 100-1; Nisbet, 1986, pp. 37-8; Parkin, 1956, pp. 32, 61-3; Willets, 1992, pp. 67, 71).

From the standpoint of early conservatism, then, if society is indeed to be thought of as a community, it is nevertheless a rather special kind of community. It is an over-arching community which is based, not on the principles of unity, homogeneity and simplicity, but on those of plurality, diversity and complexity (Nisbet, 1973, p. 416). To employ a phrase of David Willets, it is a 'community of communities' (Willets, 1992, p. 71).

It is clear, therefore, that there are many points of similarity between the conservative theory of society and that of pre-modern thought. Once again, however, we must be careful not to go too far and neglect altogether the differences. Thus, for example, conservative ideology is not completely hostile to the pursuit of individual self interest, provided that it occurs in its 'proper place'; provided that it operates within the confines of moral duty; and provided, therefore, that it always pays due attention to the interests of the community as a whole.

In the view of early conservative thinkers, what is wrong with classical liberalism is not that it advocates the principles of individualism and self-interest *per se*, but rather that it goes too far in this direction. It advocates the principles of excessive or unrestrained individualism and self-interest. It is alleged that this is a bad thing because it undermines the cohesiveness of the wider social community (Cobban, 1962, pp. 89-90; Freeman, 1980, pp. 60-1; Gilmour, 1978, p. 63).

Economics

One might expect that early conservative thinkers would be (and indeed should be) critical of both the policies and the principles associated with classical liberal economic theory. This is certainly true, for example, in the case of some of the German romantic conservatives in the late eighteenth century (Alexander, 1931, pp. 217-27; Briefs, 1941; Reiss, 1955, p. 30). On the other hand, however, it has been observed on more than one occasion that Burke himself was committed to an acceptance of the 'laissez faire' economic policies of classical liberalism. This has led to a debate over the question of whether Burke's acceptance of free market economics is actually consistent with his own conservative ideals (Auerbach, 1959, p. 37; Eccleshall, 1986, pp. 84, 99-102; Freeman, 1980, pp. 41-3; MacPherson, 1980, pp. 4-5, 7, 21-2, 51-63; Nisbet, 1986, pp. 36-7, 64-5; Vincent, 1992, pp. 65, 79; Willets, 1992, pp. 8, 10, 47, 79, 92, 96).

If one were to take the view, as Robert Nisbet does, that conservatism is essentially a form of medieval revivalism then the answer to this question is that Burke's views on economic affairs do indeed conflict with his general commitment to the values of conservatism. On the other hand, however, if one were to take the contrary view that conservatism actually constitutes an attempted synthesis of liberal ideals with those of pre-modern thought, then this alleged contradiction disappears.

We have seen, for example, that conservatism is not hostile to all pursuit of individual or 'private' self interest, provided it takes place within its own proper sphere, and provided it is subject to moral regulation and thus subordinated, ultimately, to the interests of the community as a whole. This position allows for the existence in society of corporate economic interests, or for the existence of a particular economic community operating within the wider community of society as a whole. It is Burke's opinion that this economic community should be left by the state to operate freely, always provided that this is in the interests of the wider social community. It would, however, be consistent with Burke's principles to argue that, in certain circumstances, there might well be a justification for more direct regulation of the economy by the state. In the words of M. M. Auerbach, Burke always assumed 'that liberal capitalist economics could be kept subordinate to the conservative social ethic' (Auerbach, 1959, p. 37).

Burke's attitude towards economic affairs illustrates very well the synthetic character of the ideology of conservatism. As David Willets has put it, 'modern conservatism aims to reconcile free markets' with a 'recognition of the importance of community'. It is 'the distinctive insight of British conservative thinkers' that 'these apparently contrasting ideas go together' (Willets, 1992, p. 92).

Law

In so far as questions of law and rights are concerned, once again conservative thinking is heavily indebted to that that of earlier times. As in the case of our discussion of pre-modern political thought, there are two points to note in this regard. The first of these is the conservative attitude towards the notions of natural law and natural rights.

It is commonly assumed that the notions of natural law and natural rights have no part at all to play within the ideology of conservatism. Their rejection is more or less definitive of the conservative approach to questions of jurisprudence. The classic illustration of this negative attitude towards these notions is, allegedly, to be found in the writings of Burke (Burke, 1969, p.118; Canavan, 1960, pp. 114-5; Cobban, 1962, pp. 44-5; Wilkins, 1967, p. 155).

As against this, however, it could certainly be argued that Burke does not reject the notions of natural law and natural rights *per se*. In some sense or other these notions are central to Burke's approach to political questions. What Burke actually rejects is the revolutionary interpretation of these ideas which is to be found in the liberal doctrine of the 'rights of man' (Cameron, 1973, pp. 76-80; Canavan, 1960; Freeman, 1980, pp. 84-8; Kirk, 1951; Hampsher Monk, 1987, pp. 37-40; MacPherson, 1980, pp. 16-17, 32; Montrose, 1961; Parkin, 1956; O'Gorman, 1973, pp. 12-13, 19, 103-4; Stanlis, 1958, pp. 16-17; Wilkins, 1967).

Burke's attitude towards natural law, and especially towards the relationship which exists between natural law and positive law, is in fact strikingly similar to that of the political thought of the later medieval period. As in the case of the scholastic natural law tradition, Burke takes the view that the principles of natural law are formal principles which require a 'specific determination'. Moreover, in Burke's version of natural law theory, also, this determination is to be provided, not by the conscience of the individual, but by the positive (customary) law of the particular community in which the individual lives (Canavan, 1960, pp. 18, 22, 85, 116-8; Wilkins, 1967, pp. 160-2).

The notion of natural law, then, is not at all alien to the ideology of conservatism. David Cameron is quite correct when he suggests that 'both a liberal and a conservative case may be built up on the basis of natural law' (Cameron, 1973, p. 46; also Hogg, 1947, pp. 68-75; Schuettinger, 1970, p.118).

The second point to note about the conservative approach to questions of law and rights is the priority which conservative thinkers give to customary law over statute law. In the case of English conservatism, this amounts to an acknowledgement of the moral and legal supremacy of English common law. This attitude is closely associated with a central feature of conservative thinking, namely its respect for historical tradition and what Burke refers to as the 'antient constitution' (Burke, 1969, pp. 117-8, 146; O'Gorman, 1973, p. 45; Pocock, 1973; Stanlis, 1958, pp, 37-40, 54-5, 98; Wilkins, 1967, pp. 200-1).

Conservative thinking is a form of constitutionalism. It should not be forgotten that, in the context of eighteenth century English politics, Burke was a Whig and not a Tory. Thus, like classical liberalism, early conservatism is firmly opposed to the doctrine of absolutism. Conservative thinkers are committed to an acceptance of the principle of the rule of law and even to the principle of legal equality, or equality before the law (Dickinson, 1977, pp. 57-8, 61-2, 72, 306, 317; Eccleshall, 1986, pp. 93-4; O'Sullivan, 1993, pp. 60-1; Vincent, 1992, pp. 59-60).

Moreover, conservatism also shares with classical liberalism the belief that individuals have rights as well as duties. Corporate rights are also individual rights, which the state ought to respect, and which therefore protect the individual from the state (Freeman, 1980, p. 60). In the case of conservatism, at least for all practical purposes, these rights are customary or historic rights. As Burke puts it, in the English case these rights (including property rights) are the chartered 'rights of Englishmen' (Burke, 1969, p. 118).

It might be thought that there is an inconsistency between Burke's commitment to natural law and natural rights, on the one hand, and to customary or historic rights on the other. In fact, however, there is no inconsistency here. For in Burke's thought natural law and natural rights have a formal character. According to Burke, these formal or 'metaphysic' principles of natural law and natural rights are 'modified' by positive law when they enter into 'common life'. It is Burke's view that positive or historic rights *are* in fact natural rights. That is to say, they are natural rights as they have been modified by the customs and traditions of a particular historical community (Burke, 1969, pp. 152-3; Cameron, 1977, p. 54; Canavan, 1960, pp. 18, 22, 85, 116-8; Freeman, 1980, pp. 88-9; Hampsher Monk, 1987, p. 40; O'Gorman, 1973, p. 116; Parkin, 1956, pp. 14-15; Stanlis, 1958, p. 98; Wilkins, 1967, pp. 154, 160-2).

We may begin our discussion of the conservative approach to politics by considering the attitude of conservative thinkers towards the abstract or *'a priori'* approach to moral and political questions that is adopted by classical liberal social contract theory.

This attitude is in fact quite ambivalent. It is sometimes suggested that Burke, and conservatives generally, are generally opposed to abstract speculation of this sort. They condemn it as 'metaphysical'. In Burke's words, principles derived on this basis just 'as they are metaphysically true' so also are they 'morally and politically false'. The 'science of constructing a commonwealth, or renovating it, or reforming it, is not to be taught *a priori*' (Burke, 1969, pp. 152-3). Conservative thinkers are hostile towards thinking of this sort, largely because of what they perceive to be its radical political implications.

It could therefore certainly be argued that conservatives, beginning with Burke, adopt a fundamentally empiricist and historical approach to moral and political issues. For conservatism, the only guide to follow in this area is that of wisdom and experience (Burke, 1969, p. 148; Cameron, 1977, pp. 5, 69; Canavan, 1960, pp. 23-4; Cobban, 1962, pp. 46-9, 75, 85, 89; Freeman, 1980, pp. 46-7, 90; Eccleshall, 1986, p. 100; Laski, 1961, p. 156; MacPherson, 1980, pp. 14-15, 36; O'Gorman, 1973, pp. 47-8; O'Gorman, 1986, p.13; Parkin, 1956, p. 10, 94-5, 98, 104; Pocock, 1973, pp. 203, 215; Stephen, 1962, 2, pp. 190-1). On the other hand, however, some commentators have rejected this assessment of the conservative position. Thus, to take just one example, Frank O'Gorman has argued that on one level Burke's thinking 'was just as abstract and as speculative as that of the writers whom he attacked' (O'Gorman, 1973, p.107; also Cameron, 1977, p. 39; Freeman, 1980, pp. 16-17; Kirk, 1964, p. 33; Vincent, 1992, p. 68).

At first sight these different interpretations of Burke's thought appear to be mutually incompatible. Nevertheless, it is possible for us to reconcile them by making a distinction between two different approaches to questions of morality and politics, the philosophical or metaphysical and the practical. David Cameron is quite right to claim that Burke does not object to abstract or metaphysical speculation *per se*. For Burke, such speculation is acceptable provided it is confined to its own proper sphere. What Burke really objects to is the 'misuse' of such philosophical reasoning. It is, however, Burke's opinion that such misuse inevitably occurs whenever men attempt to apply thinking of this sort within the sphere of practical political affairs (Cameron, 1977, p. 39).

A second feature of the conservative approach to politics is its attitude towards the value of liberty. Given their antipathy towards modern political thought in general. and classical liberalism in particular, and given also their predilection for the political ideals of pre-modern times, it might be thought that conservative thinkers would attach very little (if any) importance to the value of liberty. From this point of view, the supreme value for conservative thinkers is not that of liberty but that of order (Heywood, 1992, p. 60; Scruton, 1989, p. 19).

Such a view, however, is clearly mistaken. For conservative thought, from the time of Burke, has always emphasised the importance of liberty (Honderich, 1991, p. 82). Thus, for example, Burke claims that liberty is 'the vital spring and energy of the state itself', which has just so much life and vigour as there is liberty in it' (Burke, 1975a, p. 200; also Burke, 1969, p. 376). Liberty is not solely and uniquely a value which is associated with the ideology of liberalism.

Conservative thinkers, like all Whig thinkers, are opponents of absolutism and therefore associate freedom with the rule of law. As Burke puts it, freedom is 'not only reconcilable' to law but, when 'well disciplined', also 'auxiliary to law' (Burke, 1969, p.124). Law is not, therefore, perceived by conservative thinkers to be a threat to individual liberty. It is, rather, its guarantor. In Burke's words, liberty 'must be limited' by law 'in order to be possessed' (Burke, 1975a, p. 199). According to Burke, England is a 'free society' and this is so because it is a society in which the sovereign is committed to a respect for the rule of law (Dickinson, 1977, pp. 285-7; O'Sullivan, 1993, pp. 60-1).

For Burke, then, freedom, properly understood, is not simply a matter of 'doing what one wants'. It is not a 'solitary, unconnected, individual, selfish liberty', as if everyman should be left 'to regulate the whole of his conduct by his own will' (Cobban, 1962, pp. 55-6; Dickinson, 1977, p. 286; Harris, 1969, pp. 44-5). Burke does not subscribe to the 'negative' conception of freedom. For in his opinion the 'spirit of freedom', understood in this sense, must always lead to 'misrule and excess'. Rather, in his view, true freedom is a 'rational and manly freedom' (Burke, 1969, p. 121). It is 'social freedom'. Burke associates liberty in this sense with what he calls 'equality of restraint' under law, and a situation in which no one can 'find means to trespass on the liberty' of others. Understood in this way, liberty is, as Burke acknowledges, 'but another name for justice' (Cobban, 1962, pp. 55-6; Harris, 1969, pp. 44-5; Dickinson, 1977, p. 286). Burke's conception of liberty is therefore what is commonly referred to as a 'positive' conception of liberty. This interpretation of the nature of liberty is central to the ideology of conservatism (Cobban, 1962, p. 56; Heywood, 1992, p. 62).

Conservatism, therefore, actually shares with classical liberalism not only a commitment to the value of freedom but also, to some extent at least, a common understanding of what that commitment involves. The difference between the two ideologies lies, basically, in their respective views of the specific nature and content of the law which is to define and sustain, not only the rights, but also the freedom of the individual. Conservatism, unlike classical liberalism, takes the view that this law is customary law, or the law associated with the ancient constitution, and no other.

According to Burke, classical liberals adopt an abstract or metaphysical approach to the question of what a commitment to liberty actually involves in practice. Burke associates this approach with the attempt by the French revolutionaries to destroy the ancient constitution of France (Burke, 1874-78a, pp. 85-6). In his opinion, questions relating to political liberty will inevitably 'vary with times and circumstances'. They cannot, therefore, 'be settled upon any abstract rule' and 'nothing is so foolish as to discuss them upon that principle' (Burke, 1969, p. 151; Gilmour, 1978, pp. 146-7). For 'abstract liberty' is 'not to be found'. Liberty always 'inheres in some sensible object', that is to say within the constitutional framework of some particular historical community (Burke, 1975b, p. 171). Hence it takes a 'variety of forms, according to the temper and circumstances' of such a community (Burke, 1975a, p. 199). In the specific case of England, this means that those who value liberty must necessarily be devoted to liberty 'according to English ideas and on English principles', and to these alone (Burke, 1975b, p. 171; Burke, 1874-78a, pp. 129-30; Burke, 1874-78b, 3, p. 340). This, in effect, means that they should be committed to the defence of the English constitution. For it is the 'antient constitution of government which is our only security for law and liberty' (Burke, 1969, p. 117; Kirk, 1964, pp. 18-19).

It might justifiably be said that conservatives are critical of classical liberals because, in their view, classical liberalism sacrifices the value of order for the sake of that of liberty. On the other hand, however, it would be incorrect to suggest that conservatism (at least in theory) goes to the other extreme. In so far as its professed principles are concerned, the ideology of conservatism does not seek, contrariwise, to subordinate the value of liberty to that of order. It would be more accurate to say that conservative thought has, rather, always claimed to be attempting to find some sort of a balance between these two apparently contradictory political values (Canavan, 1960, pp. 90-3; Epstein, 1966, p. 17; Gilmour, 1978, p. 64; Hogg, 1947, pp. 68-9; Kirk, 1964, p. 15; Morley, 1880, p. 169; Nisbet, 1986, pp. 35-6; O'Gorman, 1973, pp. 134-5; O'Sullivan, 1976, p. 83). As Francis Canavan has suggested, the central theme of Burke's conservatism is an attempted 'synthesis of freedom and authority'. In Burke's thought, 'liberty and order' are 'not antithetical but complementary' (Canavan, 1960, pp. 90-2).

A third characteristic feature of the ideology of conservatism, which is closely associated with the second, is its attitude towards the value of privacy, and towards the theoretical distinction between the 'public' and the 'private' spheres. This distinction is usually associated with liberalism. As with the concept of freedom, however, it would be a mistake to suggest that it has no part at all to play within the ideology of conservatism.

Unlike absolutism and totalitarianism, and like classical liberalism, the ideology of conservatism does not subordinate the individual to the state. It does not demand of the individual an unconditional allegiance to the state. Conservative thinkers do not argue that the state can do no wrong, or that it can never act unjustly. Like classical liberals, conservatives acknowledge that individuals have rights against the state. The state is under an obligation to respect these rights. If it does not do so then the individual is justified in disobeying the law. These rights, therefore, serve to delineate a protected 'private' sphere, within which the individual should be left free from interference by the state.

Theoretically speaking, then, the only difference between conservatism and classical liberalism in this respect (although, of course, in practical terms it is a vitally important one) is that for classical liberalism the rights in question are natural rights which are interpreted by the reason of the isolated individual, whereas for conservatives they are natural rights which are interpreted by the laws, traditions and customs of a particular community. For conservatism, natural rights are thereby transformed into the historic rights which are associated with the ancient constitution of that community.

The similarities between the ideology of conservatism and that of classical liberalism with respect to these issues appear on the surface to be much greater than the differences. Conservatism is much closer to classical liberalism than it is to either absolutism or totalitarianism. The difference between the two does not lie in the fact that classical liberalism affirms the importance of the distinction between the 'public' and the 'private' spheres, whereas conservatism denies it. It lies, rather, simply in the fact that these ideologies draw the boundary line between these two spheres in different places (Scruton, 1989, p. 77). As Andrew Vincent has pointed out, conservative thinkers have always 'acknowledged the moral and political importance of the private realm' (Vincent, 1992, p. 76; also Goodwin, 1987, pp. 153-4; Nisbet, 1986, pp. 36-7; O'Sullivan, 1976, p. 12; Viereck, 1956, p. 11).

A fourth feature of the conservative approach to politics is its attitude towards democracy. This is clear enough. Conservative thinkers are opposed to democracy, if not in practice then certainly in theory. In the words of Disraeli, democracy is 'a thoroughly vicious form of government' (Pickles, 1971, p. 11). If conservatives have been compelled to accept democracy in practice, then they have always done so reluctantly, and in the hope that they would be able to neutralise what they consider to be its more insidious effects (Beer, 1969, pp. 95-6, 251, 255-6, 268; Buck, 1975, pp. 65-6, 90-1, 94, 116-17; Dickinson, 1977, pp. 283, 288-9; Eccleshall, 1986, pp. 87, 100-1; Gilmour, 1978, p. 211; Goodwin, 1987, pp. 145-6; Honderich, 1991, pp. 126, 132-3, 144; Kirk, 1964, pp. 53-6; Nisbet, 1986, pp. 44, 53; O'Gorman, 1973, p. 119-21; Scruton, pp. 53-6; Vincent, 1992, p. 77-8; Worsthorne, 1978).

There are two reasons for this opposition. The first is the conservative belief in natural inequality and the conservative commitment to the principle of paternalism. As in the case of pre-modern political thought, conservative thinkers reject the idea that individuals are the best judges of their own self-interest and are firm believers in the platonic notion of a 'natural aristocracy' of talents and abilities. It is this small minority who should rule in the interests of all (Beer, 1969, pp. 255-6; Brailsford, 1954, p. 19; Buck, 1975a, p. 12; Dickinson, 1977, p. 317; Eccleshall, 1986, pp. 87, 101; Eccleshall, 1990, p. 14; Gilmour, 1978, pp.

82-3; Goodwin, 1987, pp. 145-6; MacPherson, 1980, pp. 73-4; O'Gorman, 1973, p. 120; Parkin, 1956, pp. 33, 43-4; Viereck, 1956, pp. 20-2; Vincent, 1992, p. 75).

The classic expression of this view is to be found in Burke. Burke insists that there is a world of difference between the 'interest' of the 'common people' and what he calls their 'occasional will' (Burke, 1969, p. 191). For Burke, 'the will of the many and their interest must very often differ' (Burke, 1969, p. 141). It is true that the common people 'ought not to suffer oppression from the state', but in Burke's view the state itself suffers oppression if 'such as they' are 'permitted to rule'. To advocate democracy, therefore, is to be 'at war with nature' (Burke, 1969, p. 138).

This argument is, of course, based on general assumptions about the character of human nature. It is an argument which is 'both universal and ahistorical', and hence 'abstract' and 'metaphysical'(Vincent, 1992, p. 68). Occasionally, Burke shows that he is aware of this. He insists that he reprobates 'no form of government', not even democracy, 'upon abstract principles'. He even acknowledges that there may be circumstances in which the democratic form of government 'would be clearly desirable'. He denies, however, that this is so in the case any 'great country' (Burke, 1969, p. 228).

The second reason why conservatives reject democracy is that it is a threat to the ancient constitution. Hence it poses a threat to liberty (and, of course, to property). According to Burke, democracy is a form of 'despotism'. In Burke's opinion, there is in a democracy no 'fundamental law' to restrain the legislature. 'Nothing in heaven and earth can serve as a control to them' (Burke, 1969, p. 133; Nisbet, 1976, p. 416). An excellent recent illustration of the conservative attitude towards democracy is provided by Ian Gilmour. According to Gilmour, conservatives take the view that 'majorities do not always see where their best interests lie'. Thus, democracy is 'a means to an end not an end in itself'. If, therefore, it is leading to an end which is 'undesirable', namely a radical alteration in the constitution, then there is 'a theoretical case for ending it' (Gilmour, 1978, p. 211).

History

Early conservatism, as represented by the writings of Burke, evidently does possess what we have called a philosophy of history: a recognition of the occurrence, and even the inevitability, of change and development over time, and a belief that this development is in some sense meaningful or purposive. Burke's philosophy of history, like that of pre-modern times, is religious and not secular. It is closely associated with a belief in the existence of God and in Divine Providence. In this respect, as Russell Kirk has pointed out, 'Christian orthodoxy is the kernel of Burke's philosophy'. It is Burke's view that 'the course of history has been determined' by Divine Providence. God's purpose among men is thus 'revealed through the unrolling of history' (Kirk, 1964, pp. 27-30; also Brailsford,

1954, p. 20; Canavan, 1960, p. 130; Freeman, 1980, pp. 78-9; Laski, 1961, p. 150; Parkin, 1956, p. 118; Pollard, 1968, pp. 101-3; Weston, 1961, p. 220).

This leads us to the question of whether Burke also subscribe to a belief in progress. Some commentators take the view that Burke rejects this belief. According to Robert Nisbet, for example, it was conservatives like Burke who, at the end of the eighteenth century, overwhelmingly 'led the way in the assault on progress' (Nisbet, 1986, p. 91; also Cobban, 1962, pp. 83-4; Goodwin, 1987, p. 142; Kirk, p. 8; Pollard, 1968, p. 97; O'Gorman, 1973, pp. 118, 144, 146; O'Gorman, 1986, p.23; Scruton, 1989, pp. 190-1; Stephen, 1962, 2, p. 194; Nisbet, 1973, pp. 6-7, 266-70; Nisbet, 1986, pp. 89-91). As against this, however, others have maintained that the notion of progress does have an important part to play in Burke's political thought. On this interpretation, as Barbara Goodwin has put it, it seems evident that Burke's views on history do rest on a 'conception of human and social progress' (Goodwin, 1987, p. 143; Cecil, 1937, pp. 12-13, 17-19; also Freeman, 1980, pp. 32, 78-9, 98-100; Hogg, 1947, pp. 83-6; O'Sullivan, 1976, pp. 83-6; Pollard, 1968, p.103).

To suggest that Burke completely rejects the idea of progress, as the first of these interpretations does, is to go too far. What Burke actually rejects is the radical doctrine of progress that is adopted by the philosophy of the Enlightenment. Burke does not believe in the perfectibility of man and is pessimistic about both the possibility and the desirability of attempting to ameliorate the acknowledged evils of this world through a programme of radical social and political change. For Burke 'poverty, brutality and misfortune' are a necessary component element in 'the eternal order of things' (Kirk, 1964, p. 31, 9; Burke, 1969, p. 247).

As is well known, however, Burke also acknowledges both the inevitability and the desirability of historical change. He is, moreover, cautiously optimistic about the possibility of a certain degree of social and political improvement. Change of this sort is acceptable provided that it does not occur too quickly, and provided it does not pose a threat to the 'ancient constitution' (Burke, 1969, pp. 120, 282, 375). In this regard, therefore, Burke shares at least some of the presuppositions of the Enlightenment doctrine of progress. As Sidney Pollard has rightly claimed, 'Burke is, in many respects, in the Enlightenment tradition. There is evolution, and it is upwards and progressive, irreversible and inevitable' (Pollard, 1968, p. 103).

These two different assessments of Burke's views on progress have arisen because there is actually a contradiction lying at the heart of Burke's philosophy of history between its modern and its pre-modern aspects, or between what Michael Freeman has referred to as its 'progressive' and its 'backward-looking elements' (Freeman, 1980, p. 98). This is, in effect, a tension here between what Coleridge calls the two great historical principles of 'permanence' and 'progression' (Coleridge, 1972, pp. 16, 21; Calleo, 1966, pp.92-6).

Those commentators, like Nisbet, who deny that Burke believes in progress have a tendency to focus on the pre-modern or 'backward looking elements' in his thought. For these commentators what is most important in Burke is, as we have seen, his commitment to order and to stability. In their view, therefore, Burke rejects the principle of 'progress' in order to embrace that of 'permanence'. This assessment of Burke's attitude is closely associated with Nisbet's view that conservatism is essentially a form of medievalism, and hence the intellectual antithesis of classical liberalism. On this interpretation, those aspects of Burke's thought which have a resemblance to the Enlightenment doctrine of progress are an alien intrusion. They are an indication that Burke's views on history have been infected in some way by the liberal views of the Enlightenment. They are not authentically conservative.

This interpretation, however, is partial and one sided. Contrary to Nisbet's account, Burke does not sacrifice the principle of 'progression' to that of 'permanence', as does pre-modern political thought. Nor, however, does he sacrifice the principle of 'permanence' to that of 'progression', as (in Burke's opinion) do the liberal philosophers of the Enlightenment. The fact is that the principles of 'permanence' and 'progression' are both central elements in Burke's philosophy of history, and in that of conservatism in general. Burke's views on history, like those of Coleridge, are in effect based on a combination of these two principles. Coleridge's views on history merely make more explicit an idea which is already there, implicitly, in the writings of Burke. It is in this sense only that Coleridge might be said to have 'a more sophisticated understanding of change and progress than Burke had' (O'Gorman, 1986, p. 23).

The fact that the conservative approach to history has such a synthetic character has been noted by Hugh Cecil. In his view, although 'conservatism seems at first sight to be the direct opposite of progress', it is in fact 'an essential element in making it safe and effectual' (Cecil, 1937, pp. 17-18). For 'wisdom is not so anxious for progress as not to be afraid of novelty', nor is 'so afraid of novelty as to be contented without progress'. These two sentiments, therefore, 'are in fact complementary and mutually necessary' (Cecil, 1937, p. 13). These remarks are in the spirit of both Burke and Coleridge, and are quite typical of the conservative approach to history.

With respect to its views on history also, therefore, early conservatism is not to be regarded as being simply the antithesis of classical liberalism. Once again it would be more accurate to say that it constitutes an attempted synthesis of the views of pre-modern political thought with those of classical liberalism.

Conclusion

Conservatism does not have just one dominant value. Intellectually, the ideology of conservatism is based on an attempt (more or less explicit, and more or less coherent and systematic) to synthesise the values of pre-modern political thought, on the one hand, and those of classical liberalism and modern political thought on the other. In the view of conservative thinkers, where pre-modern thinking emphasises *order* without *liberty*, and liberalism emphasises *liberty* without *order*, conservatism is committed to both order *and* liberty.

Alternatively, one could say that conservative thinkers consider themselves to be seeking a balance, not only between order and liberty, but also between the values of *community* and *individualism*. Where pre-modern thought focuses on the value of *community* at the expense of *individualism*, and liberalism focuses on the value of *individualism* at the expense of that of *community*, conservatives see themselves as attaching equal importance to both the principles of community *and* individualism.

The typically pre-modern elements of conservative thought, all of which fall under the notions of *order* and *community*, include the emphasis on *religion*; the emphasis on the principles of *authority*, *hierarchy* and *inequality*; the emphasis on *paternalism* and *aristocracy*; the emphasis on *deference* and *duty*; and the emphasis on *custom* and *tradition*. As against this the typically modern elements, all of which are associated with the values of *liberty* and *individualism*, include the commitment to the *rule of law*, and to the principle of *equality before the law*; the commitment to the idea that individuals have *rights against the state*, especially *property* rights; the (implicit) recognition of the value of *privacy* and of the importance of the distinction between the *public* and the *private* spheres; and finally a qualified acceptance of the doctrine of *progress*.

Conclusion

This completes our overview of the various ideas associated with the ideologies of classical liberalism and traditional conservatism. It should, hopefully, by now be clear that although there are many differences between these two ideologies, there are important similarities also. Conservatism is not to be associated, purely and simply, with medieval revivalism or with the principles of traditionalism. These are certainly important for the ideology of conservatism. They are not, however, the whole story. They are merely just one part of it. Conservatism is a modern doctrine, and conservative thinkers actually share many of the assumptions of the liberal thinking that they are so keen to criticise. The distinctive characteristic feature of conservatism as an ideology is its synthetic character. It is the fact that conservative thinkers, either implicitly or explicitly, seek to combine what they consider to be the most important elements to be found within these two earlier traditions of political thought.

In this chapter we have seen that this synthetic approach is certainly to be found in the ideas of Burke. Burke, however, adopts this approach only implicitly. Nowhere does Burke seek to present a theoretical justification for doing so. In the next chapter we shall argue that precisely the same approach is adopted by Hegel.

The difference between the two is that Hegel makes explicit, in a theoretically sophisticated manner, that which in Burke is merely implicit.

4 Hegel and political ideology

Hegel and conservatism

We have already seen that the history of Hegel scholarship since the Second World War has been one which has seen a radical change in the conventional wisdom regarding the ideological location of Hegel's political thought. From being considered to be a reactionary defender of Prussian absolutism, and a forerunner of totalitarianism, Hegel today is thought of by most of his interpreters as being some sort of liberal thinker. However, these two ways of categorising Hegel and his ideas do not exhaust all of the available possibilities. For there is in fact a third possibility here, and that is to locate Hegel's political thought within the conservative political tradition.

It is nonsense to say, as F. R. Cristi has done, that 'nobody wants to deny that Hegel adhered firmly to a liberal *Grundkonzeption*' (Cristi, 1983, p. 601). On the contrary there are many of Hegel's interpreters who would wish to deny this. In the history of Hegel scholarship there have, in fact, been a number of commentators who have argued that Hegel is a conservative thinker. To take just one example, Robert Nisbet has insisted that, 'Hegel was, in his mature, great years of teaching and writing, conservative, and was recognised as such throughout educated Germany' (Nisbet, 1978, p. 114; also pp. 85, 88, 101; Cassirer, 1967, p. 251; Hook, 1970b, pp. 87-8, 92, 96; Lindsay, 1935, pp. 52, 57; Mannheim, 1986, 94, 144; Mehta, 1968, pp. 126-7, 130; Nisbet, 1973, pp. 24, 54-5, 113; Nisbet, 1976, pp. 418-19; Nisbet, 1986, pp. 2, 19-20, 35, 37-8, 49, 79, 89, 111; Schuettinger, 1970, p. 36, 119; Scruton, 1988, pp. 135-6, 153).

There is a marked tendency, in much of the work that deals with the question of the ideological location of Hegel's political thought, for the word 'conservative' to be used in the common or everyday sense. Either (1) it is used to refer to someone who is committed simply and unreservedly to the defence of the status quo, no matter what that might be; or (2) it is used to refer to someone who is totally opposed to social and political change; or (3) it is used to refer to someone who is a traditionalist, that is to say, someone who is anti-modern and who harks back to the past, or who has a marked preference for the old and the well established, simply on the grounds that it *is* old and well established; or finally (4) it is used to refer to someone who has such a respect for established authority that they consider it to be wrong to make any criticisms at all of existing social and political conditions. A good illustration of this popular conception of conservatism is provided by Charles Taylor. According to Taylor, 'the standard conservative position' of Hegel's time, or indeed 'of any other', is simply to 'cleave to the ancient and the traditional' or the 'long established' (Taylor, 1989, p. 424).

Now there are some commentators who consider Hegel to be a conservative in this sense. According to Harry Brod, for example, 'many commentators have claimed that Hegel's political philosophy represents a deliberate retreat from modernity, a return to the classical conceptions' of an 'ethical community' (Brod, 1992, p. 5). Fred Dallmayr has said that liberals 'are sometimes prone to dismiss Hegel simply as a traditionalist or a devotee of pre-modern life forms' (Dallmayr, 1993, p. 7). Moreover, as Ernst Cassirer has pointed out, it is not at all surprising that Hegel's interpreters should take this view. For there is, undeniably, a traditionalist dimension to Hegel's thought. According to Cassirer, Hegel's thought is conservative precisely because he 'defended the power of tradition. Custom (*Sitte*) was to him the basic element in political life'. Hegel 'always maintained and defended the same view. He does not acknowledge any ethical order higher than that which appears in custom' (Cassirer, 1967. p. 251; also Smith, 1991, pp. 70-2).

Those commentators who argue that Hegel should be considered to be a conservative for this particular reason have quite rightly picked up on an important aspect of Hegel's thinking, one which is often ignored altogether by those who consider Hegel to be some sort of liberal. Despite this, however, there is a tendency for these commentators, in their turn, to be as selective as their opponents in the interpretation of Hegel's ideas. They turn a blind eye to those aspects of Hegel's thinking which, according to their critics, lie at the very heart of Hegel's system, for example Hegel's emphasis on the value of freedom, his commitment to a distinction between the public and the private spheres, his belief in the rule of law, and so on. Thus, the line of reasoning which is adopted by those who claim that Hegel is a conservative is quite often itself partial and one sided. It does not do sufficient justice to the complexities of Hegel's political thought as a whole. This is something which Cassirer has also recognised. As he puts it, 'conservatism is, therefore, one of the most important characteristic features in Hegel's ethical theory. Nevertheless it is not all. It is only a particular and one sided aspect which we should not mistake for the whole' (Cassirer, 1967, p. 252).

It might be argued that the interpretation of Hegel that is offered by this third group of commentators is actually correct. These commentators are quite right to maintain that Hegel is a conservative thinker. They are, however, right for the wrong reason. The way to establish that Hegel is a conservative is not to show that he is simply a traditionalist, or simply a defender of the *status quo*, or that he is opposed to all forms of social and political change, or that he refuses on principle to criticise existing social and political conditions. For, as a number of commentators have pointed out, Hegel is committed to none of these things (Avineri, 1972, pp. 39, 55, 71-4, 115-17, 182-3, 208, 210, 216; Gooch, 1965, pp. 299-300; Hardimon, 1994, pp. 25-7, 29, 79; Houlgate,

1991, p. 78; Knox, 1970, p. 18, 21-2; Smith, 1991, pp. xi, 130-1; Suter, 1971, p. 65; Wood, 1990, pp. 8-9, 12-14, 196, 257-8; Wood, 1991, pp. ix-xi; Westphal, 1993, pp. 234-9). It is, rather, to show that conservatism itself is not committed to any of these things either, at least not in a simple and straightforward sense.

It is not at all clear that the popular use is in fact the most appropriate use of the terms 'conservative' and 'conservatism' when discussing the political thought of Hegel, or indeed any other conservative political theorist. For example, if we were to employ these terms in this particular sense then it would be incorrect to regard Edmund Burke as a conservative thinker. For Burke himself was not unreservedly committed to the defence of the status quo. Nor was he totally opposed to all change. Nor was he simply a traditionalist. Nor, finally, did he refuse on principle to criticise existing social and political conditions. It is certainly true that all of these things together might be said to constitute one aspect of Burke's political thought as a whole, and an important one at that. It would be wrong, however, to suggest (as some commentators do) that this is the only aspect, or that there is no more to Burke than this. Exactly the same is true, also, in the case of Hegel.

The intellectual antecedents of Hegel's political thought

Burke and Montesquieu

Alfred Cobban has suggested that Edmund Burke's impact on 'continental thinkers' was slight. Burke 'founded no school' and 'the influence of his thought as a whole was negligible' (Cobban, 1962, p. 273). It could, however, be argued that in the case of Germany and German conservatism this assessment is quite mistaken. A number of commentators have discussed the impact of Burke's ideas in Germany, and they have all concluded that, although they were not the only important influence, nevertheless they were indeed a significant influence in the development of German conservatism (Aris, 1965, pp. 251-6, 260, 267, 308-9, 312; Beiser, 1992, pp.239, 265, 288, 317; Epstein, 1966, pp. 568; Gooch, 1965, pp. 73, 789, 81, 83, 102-03, 235; Reiss, 1955, pp. 2-3, 8, 27, 29).

There are, in particular, many points of similarity between the political thought of Hegel and that of Burke. Both of these thinkers have a keen sense of history. Both of them attach a considerable degree of importance to custom and tradition. Both are hostile to the 'abstract' approach to politics adopted by the liberal philosophers and revolutionaries of eighteenth century France. Both of them deplore the excesses of the French Revolution. Both of them reject the idea of democracy, and for the same reasons. Both of them are paternalists. Both are hostile to absolutism and defend the principle of constitutionalism, together with that of the rule of law and equality before the law. Both of them are committed to some form of constitutional monarchy. And so on, and so on.

Some commentators claim that these similarities between the thought of Hegel and that of Burke are both striking and important (Hook, 1970, pp. 92, 96, 98, 105; Lindsay, 1932, pp. 52, 57; Mehta, 1968, p. 126; Suter, 1971). Thus, for example, V. R. Mehta has suggested that in its essentials Hegel's conservatism does little more than repeat what Burke has already said before. According to Mehta, 'Hegel's conservatism reaches its high water mark when he gives the customs and traditions' of a society pride of place. In Mehta's view, this is 'the same old doctrine of Burke, for whom there could be no genuine progress except when it was built on tradition' (Mehta, 1968, p. 127). Others however claim that, although these similarities do exist, nevertheless they are relatively unimportant and superficial (Avineri, 1970, pp. 125-8, 135; Avineri, 1972, pp. 55, 74; Beiser, 1993, p. 297; Brod, 1992, pp. 53, 143; Hinchman, 1984, p. 141; Kirk, 1964, pp. 7, 60, 405, 408; Pelczynski, 1969, p. 37; Smith, 1991, p. 148; Taylor, 1989, pp. 423-4). According to this second group of commentators it is a serious mistake to exaggerate the significance of these Burkean themes for our understanding of Hegel's political thought as a whole.

This group of commentators all tend to argue in the same way. Their reason for claiming that there is a crucially important difference between the political thought of Burke and that of Hegel is basically that Burke is a traditionalist and a positivist, whereas Hegel is evidently a rationalist. This point has been well made by Z. A. Pelczynski, who insists that although 'Hegel has often been compared to Burke', and although there are many superficial 'similarities and parallels in their political thought', nevertheless a closer analysis shows that in reality 'it would be difficult to find two thinkers whose basic political beliefs and preferences were more opposed', or 'whose mutual opposition went deeper'. This is so because Burke is in fact 'the greatest and certainly the most eloquent apologist for the very political attitude which Hegel is concerned to combat in his writings'. For the spirit which pervades all of Burke's political writings 'is the spirit of traditionalism and positivism' (Pelczynski, 1969, p. 37). Similarly, Charles Taylor has claimed that 'it should be obvious' that Hegel 'is poles apart from Burke'. For 'the moral drawn by Burke was that men should remain within the spirit of their 'positive' institutions'. For Hegel, on the other hand, 'the aim of philosophy is to discover the universal rationality in these institutions' (Taylor, 1989, p. 423).

There are two problems with this second assessment of the relationship between Burke and Hegel. The first is that it is based on an interpretation of Burke which ignores altogether the rationalism which underpins Burke's political thought, and which, as we have noted, other interpreters of Burke have insisted (quite rightly) is there. It is based on an interpretation of Burke which attaches no significance at all to Burke's debt to the Aristotelian natural law tradition. The second is that this assessment places too strong an emphasis on the rationalist dimension of Hegel's political thought. It is based on an interpretation of Hegel's ideas which appears to be completely oblivious to, or at least seriously understates, the importance which Hegel himself attaches to custom and tradition in his political writings. Hegel may not have been a 'traditionalist' as such, but (paradoxical though it might seem) he certainly did have a great deal of respect for custom and tradition (Beiser, 1993, p. 275).

That some commentators should be so keen to emphasise the differences between the thought of Hegel and Burke, rather than the similarities, is rather surprising, especially given the importance which the notion of *Sittlichkeit* or Ethical Life has in Hegel's political thought. For as is well known, in Hegel's eyes this notion has strong associations with the 'ethos', that is to say the values, customs and traditions of a particular historical community or 'nation' (Cassirer, 1967, p. 251; Cullen, 1979, pp. 56-8; Hardimon, 1994, pp. 334; Inwood, 1992, pp. 13, 91-93; Smith, 1989, p. 14; Smith, 1991, pp. 8-9, 130-1; Taylor, 1979, p. 83-4, 125; Wood, 1990, pp. 195-6, 206).

There is in fact no direct evidence that Hegel ever read Burke (Kirk, 1964, p. 7; Suter, 1971, p. 52). The immediate source for many of the typically Burkean themes in Hegel's political thought appears to be, once again, Montesquieu, for whom Hegel had a very high regard. We have already noted that in the early essay on natural law Hegel refers to the *Spirit of the Laws* as Montesquieu's 'immortal work' (Hegel, 1975a, pp. 128-9). He is similarly enthusiastic in the *Philosophy of Right*. There he refers once again to *The Spirit of the Laws* as Montesquieu's 'famous work' and acknowledges that 'here again, as in so many other places, we must recognise the depth of Montesquieu's insight' (Hegel, 1979, pp. 161, 177). What Hegel likes so much about Montesquieu and his ideas is the fact that it is 'Montesquieu, above all' who recognises the dependency of 'laws' on 'the specific character of the state' (Hegel, 1979, p. 161). Thus, in so far as our understanding of the arbitrary and contingent component of positive law is concerned, it is again Montesquieu above all who has proclaimed 'the genuinely philosophical position', namely that 'laws' need to be considered, not as something isolated and abstract', but in their relationship to 'all the other features which make up the character of a nation and an epoch' (Hegel, 1979, p. 16).

If we consider the specific case of the relationship between the thought of Burke and that of Montesquieu then, as C. P. Courtney has pointed out, the *Spirit of the Laws* 'reveals clearly' that Montesquieu 'is in a tradition' to which 'Burke belongs'. This is a tradition which when confronted with a problem of the constitution 'appeals not to theories of rights or the social contract, but to history'. Montesquieu represents 'a continuation of the French tradition of *droit coutumier*'. Thus in Montesquieu, as in Burke, 'we find assumptions similar to those of the common law, that the ancient constitution cannot be altered by the will of the king, and that ancient rights must be respected'. In Courtney's view, 'the similarity of Burke's opinions' to those of Montesquieu 'needs no stressing'. In all of this, however, there is 'no question' of any influence of Montesquieu upon Burke. It is, rather, the case that 'both writers are drawing on their classical' backgrounds' (Courtney, 1963, pp. 57, 162-3; Montesquieu, 1952, pp. 237, 261, 269). Much the same might be said about the relationship between Burke and Hegel.

The reason why Hegel is so impressed with the thought of Montesquieu is precisely because Montesquieu also attaches so much importance to the idea of Ethical Life, as Hegel understands the term. Given the importance of this idea for Hegel's political thought, and given the similarities which exist between both the thought of Hegel and Montesquieu, on the one hand, and that of Montesquieu and Burke on the other, it is indeed astonishing that commentators should be so keen to drive a wedge between Hegel and Burke.

Frederick Beiser has suggested that it is actually quite 'illuminating to compare Hegel with Burke'. For 'both stressed the value of historical continuity and tradition' and 'both appealed to history to undermine the claims of French radicals to change all society according to some abstract plan' (Beiser, 1993, p. 297). This is perfectly correct. Beiser goes on, however, to argue that nevertheless 'Hegel, unlike Burke, saw history as an argument for, rather than against, a new constitution based upon reason'. This statement is somewhat misleading. For Hegel certainly did not advocate the construction of completely new constitutions based upon reason. To argue that he did would involve mistakenly attributing to Hegel the view that the *Philosophy of Right* itself is a blue print for radical constitutional reform guided solely and exclusively by *a priori* principles. And this is, as Beiser himself acknowledges, something which Hegel explicitly rejects. What Hegel actually advocates is not the construction of completely new constitutions, but the modification or reform of old ones. For Hegel, constitutional reform of this sort is based, not on *a priori* principles, or abstract reason, but rather on the lessons of history and of historical reason.

According to John Plamenatz, Hegel 'like Burke and like Montesquieu' wanted 'a balance of power within the state, with some groups and classes having much more power than others on the ground that, by tradition and education, they were more responsible, less narrow, and more competent' (Plamenatz, 1976, p. 264). The conclusion which Plamenatz draws from this is similar to that of Z. A. Pelczynski. It is that we 'might call' Hegel 'a Whig'. It would, however, be much more accurate to go all the way here and acknowledge that if Hegel is a Whig then he is a Whig of a particular kind. His intellectual affinities lie, not with the Whiggism of Locke, but with that of Burke (Dickinson, 1977, pp. 57-79).

Needless to say, in so far as possible influences on the political thought of Hegel are concerned, behind Montesquieu stands the figure of Aristotle. The influence of Aristotle and the Aristotelian conception of natural law on Montesquieu's political thought is as great as it is upon the thought of both Burke and Hegel (Klosko, 1980; Mason, 1975; Meyer, 1967; Price, 1947; Waddicor, 1970). Thus, for example, Michael Waddicor has quite rightly claimed that, where matters of justice are concerned, 'Montesquieu developed and completed an ancient tradition' associated with the thought of Aristotle (Waddicor, 1970, pp. 132, 126-28). The similarity between the ideas of all three of these modern thinkers can easily be explained by the fact that they are all associated with the eighteenth century attempt to revive an interest in the political thought of pre-modern times, and especially that of ancient Greece (Courtney, 1963, pp. 25, 57, 162-3, 182-3; Plant, 1973, pp. 16-40; Taylor, 1976, p. 125).

Hegel and human nature

The influence of Aristotle and Kant

Hegel's political thought is also greatly influenced by the ideas of Aristotle and Kant. One way of characterising this influence would be to say that Hegel's ideas are based on an attempt to synthesise two quite different conceptions of human nature, and two quite different approaches to the study of politics. The first of these is fundamentally pre-modern and is derived from Aristotle. The second is modern and is derived from the ideas of Kant.

One would expect that, given his general approach to politics, Hegel's view of human nature would be in its essential respects greatly influenced by pre-modern political thought, especially by that of the ancient Greeks, and even more especially by that of Aristotle. The general tenor of Hegel's thought suggests that he would have a great deal of sympathy for the view that man is by nature a social and political animal. As more than one commentator has noted, it seems almost self-evident that, in Hegel's view, man is a being destined to realise his own essential nature by living together with others in a particular ethical community. In at least some sense, therefore, such a life must be considered to be natural to man, a realisation of man's potential as a human being (Mehta, 1968, p.119; Hardimon, 1994, p. 119; Ritter, 1982, pp. 147, 163-5; Smith, 1991, pp. 72, 135-6).

There is clearly an Aristotelian dimension to Hegel's political thought, which is certainly discernible in Hegel's early writings (such as the essay on *Natural Law*), and which is retained even in the *Philosophy of Right*. The title *Natural Law and Political Science in Outline*, which Hegel gave to his major work on politics when he published it in 1821, serves as a register of Hegel's debt to this Aristotelian approach to politics.

Side by side with this, however, there is another dimension to Hegel's political thought, one which is based on different principles, on a quite different conception of human nature, and which Hegel derives from the work of Kant (Dallmayr, 1993, pp. 88-91; Riedel, 1984, pp. 57-67, 69-71, 73). Thus, for example, in the *Philosophy of Mind* (1817) Hegel follows Kant in maintaining that 'the whole law and its every article are based on free personality alone', that is to say on 'self-determination or autonomy', which is 'the very contrary of determination by nature'. Here Hegel associates 'right', and hence also ethical life, with society and the social state, and he contrasts both of these with 'nature'. From this point of view, behaviour in accordance with nature is behaviour in accordance with the principle of egotism, 'wilfulness and violence'. Hence moral and social life is most definitely not natural to man. It is in the social state alone that 'right has its actuality' (Hegel, 1971, p. 248). From this point of view, ethical behaviour is in a sense clearly not natural. This is so because it is something which is freely chosen and hence determined solely by an act of the human will.

Hegel explicitly acknowledges the existence of these two quite different conceptions of human nature, and these two quite different approaches to politics, in the same passage in the *Philosophy of Mind*. He says there that 'the phrase 'Law of Nature', or Natural Right' involves 'the ambiguity that it may mean either right as something existing already formed in nature, or right as governed by the nature of things, i.e. by the notion' (Hegel, 1971, p. 248). What Hegel means by this is that we can make a distinction between human conduct which is natural in the sense that this is how human beings happen to behave now, and human conduct which is natural in the sense (already noted) that it corresponds to how human beings could behave, and would behave, if they fulfilled their potential and came to live a fully human life, that is to say, a life which expressed their essential nature as human beings. It is clear that the same behaviour might be considered to be natural from one of these points of view, but not from the other. In the passage cited Hegel appears to commit himself unreservedly to the first of these two perceptions of what it is for human conduct to be natural. Thus, on this occasion at least, he completely disassociates himself from the Aristotelian conception of human nature.

The view of human nature expressed by Hegel in this passage is decidedly modern. What is more, these views are not an isolated aberration. They recur in the *Philosophy of Right* itself. For there Hegel insists that the 'basis of right' is 'mind', and its 'precise place and point of origin' is not nature but 'the will'. According to Hegel (following Kant and Rousseau) the human will is not determined by nature. It is 'free'. Hence it is 'freedom' (and not nature) that is 'both the substance of right and its goal' (Hegel, 1979, p. 20; also. p. 156).

The existence and importance for Hegel's own thinking of this Kantian view of human nature and politics is clearly registered by the fact that Hegel did choose to give his major work on politics two titles and not one, and by the fact that the second of these titles, *Elements of a Philosophy of Right,* makes no reference at all to the notion of natural law, and hence no allusion to the Aristotelian political tradition.

Some commentators have noted the existence of this tension between two quite different conceptions of human nature in Hegel's thinking. Unlike Hegel, however, these commentators are of the opinion that these two conceptions do not sit at all well together. As a result, they have come to the conclusion that Hegel's thinking on this subject is not an attempted synthesis of two opposing (but complementary) standpoints. It is simply contradictory and confused.

One way of explaining the existence of this (apparent) contradiction would be to suggest that Hegel's views on human nature evolve over time. Thus for example one could argue, as Manfred Riedel has done, that when Hegel wrote his essay on *Natural Law* (1802) he was greatly influenced by the Aristotelian conception of human nature. At this time, therefore, his conception of nature 'is the traditional teleological one, which Hegel attempts to renew as a fruitful basic principle of natural law' (Riedel, 1984, p. 81). In Riedel's view, however, 'Hegel did not adhere long' to this particular notion of 'ethical life', the structure of which clearly mirrors 'the outlines of the Attic *polis*'. Hegel 'modified this view almost immediately' and finally 'towards the end of the Jena period he gave it up entirely' (Riedel, 1984, p. 88). At this later date, Hegel's political thought 'no longer has for its object 'ethical nature' and its law, which Hegel clearly identifies with the substantive ethical life of the Greek *polis*'. Its object, rather, is 'the 'concept' of law' (Riedel, 1984, p. 96). This is a judgement with which both Bruce Haddock and Stephen Smith concur. According to Haddock, as we have already noted, 'Hegel saw the whole panoply of institutions, laws, social procedures, practices, and relationships as an expression of the human will'. Thus, in Haddock's opinion, it is 'will and personality', rather than 'nature', which are 'crucial to Hegel's wider account of politics and the state' (Haddock, 1993, pp. 120-1). And according to Smith, Hegel takes the view that 'political life is not natural to men but a requirement to rectify the inadequacies of nature' (Smith, 1991, p. 115; also pp. 113-14; Smith, 1989, p. 8).

From this point of view, then, Hegel's political thought shows a clear pattern of development over time. It moves away from the older, Aristotelian conception of politics and towards the modern, Kantian conception. On this interpretation, the Aristotelian elements which we find in Hegel's later writings are not really authentically Hegelian at all. They are an aberration or throwback to an earlier period of Hegel's intellectual development. They are the last remnants of a vision of politics which Hegel has long since been struggling to abandon. It is, therefore, extremely unfortunate that Hegel should have called his major work of politics *Natural Law and Political Science in Outline*. This is an indication that he has not yet quite succeeded in shaking off the influence of Aristotle.

It is of course certainly correct to say that Hegel's understanding of the nature of 'ethical life' alters between 1802 and 1821. Hegel does indeed come to acknowledge that the ethical life which is appropriate in a modern society is not to be regarded as identical as that which was appropriate in the ancient Greek *polis*. The difference between the two is precisely the fact that in the former, unlike the latter, there is and must be a recognition of the value of 'subjective freedom', understood in the Kantian sense. To suggest, however, that this implies that Hegel abandons altogether the central insight that is provided by ancient Greek political thought, namely its view of human nature, and that he later attempts to construct an alternative approach to politics which is based upon entirely different principles, is to go much too far.

Fred Dallmayr has pointed out that Hegel's major work of political thought 'was initially titled *Naturrecht und Staatswissenschaft im Grundrisse*' and that 'it was later renamed *Grundlinien der Philosophie des Rechts*' (Dallmayr, 1993, p. 21). This appears to support Riedel's contention that there is a shift in Hegel's view of human nature between 1802 and 1821. It may well be, of course, that such a shift did indeed take place. No matter what was to happen later on, however, the fact remains that when Hegel first published this work he gave it two titles and not one. And the first of these titles clearly indicates that, even at this later stage, Hegel's political thought still attaches a considerable degree of importance to the classical Aristotelian approach to politics, and hence also to the classical Aristotelian conception of human nature.

Joachim Ritter has also drawn attention to this tension between the Aristotelian and the Kantian dimensions of Hegel's political thought. He points out that 'the *Philosophy of Right can be* understood' simply as the 'philosophical theory of the realisation of freedom'. If we look at the work solely from this point of view then we must recognise that Hegel evidently goes 'beyond' Aristotle and the Aristotelian approach to politics (Ritter, 1982, p. 128). In Ritter's view, however, we really ought not to do this. For what Hegel is seeking to do in the *Philosophy of Right* is to construct a theoretical approach to politics which actually combines the important insights provided by the Aristotelian tradition on the one hand and the Kantian tradition on the other. His political thought is a theory which is based both on the notion of 'the realisation of freedom' *and* the notion that political life is a reflection of essential 'human nature'.

Ritter argues, quite rightly, that in Hegel's view these two principles are actually complementary to one another. Moreover, the belief that they are complementary is fundamentally an Aristotelian insight. For it amounts to saying that 'the "world of spirit" is a "second nature"' to man'. Indeed, Hegel explicitly acknowledges that such is the case. In the Introduction to his *Lectures on the Philosophy of History*, he points out that 'the first nature of man is his immediate, animalic existence'. On the other hand, however, 'morality' or 'duty', Hegel suggests, 'has been rightly called' his 'second nature' (Hegel, 1953, p. 53). Moreover, Hegel takes a similar view in the *Philosophy of Right*. Here Hegel begins paragraph four by saying that the system of right is 'the realm of freedom made actual'. He concludes the paragraph, however, with the remark that, at the same time, it is 'the world of mind brought forth out of itself like a second nature' (Hegel, 1979, p. 20). According to Ritter, therefore, it is entirely understandable that Hegel should have given his major work on politics not one, but two titles. For this is something which consciously and explicitly registers his own indebtedness to both the Aristotelian and the Kantian traditions at the same time.

Before turning to discuss Hegel's theory of society, we may end this discussion of the influence of Aristotle and Kant on Hegel's political thought generally, and on his view of human nature in particular, with a few comments regarding Hegel's attitude towards the question of human equality. As might be expected, this is ambivalent. Hegel's debt to Aristotle in this regard is indicated by the fact that he is a firm believer in the principle of natural inequality. In his view, 'men are made unequal by nature'. What Hegel means by this is that human beings are 'dissimilar' with respect to 'natural, bodily and mental characteristics'.These 'differences' are 'conspicuous in every direction and on every level', and they have as their inevitable consequence 'disparities of individual resources and ability' (Hegel, 1979, p. 130; Hegel, 1971, p. 265). On the other hand, however,

Hegel's debt to Kant is indicated by the fact that, although he believes that people are by nature unequal with respect to their possession of basic talents and abilities, nevertheless he accepts the Kantian dictum that despite this they all have an equal value or worth as 'persons', and hence ought to be treated equally in similar circumstances. Thus for Hegel, as for Kant, the 'imperative of right' is 'Be a person and respect others as persons' (Hegel, 1979, p. 37). Politically speaking, the practical implications of this dual conception of human nature are an hostility to democracy, on the one hand, and an acceptance of the principle of equality before the law on the other.

Hegel's theory of society

Society and the state

There is a close relationship between Hegel's use of the term 'society' and his use of the term 'state'. In the *Philosophy of Right* Hegel employs each of these terms in two quite different senses: a narrow sense and a broad sense. As a result, Hegel's political thought contains two quite different views of the nature of society.

In the narrow sense the term 'state' refers to those bureaucratic institutions which, in modern societies, are associated with the process of making and enforcing statute law. This is in effect the 'government', or what Hegel calls 'the strictly political state' (Hegel, 1979, p. 163; Pelczynski, 1971a, p. 11). In this sense the state is clearly to be distinguished from 'society', or what Hegel refers to as 'civil society'. In this narrow sense, the state and society', together with the family, constitute the sphere of 'ethical life'. They are integral component elements within the overall structure of a particular historical community. From this point of view, therefore, society and civil society are one and the same thing.

In the broader sense of these two terms, 'state' and 'society' are not separate from one another. On the contrary, they are identical with one another. Here the word 'state' is used by Hegel to refer much more widely to society as a whole. In this second sense the state *is* that wider social community which Hegel identifies as the sphere of ethical life. Thus, from this second point of view, society and civil society are not the same thing. Here civil society is just one of the elements of which society as a whole is composed.

Hegel draws attention to these two different uses of the word 'state' quite explicitly in his *Lectures on the Philosophy of History*. He says there that the term 'state' 'is ambiguous' because when one employs it 'one usually means the simple political aspect' as distinct from the other aspects of social or ethical life. He emphasises, however, that this is not the sense in which he proposes to use the term. For 'we understand the term 'state' in a more comprehensive sense' than this (Hegel, 1953, p. 52; also p. 63). That Hegel employs the term 'state' in this broad sense to refer to society as a whole, or to the wider ethical community, is something which has been noted by a number of his interpreters (Pelczynski, 1971a, p. 13, also pp. 10-12, 14; Singer, 1983, p. 42; Brod, 1993, p. 8; Hardimon, 1994, p. 213; Inwood, 1992, pp. 277-80; Westphal, 1993, p. 259).

There is also a close relationship between Hegel's use of the terms 'state' and 'society', on the one hand, and his use of the term 'constitution' on the other. Hegel tends to employ the word 'constitution', also, in two different senses, a broad sense and a narrow sense. In the narrow sense, as one might expect, a constitution for Hegel is that set of institutional structures which are associated with the 'political state' of a particular society. In the broad sense, the constitution of a state is more or less identical with what Hegel (following Montesquieu) calls the 'collective spirit of the nation'. This 'collective spirit' is manifested in the customs and traditions which are associated with the ethical life of that society (Hegel, 1953, p. 59; Smith, 1991, p. 146). Here Hegel employs the term 'constitution' again very loosely to refer to society as a whole. In this broad sense the term 'constitution', like the terms 'state' and 'society', is used by Hegel to refer to the sphere of ethical life associated with a particular historical community or nation.

Society as a community

It is evident that Hegel considers society in the broad sense as being some sort of community. He quite clearly rejects the classical liberal theory of society. In his view this theory is erroneous because it sees society as being merely an 'agglomeration of atomic individuals'. It does not see, therefore, that society in general, and hence also the 'constitution of the state', is an 'organism', a whole greater than the sum of its individual parts (Hegel, 1979, pp. 164, 282; Mehta, 1968, p. 8).

A good illustration of Hegel's views on this subject is provided by his essay on the *Proceedings of the Wurtemberg Estates* (Hegel, 1969). Here Hegel says that society is best seen as an 'organic order'. In this text Hegel explicitly distinguishes his own view of society from the view adopted by classical liberalism and the ideals of the French Revolution. For the latter is based on quite different principles. It sees society as being composed of 'isolated atoms'. The people as a whole, therefore, is 'dissolved into a heap'. Hegel insists that such 'French abstractions', which are based on 'mere numbers', must be 'discarded'. To see society in this way is not to see it as it should be seen, as a community. The 'abstract provisions' of classical liberalism are 'most unworthy of the community and most in contradiction with its concept as a spiritual order'. Principles of this sort spell 'death to every rational concept, organisation and life' (Hegel, 1969a, pp. 262-63).

Robert Nisbet is quite right, therefore, when he says that Hegel attaches a considerable degree of importance to the value of community (Nisbet, 1973, p. 55). Nisbet claims, however, that like all conservatives what Hegel values is the 'traditional community'. According to Nisbet, all early conservatives (Hegel included) are opposed to 'modernism'. Thus 'the rediscovery of the traditional community and its values is central' to their thought. This judgement, although not exactly incorrect, is certainly partial and one sided. It captures only one aspect of the thinking, not only of Hegel, but also of conservatism generally. It is true that Hegel insists that society should be seen as a community. However, for Hegel this is a community of a rather special kind. It is a modern community and not simply a traditional one.

In Hegel's view, society as a whole should be seen, not as a simple community such as (allegedly) existed in pre-modern times, but as a complex or 'articulated' community. It is, in effect, an over-arching 'community of communities'. Thus, for example, in the essay on the *Wurtemberg Estates*, Hegel says that society understood as an 'organic order' should be considered to be an 'articulated whole' whose component parts 'themselves form particular subordinate spheres'. Hegel likens these 'subordinate communities' to the corporate groups of the Middle Ages and suggests that structures of this sort should actually be revived, in a modified form, in early nineteenth century Germany. It is now time to bring these 'lower spheres back again into respect' and 'purged of privileges and wrongs, to incorporate them as an organic structure in the state' (Hegel, 1969, pp. 262-3).

Hegel also expresses this corporatist theory of society in the *Philosophy of Right*. There he suggests that 'the circles of association' which exist in society are 'already communities' (Hegel, 1979, p. 198). He refers to it again in his *Lectures on the Philosophy of History*, when he says that the preservation of a 'state', that is to say of 'ethical life', is one and the same as the preservation of the various, different 'well ordered spheres of life' (Hegel, 1953, p. 38).

That Hegel sees society as being an 'articulated community' has been noted by more than one commentator. Thus, for example, Andrew Gamble refers to Hegel's view of society as being that of a 'morally united and yet internally differentiated community' (Gamble, 1983, p. 98). And Shlomo Avineri has suggested that for Hegel society as a whole is 'a highly sophisticated and differentiated pluralistic system' (Avineri, 1972, p. 47; also pp. 171-72; also Brod, 1992, p. 98; Dallmayr, 1993, p. 250; Hardimon, 1994, pp. 34-6, 40; Houlgate, 1991, p. 118; Mehta, 1968, p. 79; Nisbet, 1976, p. 418-20; Pelczynski, 1971a, p. 11; Plant, 1973, p. 109).

Hegel's theory of society, then, is one which is pluralist or corporatist in nature (Hegel, 1979, pp. 152-5). It sees society as being a complex community composed of a variety of different groups and institutions. Each one of these has a fundamentally hierarchical structure. It also has its own particular function, the performance of which is necessary for the well being of society as a whole. The individuals who compose society as a whole are all members of these various different corporate groups. They each have their own particular place or station, with is attendant duties.

It is Hegel's view that harmony and well being in such a society depends on individual virtue. That is to say, it depends on the fact that each individual should be willing to carry out (voluntarily) the duties associated with their own particular station in society. (Hegel, 1953, p. 37). According to Hegel, in an 'ethical community' of this sort it easy to say what are 'the duties he ought to fulfil in order to be virtuous'. He has 'simply to follow the well known and explicit rules of his own situation' (Hegel, 1979, p. 107). The basis of these duties is 'civil life'. Individuals 'have their assigned business and hence their assigned duties. Their morality consists in acting accordingly' (Hegel, 1953, p. 37; also Houlgate, 1991, p. 100; Mehta, 1968, p. 125).

It might be thought that there is a contradiction between Hegel's view of society as an ethical community based on the principle of spiritual unity, on the one hand, and his recognition that this ethical community is actually separated into subordinate spheres(and especially the two main subordinate spheres of state and civil society) on the other. However, it is Hegel's view that unity does not actually preclude certain forms of separation. On the contrary, the sort of unity which Hegel feels his appropriate for society in the modern age is precisely a unity which (paradoxically) at the same time recognises the value and importance of separation. It is this idea of 'unity-in-separation' that Hegel has in mind when he refers to the community as being an 'articulated' community. As Z. A. Pelczynski has pointed out, the two spheres of state and civil society are considered by Hegel not only to be separated but also to be 'organically connected', that is to say, 'interacting and interdependent'. For the concept of an organism 'implies also differentiation or "articulation"' (Pelczynski, 1971, p. 11).

The idea of society as a community based on the principle of 'unity-in-separation' or 'unity-in-difference' provides us with a good insight into Hegel's understanding of the specific form of ethical life which is appropriate in the modern era. As Michael Hardimon has suggested, in Hegel's view the ethical life of pre-modern society is based on a 'primitive' unity, that is to say, the 'absence of separation and division between community members'. The ethical life appropriate to a modern society, however, must necessarily be based on 'a form of unity that preserves difference'. Such a unity is what Hardimon calls a 'concrete unity'. This is 'not unity *without* difference but unity *in* difference' This is not a 'simple' unity, but a 'higher unity', 'one that preserves and embraces division, conflict and otherness' (Hardimon, 1994, pp. 34-36, 40; also Cassirer, 1967, pp. 265, 275; Dallmayr, 1993, p. 59; Scruton, 1988, p. 150).

The public and the private spheres

Hegel's theory of society as an articulated community has clear implications for our understanding of his attitude towards the distinction between the public and the private spheres. Some of Hegel's interpreters, like Karl Popper, have argued that Hegel is a totalitarian thinker. These commentators, therefore, evidently believe that the distinction between the public and the private spheres has no part at all to play in Hegel's political thought. As we have seen, however, other commentators have (quite rightly) rejected this view (Avineri, 1972, pp. 51, 180-1; Gamble, 1983, p. 97; Gooch, 1965, pp. 298-9; Heiman, 1971, pp. 130, 133-5; Smith, 1991, pp. 6, 236).

Thus, for example, Avineri has maintained that, in Hegel's opinion, the most distinctive characteristic feature of political life in the modern era is the fact that 'private life and public activity became distinct from one another'. This is a distinction which Hegel is keen to preserve in his own political thought. According to Avineri, then, 'Hegel insists on the necessity of autonomous' bodies and various 'non-political spheres of human life'. These should 'lead a life that is separate from and independent of the state' (Avineri, 1972, p. 51; also pp. 180-1).

It is certainly true that Hegel associates the rise of the modern state, and the separation between 'state' and 'civil society', with the breakdown of the traditional community and the dissipation of the pre-modern form of ethical life. It is also true that one of the principal tasks of Hegel's political thought is in some way to heal the rift that exists between these two spheres. In an important sense the Hegelian project is indeed an attempt to re-create a sense of community which has been lost. However, this is so only in a sense. For the type of community which Hegel wishes to create is not the 'traditional' one. Hegel does not think that we can go backwards. Nor is he completely anti-modern. The type of ethical life which Hegel has in mind in the *Philosophy of Right* is a form of ethical life that, in his view, would be best suited to modern times, in which the principle of individualism and autonomy has risen to a position of predominance. Hegel is, therefore, especially keen to integrate a commitment to this principle (at least in some form) within his own system of political thought.

What this amounts to is that in theory the community which Hegel seeks to create is one which seeks to heal the rift between the public and private spheres without actually abolishing this distinction altogether. As Andrew Gamble has insisted, 'Hegel was concerned that both state and civil society should retain their separateness, otherwise the distinctive quality of modern life and the possibility of full individual freedom would be lost' (Gamble, 1983, p. 97; also Cullen, 1979, pp. 94-6; Gooch, 1965, p. 299; Nisbet, 1986, pp. 38, 49, 84; Scruton, 1988, pp. 149-50; Smith, 1991, p. 236).

Hegel's attitude towards the distinction between the public and the private spheres is closely associated with his corporatist theory of society (Cullen, 1979, 91-4; Heiman, 1971). We have seen that, according to Hegel, the sense of community in modern times has become weaker. In Hegel's view, this weakening of the ties of community is a threat to the existing social order. This is so because it undermines the moral fabric of society, that is to say a society's 'ethical life'. This development goes hand in hand with that of the separation between civil society and the state. It is, therefore, associated with both a concentration of power and authority in the hands of the 'political state', on the one hand, and the 'atomisation' of the relationships between individuals in civil society on the other.

One of Hegel's proposed solutions to the problem of the loss of community is, as we have noted, to create a new form of social order based on a revival of the medieval notion of the corporation in a modified form. There are a number of things about medieval society (as he understands it) which Hegel likes. In particular he likes the fact that it is based on an acceptance of the principle of the decentralisation of political power. The corporate structure of medieval society acts as a bulwark against the excessive concentration of political power in the hands of any one individual or group. It provides, therefore, a certain degree of protection for the rights and liberties of society's various corporate institutions. As Hegel himself puts it, corporate institutions 'are the components of the constitution'. They are 'the pillars of public freedom' (Hegel, 1979, p. 163; also Heiman, 1971, p. 116).

It is Hegel's view that excessive concentration of power in the hands of the state is certainly undesirable. In addition, however, such a concentration of power is also not necessary for the preservation of social order. Or rather, it would not be necessary, if only we could re-create that sense of community which has been lost, by other means. The key to this is the revival of the idea of the corporate group. Such groups bind individuals more closely, not only to one another but also to the community of which they are a part. They are 'the firm foundation not only of the state but of the citizen's trust in it' (Hegel, 1979, p. 163). They are mediating structures which lie between the individual and the political state, and which protect the individual from the state (Brudner, 1981, pp. 134-6). In a society which is composed of corporate groups order is preserved less by the coercive power of the state, and more by the existence of a spiritual consensus based on values which are shared by every member of the community. In such a situation every member of society will be more likely to perform the duties associated with their station voluntarily, simply because they recognise that this is their duty. Thus, for Hegel, it is the articulation of society into various corporate groups which serves to create both a new form of order, on the one hand, whilst at the same time protecting the liberty of the individual members of society on the other.

An important implication of this view is that it is clearly inappropriate to regard Hegel as a totalitarian thinker who seeks to subordinate the individual to the political state, and who does not recognise the validity of any distinction between the public and the private spheres, or between civil society and the state. Hegel's view of society as an articulated community contains within it a recognition of the validity and importance of a private sphere within which individuals and corporate groups are left free to pursue their own particular interests, unhindered by the state.

This is, indeed, the crucial distinction between Hegel's version of corporatism and that associated with Italian fascism. As G. Heiman has quite rightly pointed out, 'fascism was essentially monolithic, claiming pre-eminence in all aspects of human existence'. Hegel's corporatism, or his 'legal-political pluralism', did not do this. For Hegel, the individual's 'corporate existence' had 'nothing to do with the individual's private life'. The various private aspects of human existence 'were not absorbed by the state, nor its laws, nor its constituent groups'. It is, therefore, a mistake to equate Hegel's corporatism with the 'pseudo-corporatism of twentieth century fascist Italy' (Heiman, 1971, p. 134; also Brod, 1992, p. 98; Cassirer, 1967, p. 275; Pelczynski, 1969, pp. 56-68; Scruton, 1988, pp. 149-50; Smith, 1991, pp. 142-4; Wilford, 1986, p. 221).

Most of these commentators take the view that, because Hegel's corporatism is quite different from that associated with the ideology of fascism, then it follows that Hegel must be some sort of liberal corporatist, or a liberal pluralist. There is, however, nothing specifically liberal about corporatism, about a commitment to constitutional government, or about resistance to excessive state centralisation in the name of freedom. Hegel's views on this issue are in fact strikingly similar to those of Burke and traditional conservatism. In practice, of course, it is certainly correct to say that the scope for 'free activity' which is afforded to individuals by conservatives like Hegel or Burke, at least with respect to certain issues, may well 'stand in comparison with that assigned to them by many liberal thinkers of the age' (Pelczynski, 1969, p. 68). Clearly, however, that is beside the point. Moreover, in making this point Pelczynski implicitly acknowledges that Hegel is not actually a liberal thinker at all.

Noel O'Sullivan has argued that a central characteristic feature of German romantic conservatism in the early nineteenth century is that it rejected the theoretical distinction between the public and the private spheres. As O'Sullivan puts it, 'no artificial distinctions' were 'then drawn between the state and the individual' or 'between public and private life'. This is one reason why the German romantic conservatives 'tended to admire the ancient world'. For that, too, 'was a world in which there was no fragmentation of human existence, and no cleavages within the social order' (O'Sullivan, 1976, p. 61). Thus, according to O' Sullivan, 'from the start, German conservatives set out to make the state encompass every sphere of life, and so confine man within the single role of citizenship'. In short, they made the state 'a total institution' (O'Sullivan, 1976, p. 66).

If this assessment of the general character of German conservatism were correct then it would of course follow that Hegel could not be considered to be a conservative thinker, at least not if we insist on examining his ideas within their German context. It is not surprising, therefore, that O'Sullivan should arrive at this very conclusion himself. There are, however, two reasons for objecting to this line of reasoning. Firstly, it is not at all clear that Hegel's views really should be located against this particular context. Secondly, it is quite wrong simply to identify (as O'Sullivan does) early German conservatism with the ideas of the Romantics. For there were other schools of Conservative thought in Germany at this time which differed from Romanticism on a number of points, for example the 'Hanoverian School' of conservatism, as represented by the ideas of Ernst

Brandes and August Wilhelm Rehberg (Aris, 1965, pp. 55-7; Beiser, 1992, pp. 303-9; Epstein, 1966, pp. 549-90; Gooch, 1965, pp. 73-88).

The members of the Hanoverian School of German conservatism were opposed to absolutism and in favour of a constitutional monarchy. Their commitment to the principles of constitutionalism and the rule of law has the implication that they did not reject the distinction between the public and the private spheres (Aris, 1965, pp. 55-6; Beiser, 1992, p. 303; Epstein, 1966, pp. 549, 568, 570-2; Gooch, pp. 78-9). In this respect, their political thought reflects an admiration for the English constitution. The ideas of Brandes and Rehberg are in fact strikingly similar to those of Burke. More to the point, however, with respect to the distinction between the public and the private spheres, their ideas are also strikingly similar to those of Hegel.

It is interesting to note, in this regard, that O'Sullivan's reason for thinking that Hegel is not a conservative thinker is not because Hegel is an advocate of totalitarianism. On the contrary, it is that Hegel actually rejects totalitarianism whereas the German romantic conservatives embrace it. In making this judgement O'Sullivan contradicts his own earlier characterisation of conservatism as being an ideology for which the 'primary aim' is 'the preservation of the distinction between private and public life' (O'Sullivan, 1976, p. 12). From the standpoint of this general characterisation of conservatism (which is clearly an exaggeration) there is more reason for considering Hegel to be a conservative thinker than there is for considering the members of the German Romantic school to be so.

Hegel and economics

To say that the distinction between the public and the private spheres ought to be valued and preserved is one thing. The question of where exactly the dividing line between these two spheres ought to be drawn is quite another. The answer to this question has significant implications for Hegel's attitude towards economic affairs (Avineri, 1972, pp. 87-99, 132-154; Cullen, 1979; Pelczynski, 1969, pp. 55-68)

On this question, as Pelczynski puts it, 'Hegel is not dogmatic about the limits of state activity and he forgoes the laying down of any rigid and absolute principles in that sphere' (Pelczynski, 1969, p. 67). Thus, in his essay on *The German Constitution* (1799-1802), Hegel goes so far as to say that the government 'must leave to the freedom of the citizens whatever is not necessary for its appointed function of organising and maintaining authority and thus for its security at home and abroad'. For 'the freedom of the citizens is inherently sacrosanct' (Hegel, 1969b, pp. 161-2). This amounts in practice to the advocacy of a free market economy. Pelczynski has noted that, at the time he wrote this essay, Hegel was 'greatly interested in Britain'. He wrote a commentary on Sir James Steuart's *An Inquiry Into The Principles of Political Economy*, in which he (Hegel) defends 'the principles of free competition'. He was, generally speaking, greatly impressed by what he took to be the British experience and especially by the idea of an 'autonomous' or 'dynamic' civil society (Pelczynski, 1969, pp. 63, 67; also Cullen, 1979, pp. 70-2)

In his later essay on *The Wurtemberg Estates* (1817), however, as again Pelczynski notes, Hegel 'abandons the minimalist position' which he had taken up earlier, without however going so far as to advocate a position of 'centralism'. Here the state is simply viewed 'as playing a more active and direct part in the affairs of civil society' (Pelczynski, 1969, p. 64). This later position is reaffirmed in Hegel's essay on *The English Reform Bill* (1831). In this essay, written towards the end of his life, 'Hegel admits the necessity of considerable government interference' in order to 'provide employment and subsistence to whole classes of the population' (Pelczynski, 1969, p. 67).

This is also the view which Hegel adopts in the *Philosophy of Right* (Hegel, 1979, pp. 147-52; 275-7). Here Hegel points out that there are two 'extreme' positions regarding the issue of state regulation of the economy. The first is complete 'freedom of trade and commerce'. The second is 'public organisation to provide for everything and determine everyone's labour' (Hegel, 1979, pp. 147, 276). In practice, the position to which Hegel commits himself here is one which lies somewhere in between these two extremes. It is therefore to some degree an interventionist one. Hegel's suggests that a free market economy leads to the generation of too much social inequality, and hence poverty. In such circumstances, intervention by the 'public authority' is justified. For society 'has the right and duty' to act as a 'trustee' for those whose 'extravagance' destroys the 'security of their own subsistence or their families' (Hegel, 1979, pp. 148-49). In particular, it has the duty to prevent the creation of a 'rabble of paupers' (Hegel, 1979, p. 150).

At first sight it is not clear what to make of this apparent shift in Hegel's position with respect to economic issues. One possibility of course, as usual, is that his views are inconsistent. It is certainly possible that, over a period of time, Hegel simply changed his mind regarding the question of state intervention in the economy. The earlier view is, of course, strikingly similar to that advocated by Adam Smith and the ideology of classical liberalism. It might, therefore, be suggested that this shift in position with respect to economic issues is consistent with a general drift throughout Hegel's life away from an earlier commitment to the standpoint of liberalism and towards a later commitment to the standpoint of conservatism. More than one commentator has suggested that such a shift did in fact take place (Dallmayr, 1993, p. 93; Gooch, 1965, pp. 297-300).

This view takes it for granted that when he takes the earlier position Hegel is adopting a liberal standpoint. It is assumed automatically that, in the late eighteenth and early nineteenth centuries, a commitment to free market economics is necessarily associated with a commitment to the principles of classical liberalism. This commitment has no part to play within the ideology of conservatism. We have, however, already seen that such a view is mistaken. For

Burke himself was a clear advocate of the idea that under certain circumstances it might be beneficial to the national community that the state should not regulate the economy.

Hegel's lack of dogmatism regarding the issue of regulation of the economy is in fact entirely consistent with the standpoint of traditional conservatism. Like Burke, Hegel is neither for or against such regulation *per se*. For Hegel, as for Burke, whether or not the state should intervene in the economy depends on whether the operation of a free market is perceived to be in the interest of the wider social community as a whole. If it is, then the state should not intervene. If it is not, then the state should intervene. For, in the latter case, to permit an unregulated freedom within the economic sphere would be undermine the moral fabric of society. In these circumstances the balance between liberty and order has clearly shifted too far in the direction of liberty at the expense of order. The necessary equilibrium between the two principles, therefore, needs to be restored by the intervention of the state. As Houlgate has pointed out, for Hegel 'the freedom of economic enterprise which underlies civil society' is 'not absolute'. This is so because 'the public has the right to demand that the economic system be maintained as a place where freedom, right and welfare remain available to all'. This means that 'individuals do not have the right to violate the rights or destroy the welfare of others in the pursuit of their own interests' (Houlgate, 1991, p. 108; also Plant, 1973, p. 116).

Like Burke, then, Hegel considers the economic system of society to be a 'subordinate community'. It is a corporate sphere within the overall system of Ethical Life. It is an integral element in the articulated structure of the wider community that is society as a whole. Hegel associates the economic system with what he calls 'civil society', the economic system falls, generally speaking, within the private sphere. It is desirable that, in so far as this is possible, it should not be directly regulated by the state. However, the interests of the economic sphere are and must be always subordinated to the needs of the wider social community as a whole. They are, therefore, subject to regulation by the state should the circumstances require it. This is something which has been appreciated by Fred Dallmayr. According to Dallmayr, as a consequence of his reading of Steuart, Hegel 'gained an appreciation of modern free enterprise and market economics'. And yet at the same time 'he was also critical or apprehensive of a narrow economism'. He rejected any 'exclusive focus on private self-interest to the detriment of public and moral bonds' (Dallmayr, 1993, p. 19).

This judgement is supported by Hegel's comments on economic intervention in the *Philosophy of Right*. The theoretical justification which Hegel gives for his advocacy of state regulation of the economy here is that each of the two 'extreme' attitudes towards state intervention referred to above has its strong points, and 'both points of view' must therefore 'be satisfied'. Hence we should balance the two principles of liberty and order. For 'freedom of trade should not be such as too jeopardise the general good' (Hegel, 1979, p. 276).

Hegel's approach to politics

Hegel and liberty

A superficial reading of the *Philosophy of Right* might well lead the unwary reader into concluding, very quickly, that Hegel surely must be considered to be some sort of liberal thinker, if only because of the great importance which he attaches, throughout the work, to the value of freedom or liberty. Thus, for example, the whole of the Introduction to this work is devoted to a discussion of the concept of freedom. Indeed, Hegel defines the concept of 'right' by reference to that of freedom. For Hegel, 'freedom is both the substance of right and its goal, while the system of right is the realm of freedom made actual' (Hegel, 1979, p. 20; also p. 33).

However, to conclude on these grounds that Hegel's political thought represents the standpoint of classical liberalism would be a mistake, for two reasons. The first is that, as we have seen, liberty is not simply and solely a liberal value. It is a value which has an important part to play in the ideology of conservatism also. We have already seen that this is so in the case of Burke, and what is true of Burke is also true of conservatism generally, and especially of German conservatism.

For example, G. P. Gooch has pointed out that Friedrich Gentz, the German conservative responsible for translating Burke's *Reflections* was firmly of the belief that freedom is an important political value. Indeed, next to order, it is the most important value of all. Gentz, like Burke, insists that 'political freedom' is necessarily 'limited freedom'. Liberty is necessarily an 'ordered liberty'. Gentz believes that states 'may have an excess or liberty, or of rule'. It is, however, the former which 'is more dangerous'. For 'a little freedom combined with order is better than a great deal without it'. In Gentz's view, 'equilibrium' between these two principles of liberty and order 'is most nearly approached in England, whose constitution should be studied by every publicist' (Gooch, 1965, pp. 96-7; also Beiser, 1992, pp. 317-22; Reiff, 1912, p. 46).

The claim that freedom is an important value for conservatism, and especially German conservatism, has been made by Karl Mannheim. According to Mannheim, it is necessary to make a distinction between 'the liberal and conservative concept of freedom'. For early conservatism in Germany 'could not fail', as a consequence of 'political necessity', to 'set up an explicitly conservative concept of freedom', which might stand 'in opposition to the revolutionary concept' of classical liberalism (Mannheim, 1986, p. 91). For Mannheim, early German conservatism 'does not attack 'freedom' itself'. What it rejects is the classical liberal conception which understood freedom to mean 'the right of the individual to do as he wishes' (Mannheim, 1986, p. 91).

Some commentators have suggested that there is something particularly 'Germanic' about this tendency to re-define the concept of freedom in a way which differs from the classical liberal conception. That is to say, there is something uniquely 'German' about the 'positive' conception of freedom. Thus, for example, John Sheehan has argued that 'modernisers' in Germany at the beginning of the nineteenth century had to 'translate western ideas and experience into their own terms'. And 'as so often happens in the process of translation, the original had to be adapted, perhaps even distorted' before it could 'become comprehensible to the translator and his audience' (Sheehan, 1978, p. 1; also Krieger, 1957, pp. ix, 4-5). As a matter of fact, though, there is nothing peculiarly German about this at all. For the tendency to redefine the concept of freedom so that it might be incorporated within an anti-liberal approach to politics is something which is central to the conservative tradition generally. In this respect there is no significant theoretical difference between the views of Hegel (and of German conservatism generally), on the one hand, and those of Burke on the other.

The second reason why Hegel's commitment to the value of freedom does not entail a corresponding commitment to the values of classical liberalism is that, like Burke, Hegel rejects the 'negative' conception of freedom, and for much the same reasons (Berlin, 1973; Houlgate, 1991, pp. 70-84; Mehta, 1968, pp. 50-70; Parkinson, 1983; Pelczynski, 1984; Plamenatz, 1971; Schact, 1972). For Hegel, as for Burke, true freedom is not the freedom simply to do what we want or choose to do. This is the popular conception of freedom, the view of 'the man in the street' (Hegel, 1979, p. 230). This is 'negative freedom' or 'freedom as the understanding conceives it' (Hegel, 1979, p. 22; Hegel, 1953, p. 50; Hegel, 1971, p. 266). A truly free act, for Hegel, requires self-restraint. It requires a decision to limit one's own freedom in order to respect the freedom of others. All truly free action is a form of moral action, which is based on a respect for the principle of 'equal freedom' or 'equal liberty'. A truly free act, therefore, is the act of 'a free will which wills the free will' (Hegel, 1979, p. 32). In contradistinction to the 'negative' conception of freedom, Hegel describes this view as 'positive freedom' (Hegel, 1979, pp. 259-60).

In saying this, Hegel is saying little different from what Kant (and Burke) had already said before him. The difference between Hegel and Kant (at least as Hegel sees it) has to do with the source for the content which is to be ascribed to the formal principle of equal liberty. Hegel is strongly opposed to the idea that the content for this principle should come from the conscience of isolated individuals, and he criticises both Rousseau and Kant for suggesting otherwise (Hegel, 1979, pp. 27-8, 33, 90-1, 96-7, 253). As we have already noted, Hegel believes that such a view is an 'empty formalism' by means of which 'any wrong or immoral line of conduct may be justified' (Hegel, 1979, p. 90).

It is Hegel's view, therefore (as again we have noted), that the principle of equal liberty has a definite 'objective content'. It is associated with 'fixed principles' and 'objective duties' (Hegel, 1979, p. 91). In the first instance these are the principles of 'abstract right', such as the principles forbidding the act of theft and murder (Hegel, 1979, pp. 96-7). However, once these abstract principles have themselves been provided with a definite content by being incorporated into the laws of a particular historical community, then the duty to act in accordance with them is transferred to the customs, traditions and laws of that community.

In the final analysis, then, it is Hegel's view that one can only be truly free by living together with others in such a community under a system of law. What Hegel's 'positive' conception of freedom amounts to is nothing more than an advocacy of the rule of law. For Hegel, 'every genuine law is a liberty' (Hegel, 1971, p. 266; also Hegel, 1953, p. 55; Avineri, 1972, pp. 190-3; Smith, 1989, p. 5; Smith, 1991, pp. xi, 8-9, 124).

It is sometimes suggested that Hegel's 'positive' view of freedom signifies that he is a totalitarian thinker. Nothing could be further from the truth. As Allen Wood has rightly pointed out, there is nothing really at all sinister about Hegel's view of freedom. For it is a well established principle, even within the ideology of classical liberalism, that an important distinction needs to be made between 'liberty', properly understood, and 'license'. Even Locke admits that a framework of law, and hence obedience to law, is a necessary precondition for the existence of political freedom in any society (Scott, 1956; Wood, 1990, pp. 40-2). It is this and this only which Hegel has in mind when he says that 'really, every genuine law is a liberty'.

It might be thought that what this shows is that, like Locke or Kant, Hegel is a liberal thinker. However, this is not the case. For the law which, in Hegel's view, is to provide the specific content for the formal principle of equal liberty, is most emphatically not natural law as interpreted by the conscience of the individual moral agent. It is, in the first instance, the customary law associated with the constitution of a particular historical community. In this respect, therefore, Hegel's views are much closer to those of Montesquieu or Burke than they are to those of Locke or Kant. In short, Hegel's views are neither totalitarian nor liberal. They are quite typically conservative.

For Hegel then, as for Burke, the liberty which has value is actually a form of 'ordered liberty'. It is a liberty which is associated with a particular framework of laws and hence a specific moral and legal order. This framework and this order are themselves, at least in their concrete details, specific to a particular historical community and hence to the existing political constitution of that community. Individuals are free, and can be free, only in such a community. Moreover, individuals are only truly free to the extent that they voluntarily obey the laws of that community. As Pelczynski has put it, for Hegel 'freedom in the ethical sphere' is associated with 'the guidance of one's actions by the living, actual principles of one's community, clearly understood and deliberately accepted, and in secure confidence that other community members will act in the same way' (Pelczynski, 1971a, p. 9).

Hegel's political thought, like Burke's, is therefore based on an attempt to synthesise the apparently contrasting values of order and liberty. This is something which has not gone unnoticed. Andrew Gamble, for example, has maintained that Hegel's political ideal is that of 'a morally united yet internally differentiated community' which would 'make possible a balance between liberty and order' (Gamble, 1983, p. 98; also Gooch, 1965, pp. 298-300). Such a view, as we have seen, is the watchword of traditional conservatism.

Hegel and constitutionalism

We have seen that Hegel associates freedom with a situation in which individuals live under a framework of law and collectively respect the principle of the rule of law. In short, for Hegel, freedom is a matter of obedience to the laws of the state. At first sight this seems very sinister. It is, therefore, important that we understand exactly what this means for Hegel.

Hegel's theoretical distinction between the two different senses of the term 'state' is of some significance here. It is important to note that, in the first instance, the reference to the state in this context is a reference to the 'state' in the broader of the two different senses of this term, not the narrower. This amounts to saying that the laws which, for Hegel, regulate individual conduct and thereby sustain individual freedom are to be associated with the customs and traditions of a particular ethical community rather than with the statute law of that community's 'political state'.

For Hegel then, as for Burke and Montesquieu, in theory these customary laws might be said to provide the individual with a certain measure of protection against the political state. Hegel is committed to the principle of constitutional rule. He is not a defender of Prussian or of any other kind of absolutism. In his view, the constitution is a guarantor of individual liberty. As V. R. Mehta has rightly pointed out, for Hegel 'the constitution of the state stands as a bulwark against the abuse of government. It defines the authority of the government and also sets a clear limit to it'. The belief that Hegel 'entrusts absolute powers to the state' is, therefore, simply 'a misunderstanding' (Mehta, 1968, p. 74, 81).

We have seen that, from the standpoint of Hegel's natural law theory, the particular content that is to be given to the formal principles of natural law are not a matter of moral necessity. The specific nature of these principles is arbitrary, contingent and historically conditioned. They are accidental features of the constitution of a particular historical community. They are, therefore, closely associated with, and indeed have a specific character which is determined by, the customs, traditions, sentiments, values and attitudes of mind which are associated with that community and its culture or national character. The inspiration which lies behind this view is, as Hegel freely admits, provided by Montesquieu (Hegel, 1979, p. 16). A commitment to this principle, considered in isolation, leads to what might be called a form of constitutional relativism. From this point of view, the way in which rights are defined by the political constitution of one society is no better and no worse, morally speaking, than the way in which those rights are defined by that of another (Wood, 1990, p. 205).

Hegel's views on this issue may be illustrated by considering his attitude towards the abstract, 'a priori' approach adopted to constitutional issues by the liberal thinkers of the Enlightenment. In the *Philosophy of Right* Hegel is extremely critical of this approach to 'constitution building'. He suggests that to attempt to 'give a constitution' (even if this is one 'more or less rational in content') to any nation 'a priori' is to overlook the fact that all constitutions must inevitably contain an arbitrary, contingent and historical element. It is to overlook 'that factor in a constitution which makes it more than and *ens rationis*'. In Hegel's view, therefore, 'every nation has the constitution appropriate to it' (Hegel, 1979, p. 177, 286-7; Hegel, 1892-96, 2, pp. 97-8; Wood, 1991, p. 203). Elsewhere Hegel suggests that the different types of constitution 'must be discussed historically or not at all' (Hegel, 1979, p. 177).

In Hegel's view, the idea that a constitution might be constructed *a priori* is associated with a theory of society which sees society as being merely an 'agglomeration of atomic individuals'. As we have seen, Hegel considers this theory of society to be false. For Hegel society, and hence also the 'constitution of the state' itself, is an 'organism', a whole greater than the sum of its individual parts (Hegel, 1979, pp. 164, 282). Thus constitutions exist in their own right and prior to the existence of individuals. As Hegel puts it himself, to ask 'Who is to frame the constitution?' is to ask a 'meaningless' question. Constitutions should be thought of as things which are 'simply existent'. In some important sense they are 'constant'. Hence they are 'divine' and 'exalted above' the things that are made by men (Mehta, 1968, p. 77; Suter, 1971, p. 66).

We have already observed that Hegel uses the term 'constitution' in two different senses. When he uses it in the narrow sense he is referring to the political constitution of a particular historical community. When he uses it in the broad sense he is referring to society as a whole, or (following Montesquieu) to the unifying spiritual principle which underpins the ethical life of such a community. It follows from this that, for Hegel, the question 'who has the power to make a constitution?' is one and 'the same as the question, Who has to make the spirit of a nation?'. For to 'separate our idea of a constitution from that of the collective spirit' is to show how superficially we have 'apprehended the nexus between the spirit in its self-consciousness and in its actuality' (Hegel, 1971, p. 268). Once again, therefore, it makes no sense, in Hegel's opinion, to talk about our 'making' a (narrow political) constitution. For such a constitution 'only develops from the national spirit identically with that spirit's own development'. It is only by 'the indwelling spirit and the history of the nation' that 'constitutions have been and are made' (Hegel, 1971, pp. 268-9).

In so far as constitutional issues are concerned, therefore, it is Hegel's opinion that the only meaningful question to ask is not be 'about framing' a new constitution, 'but only about altering' an already existing constitution (Hegel, 1979, p. 178). And this implies that any such alteration should respect the integrity of the constitution which is being altered. The 'very presupposition of a constitution directly implies that its alteration may come about only by constitutional means' (Hegel, 1979, p. 178). This is a view which clearly rules out any radical social or political change, but which does allow for the possibility of constitutional reform. Indeed, it not only allows for it but also recognises that changes of this sort are more or less inevitable. For constitutions, like natural organisms, grow and develop over time. A constitution 'advances and matures'. Thus it 'changes over a long period of time into something quite different from what it was originally' (Hegel, 1979, p. 291; Mehta, 1968, p. 77).

Hegel and constitutional reform

We have suggested that Hegel is not opposed to constitutional reform. On the contrary, he is strongly in favour of it. This raises the question of what guidelines ought to be followed by those seeking to introduce such reforms. In Hegel's view, there are two basic principles which need to be borne in mind here. Both of these principles are historical. They are, however, historical in different senses.

The first of these principles is historical in what might be said to be a 'local' sense. We have seen that Hegel makes a distinction between two senses of the term 'constitution'. This distinction has important implications for his attitude towards such constitutional reform. For these two senses are closely related to one another. In Hegel's view a constitution in the narrow sense, the political constitution, is simply 'the actual organisation and development' of the collective spirit of the nation 'in suitable institutions' (Hegel, 1971, p. 268). It follows from this that, for Hegel, a state (in the broad sense) 'is an individual totality from which no particular aspect, not even one as highly important as the constitution, can be separated and considered by itself alone' (Hegel, 1953, pp. 59-60). The political constitution should not 'be considered, discussed, and selected in isolation'. For not only is this constitution 'intimately connected with those other spiritual forces and dependent on them, but the determination of the whole spiritual individuality' is 'only a moment in the history of the whole'. It is 'this which gives to the constitution its highest sanction and necessity' (Hegel, 1953, p. 60.

It follows from this that one of the guidelines which must be followed when altering the constitution of a particular historical community is that provided by the 'national character', or the 'spirit of the laws', associated with the community in question. According to Hegel, all constitutional reform must necessarily respect the values, customs and traditions which underpin the constitution that is being reformed. This sets clear limits to the both the extent and the pace of the reforms. In the *Philosophy of Right*, Hegel illustrates this point with an example. 'A nation's constitution must embody its feeling for its rights and its position'. For example, the new constitution which Napoleon gave to the Spaniards 'was more rational than what they had before'. The Spaniards, however, rejected it. They 'recoiled from it as something alien, because they were not yet educated up to its level' (Hegel, 1979, p. 287; Wood, 1990, pp. 207-08). Hegel's attitude with respect to this aspect of constitutional reform has been well captured by V. R. Mehta. In Mehta's view, Hegel follows Burke in arguing 'that speculative thinking has no relevance to the process of practical politics'. It is Hegel's view that 'change is inevitable'. So also, therefore is constitutional

142

reform. This, however, 'should not be alien to the spirit of the nation'. Nor should it 'constitute a threat to the stable order of society'. For 'there can be no progress without order'. Such reform, therefore, should always respect 'the customs and traditions of the particular society', whilst at the same time 'scrutinising their rationale with the help of reason' (Mehta, 1968, pp. 18, 131). Thus, according to Mehta, one of the guidelines for such reform is what Hegel (following Montesquieu) calls 'the collective spirit of the nation' (Mehta, 1968, p. 85).

The second principle which, in Hegel's view, provides the guidelines for all would be constitutional reformers is also provided by history. However, this is not 'local' history, or the history of a particular ethical community. It is rather what in his *Lectures on the Philosophy of History* Hegel calls 'world history' (Hegel, 1953). To be more precise, it is the historical example (as selectively interpreted by Hegel himself) that has been provided by the French Revolution (Mehta, 1968, p. 76).

A number of commentators have been misled by Hegel's commitment to constitutional reform into thinking that he must subscribe to the stoic conception of natural law. For such a commitment seems to imply that Hegel thinks that natural law constitute some sort of 'rational ideal' which might serve as 'a measuring rod of actual laws' (Pelczynski, 1969, p. 49). However, this is not what Hegel means when he talks about existing positive laws being 'irrational'. When Hegel talks in this way what he usually means is simply that the positive laws in question are 'hopelessly out of date' when considered from the standpoint of world history, and hence in comparison with the legal systems of other countries, especially post-revolutionary France (Avineri, 1972, p. 54).

If Pelczynski's judgement were correct, then it would follow that the *Philosophy of Right* itself might legitimately be considered to be a blue print for constitutional reform constructed upon 'a priori' rational principles. It seems clear enough, however, that Hegel did not view the constitutional framework which he sets out in the *Philosophy of Right* in this light. In his view, the *Philosophy of Right* is, rather, a distillation of the historical lesson that is provided by the French Revolution. It does, of course, provide a guideline for constitutional reform. In Hegel's view, however, such reform must always also pay very close attention to local conditions, and to local customs and traditions. The lessons of the French Revolution cannot be applied mechanically in the manner of the abstract reasoning of the eighteenth century liberal reformers.

The commitment to reform which undoubtedly exists in Hegel's political thought derives, not as one might expect from the fact that he embraces the notion of natural law, but rather from Hegel's philosophy of history. It is history and not natural law which, in Hegel's view, provides us with a critical standard for the evaluation of positive law. The reason which underpins Hegel's commitment to reform is above all an historical reason.

We have seen that for Hegel, when considered from the standpoint of local history all constitutions are equally valid. At this level the principle of constitutional relativism rules. Things are quite different, however, when we look at the situation from the standpoint of world history. It is Hegel's view that, when examined in this light, the constitutional systems of different societies certainly can be compared with one another and hence evaluated. What was arbitrary from the standpoint of morality, or moral reason, ceases to be so when considered from the standpoint of world history, or historical reason. From the world historical standpoint, some constitutions are definitely more 'rational' than others. As Hegel himself puts it, 'the absolute judge of states' is 'the mind which gives itself actuality in world history' (Hegel, 1979, p. 279). Pelczynski has pointed out that, 'almost invariably Hegel invokes history rather than reason whenever any institutional questions' are involved. 'By 'history', however, is meant' not the 'chronicle type of history', but the 'wider and more speculative approach'. That is to say, the approach usually associated with Hegel's own philosophy of history (Pelczynski, 1969, p. 35; Wood, 1991, pp. 205-8, 223-5). This point is sound. However, by acknowledging it Pelczynski undermines his own claim that Hegel believes in the existence of moral principles which are abstract, universal and rational, and which might be used to critically evaluate positive law.

Hegel's views on this critical aspect of the subject of constitutional reform have been captured by L. P. Hinchman. Like Foster, Hinchman recognises the apparently contradictory nature of Hegel's overall position with respect to natural law. For 'while Hegel does reject abstract theories of natural right that measure existing states against a nonactual "beyond"', nevertheless 'he refuses to abandon the principle that right differs in its very essence from mere positive existence or historical longevity' (Hinchman, 1984, p. 188). In Hinchman's view this leaves Hegel with a serious problem. For 'if we do not judge the rationality of existing institutions according to a transcendent, nonactual standard, how can we avoid identifying right with positive law and existing institutions?' (Hinchman, 1984, pp. 188-9). Hegel's solution to this dilemma, according to Hinchman, is to attempt to 'demonstrate that historical development has finally led to the creation of actual states that incorporate the institutions and principles which the "idea of right" would require' (Hinchman, 1984, p. 189).

The sentiment expressed in the final sentence here is not quite accurate. There are no specific institutions or principles which the "idea of right" (and hence also that of freedom) as such requires. For this is a purely formal principle, which has to be given a specific content in and through history. It would be more accurate to rephrase Hinchman's remarks and say that , for Hegel, historical development has finally led to the creation of actual states that incorporate the institutions and practices which world history itself requires. Nevertheless, that aside, Hinchman does succeed here in grasping the essence of this particular aspect of Hegel's attitude towards constitutional reform.

It might be said, then, that Hegel's attitude towards constitutional reform is one which seeks to balance the strong feeling that (in the light of the onward march of world history) such reforms are certainly necessary, with the equally strong feeling that nevertheless reforms of this sort should not be too radical. They should not go too far, too fast, and they should certainly respect existing customs and traditions in so far as this is possible. In short, like Burke and Coleridge, what Hegel is seeking to do in his remarks on constitutional reform is balance the two principles of 'permanence' and 'progression', or alternatively the two values of 'order' and 'liberty'.

This is something which has been noted by G. P. Gooch. Gooch has suggested that Hegel's views on constitutional reform are best seen as an attempt to compromise between the respective positions of traditionalism, on the one hand, and the liberal ideals of the French revolution on the other. In his opinion Hegel took the view that both 'the rigid maintenance of vanished conditions and the rival extreme of abstract theory are alike the sources of misfortune in every land'. The *via media* between these two extreme positions is to abandon a position of 'pedantic traditionalism' and embrace a programme of 'rational reform' (Gooch, 1965, p. 300). Thus, according to Gooch, Hegel believed that 'the supreme lesson of the French Revolution' was that 'order and liberty must be combined' (Gooch, 1965, p. 298).

Hegel and the Prussian reforms

In support of their claim that Hegel is not a conservative, a number of commentators cite as evidence his sympathetic attitude towards the Prussian reforms introduced by Stein and Hardenberg between 1806 and 1819 (Avineri, 1972, pp. 64, 73, 116-17; Dallmayr, 1993, pp. 79-80; de Ruggiero, 1981, p. 217; Hardimon, 1994, pp. 27, 29, 65, 79; O'Sullivan, 1976, p. 59; Singer, 1983, p. 24; Smith, 1991, p. 132; Weiss, 1977, p. 29; Westphal, 1993, pp. 238-9; Wood, 1990, pp. 13, 257-8; Wood, 1991, p. x). In almost every case these reforms are referred to as liberal reforms. It is simply assumed by most of these commentators that a commitment to reform is, and must be, by its very nature an indication of liberal sympathies. From this point of view, all reforms are necessarily liberal reforms. It is, however, evidently a mistake to make this assumption. For a recognition of the need for reform is an important feature of the history of conservatism also. From the time of Burke onwards, conservatives have been opposed, not to reforms as such but to radical reforms, or to reforms which challenge the integrity of the ancient constitution.

It is in fact not at all clear that the Prussian reforms of 1806-1819 are best described as liberal reforms. More than one historian has denied this (Aris, 1965, pp. 10, 317, 361, 366-7, 370-2, 376-9 400-2; Gooch, 1965, pp. 519-29; Nisbet, 1980, p. 278; Sorel, 1969, pp. 458, 468-9; Taylor, 1976, p. 37). For example, it seems quite clear that the political sympathies of Stein were not liberal but conservative. In political affairs, Stein is on record as having acknowledged himself to be in 'perfect agreement' with 'the ideas and sentiments' of Rehberg (Epstein, 1966, p. 565; also p. 549). Rehberg, however, was a conservative and not a liberal reformer. Together with Brandes Rehberg represents the Hanoverian School of German conservatism. As Gooch has pointed out, 'Hanoverian opinion was neither liberal nor reactionary, but stood for a not wholly unprogressive conservatism' (Gooch, 1965, p.73). Rehberg, like Brandes, was also greatly influenced by the thought of Edmund Burke. Aris has claimed that throughout Rehberg's writings what 'we hear is Burke's voice' (Aris, 1965, p. 57). This assessment is shared by Epstein, who has insisted that Rehberg's outlook 'was similar to that of Edmund Burke' (Epstein, 1966, p. 559, 590). According to Epstein, Rehberg saw his principal task as 'stating the conservative case for reform', the purpose of which was to develop 'a constructive synthesis of the old and the new' (Epstein, 1966, pp. 337, 561).

Given the nature of Rehberg's basic approach to politics, and given the fact that Stein considered himself to be substantially in agreement with Rehberg on all important issues of principle, it is not too surprising that Stein himself should have been so enthusiastic about the Burke's *Reflections*, which he considered to be 'the work of a great and experienced statesman who, with deep knowledge and splendid eloquence, defends the cause of civil order, religion and morality against empty and criminal innovations' (cited by Gooch, 1965, p. 520).

A very good case could be made, therefore, for the view that the Prussian reforms of the early nineteenth century were not liberal reforms at all. On the contrary, they were conservative reforms. That is to say, they were reforms introduced from above with the express purpose of defusing political tension and averting the possibility of more radical political change inspired by the French Revolution. Their purpose was, as is usually the case with conservative reforms, to preserve as much of the existing social order as possible whilst, at the same time, recognising the need for at least some social and political change.

An excellent illustration of this particular attitude towards the Prussian reforms is provided by Albert Sorel. In his view, the 'great German statesmen, the 'Steins, Hardenbergs, and Humboldts', all acted according to the same principles. They all saw 'the spirit of tradition and the spirit of reform as complementary and mutually corrective' (Sorel, 1969, p. 459). In the case of Stein, in particular, the purpose of reform was that of 'robbing the Revolution of all motive by forestalling it with reforms better suited to the ways of the country' (Sorel, 1969, p. 468). More or less the same view is taken by A. J. P. Taylor. According to him, 'the great Prussian reforms of 1807-1812' were all 'designed to strengthen authority'. That this has not always been appreciated is because 'the reforms were accompanied by a cloud, or a smoke screen, of liberating, if not liberal, phrases and ideas' (Taylor, 1976, p. 37).

Once we recognise what the conservative attitude towards constitutional reform really is, it becomes evident that it is simply not true to say, as Kenneth Westphal has done, that 'Hegel opposed all the conservative forces of his day' (Westphal, 1993, p. 239). For Stein and Hardenberg themselves were actually a 'conservative force', in the strict sense of the term. Hegel certainly did oppose the crude defenders of the local *status quo*, together with all of the forces of reaction. Jean Hyppolite is quite right to say that 'by temperament' Hegel was 'primarily a reformer' (Hyppolite, 1969a, p. 39; Cullen 1979, p. 40). But that is another matter entirely. As Sidney Hook has pointed out, 'the fact that a conservative is attacked by reactionaries does not transform him into a liberal' (Hook, 1970, p. 92).

Although he is not opposed to a certain degree of popular participation in the legislature, Hegel certainly is, as most commentators have recognised, opposed to democracy (Avineri, 1972, pp. 125, 162, 184; Brod, 1992, p. 142; Brudner, 1981, pp. 122-3; Cristi, 1983, p. 603; Hardimon, 1994, p. 219; Hook, 1970, p. 60-1; Hartman, 1953, p. xxxiii; Levin and Williams, 1987, pp. 105-6, 108, 114; Mehta, 1968, p. 77, 111, 118; Plamenatz, 1976, pp. 211-13, 264; Smith, 1991, pp. 129, 238; Singer, 1983, p. 41; Taylor, 1989, pp. 444-6; Westphal, 1993, pp. 261-2). Like most pre-modern political thinkers, and like most conservatives, Hegel objects to democracy on principle. Moreover, the reason for Hegel's rejection of democracy is basically the same as that of his predecessors. It is his belief in natural inequality and his commitment to the principle of paternalism. Hegel does not believe that individuals are the best judges of their own self interest. Thus he believes that society really ought to be governed by a wise elite who know best and who can be relied upon to rule benevolently in the universal interest of the whole community (Hegel, 1953, p. 57, 61-2; Hegel, 1956, p. 456; Hegel, 1979, pp. 33, 130, 156-7, 175, 182-3, 186, 195-6, 198, 200-5, 227, 295).

In Hegel's view, therefore, any demand for political equality, or democracy, must be deemed to be 'a folly of the understanding' (Hegel, 1979, p. 130). A belief in natural equality is the fundamental error upon which the principles of classical liberalism, and the false ideals of the French Revolution, are based. According to Hegel, 'current opinion' has it that 'the people must know what is in their best interests'. However, contrary to this belief, the truth of the matter is that 'the people' is precisely that section of society which does not know this. Knowledge of this sort 'is the fruit of profound apprehension and insight', that is to say, of 'precisely the things which are not popular' (Hegel, 1979, p. 196). For Hegel, democracy is a form of government which is 'grounded on the will interpreted as the whim, opinion and caprice of the many'. It is an 'atomistic and abstract view' which 'stands opposed to the Idea of ethical life' (Hegel, 1979, pp. 186, 198, 202; Taylor, 1989, p. 445).

In the 'ideal' constitution outlined by Hegel in the *Philosophy of Right* the various corporate groups or 'classes' in society are represented in the legislature by what Hegel refers to as the 'estates' (Hegel, 1979, pp. 131, 198). Hegel acknowledges that these estates are a 'guarantee of the general welfare and public freedom'. He insists, however, that this is not so because the representatives who sit in the estates have any 'particular power of insight'. On the contrary, it is the 'highest civil servants' who make up the executive, and who advise the monarch within the legislature, who possess an understanding of what is in the 'universal interest'. It is they who 'necessarily have a deeper and more comprehensive insight into the nature of the state's organisation and requirements'. This true to such an extent that, 'even without the estates' these civil servants would be 'able to do what is best' (Hegel, 1979, p. 196; Taylor, 1989, p. 444).

In Hegel's constitution, although the estates do indeed help to provide a guarantee of general welfare and freedom, nevertheless their role in the legislative process itself is very strictly limited (Westphal, 1993, p. 261). According to Hegel, there are two basic reasons why the estates might be seen to perform a useful political function. The first is because the representatives who sit in the estates engage in public debate. They are allowed to 'deliberate and decide on public affairs'. In this way they are able to subject the activities of the bureaucracy and the higher civil servants to scrutiny and to public 'criticism'. In this sense at least, therefore, they act as a check on their activities (Hegel, 1979, p. 196).

The second reason is because the estates operate as a 'mediating organ', or a line of communication, between the monarch and the executive, on the one hand, and 'the people' on the other (Hegel, 1979, p. 197). Their principal task is to 'vindicate the universal interest' to those who have elected them. As Hegel puts it, the 'real significance of the estates lies in the fact that it is through them that the state enters the subjective consciousness of the people and that the people begin to participate in the state' (Hegel, 1979, p. 292; Mehta, 1968, pp. 78-9).

Some commentators, having noted that Hegel does at times make some quite positive remarks about the virtues of popular participation in the legislature, have taken the view that Hegel is actually in favour of democracy, or at least that he is not completely opposed to it at all times. Thus, for example, Pelczynski has maintained that 'it would be wrong' to regard Hegel 'as being opposed to democracy in any sense'. Pelczynski's reason for holding this view is precisely because Hegel actually welcomes 'popular influence', as long as it 'forms only one element of the constitutional structure of the modern state' (Pelczynski, 1969, p. 77; also Bosworth, 1991, pp. 8, 11-13, 54, 109, 123; Cristi, 1983, pp. 601-2, 607).

This view, however, is based on a misunderstanding of the nature of democracy. For although they are quite closely related, democracy and popular participation are clearly not identical. A commitment to popular participation is not necessarily associated with a commitment to democracy. Hegel's attitude towards the line of communication to which we have just referred is very much that it operates from the top down, and not from the bottom up. Far from implying a commitment to democracy, Hegel's emphasis on the need for popular participation actually implies the reverse. In words which echo very closely Burke's *Speech to the Electors of Bristol*, Hegel argues that the task of the representatives sitting in the estates is most definitely not to serve 'the particular interest' of the society or corporation which elected them. Their 'relation to their electors' is most emphatically 'not that of agents with a commission or specific instructions'. It is, rather, to serve the universal interest of the community as a whole, as that is interpreted by others (Burke, 1975, pp. 156-8; Hegel, 1979, p. 201; also, p. 202; Brod, 1992, pp. 137-43).

In Hegel's view, then, the purpose of popular participation in the legislature is not to influence the actions of those who rule society, but rather to influence the opinions of those who are ruled. Hegel approves of estates assemblies being open to 'the public' because they 'are a great spectacle' and provide 'an excellent education for the citizens'. It is from the estates that 'the people' learns best 'how to recognise the true character of its interests'. The estates are 'the chief means of educating the public in national affairs' (Hegel, 1979, p. 294; also Brod, 1992, p. 131; Levin and Williams, 1987, p. 110; Westphal, 1993, p. 261).

Hegel considers this to be important because he recognises that 'the principle of the modern world' is that of 'subjective freedom', or the principle that individuals will only recognise that which they can reconcile with their own conscience. The legitimacy of the state depends, therefore, on the fact that it is actually freely acknowledged by those who have to render obedience to its laws. This is only possible if the state reveals itself 'as something entitled to recognition'. Hence the need for a line of communication between the state and civil society.

There is, of course, all the difference between consultation and legislation. Having a right to state publicly one's opinion regarding matters of legislation is one thing. Having the right to take part in actually making the law oneself is quite another. Hegel is quite clear that in his preferred constitution, 'everyone wishes to have some share in discussion and deliberation'. However, 'once he has had his say', and hence his 'subjectivity has been satisfied', each individual should then be content to put up with his lot (Hegel, 1979, p. 294; also p. 195).

Hegel's attitude towards democracy is, of course, closely associated with his attitude towards the French Revolution (Avineri, 1972, pp. 8, 125, 184; Brod, 1992, pp. 11-12, 45, 47-8, 123; Cullen, 1979, pp. 14-16; 30-1; Dallmayr, 1993, p. 253; Hyppolite, 1969; Mehta, 1968, pp. 16-19, 52; Plant, 1973, pp. 51-5, 73, 82; Suter, 1971; Ritter, 1982; Singer, 1983, pp. 1, 20-1, 35-6; Taylor, 1989, pp. 403, 416-8). His assessment of the Revolution itself, however, is actually quite ambivalent. In so far as the Revolution was associated with democracy, Hegel was opposed to it. In his view it was precisely a commitment to political equality and democracy, or 'the outlook of the rabble', which led to 'the maximum of frightfulness and terror' (Hegel, 1979, pp. 175, 156-7, 227-8). On the other hand, however, Hegel saw the Revolution as a world historical event. It was a significant turning point in world history, after which the world could never be the same again (Hegel, 1956, p. 447). It signified the death knell of the 'old' order. After the French Revolution there could be no question of going back to the *status quo ante*, or of resisting the pressure for social and political reform. It was the the French Revolution which in Hegel's view, set the historical standard for other countries to follow in their pursuit of such reform (Cullen, 1979, pp. 14-15). Hegel's interpretation of the significance of the French Revolution is, however, highly selective. In his view, the vital historical lesson to be learned as a consequence of the Revolution is that the most appropriate political constitution for the modern era is one which is based, not on the principle of democracy (or democratic republicanism), but on that of constitutional monarchy. For Hegel, 'the development of the state to constitutional monarchy is the achievement of the modern world' (Hegel, 1979, p. 176; also p. 288; Brudner, 1981; Cristi, 1983).

Hegel's views on legislation

Generally speaking, as we have noted, Hegel takes the view that the function of positive law is to provide a specific 'determination' of the abstract principles of natural right. A system of positive law must, therefore, 'necessarily involve the application of a universal concept' to 'particular cases' (Hegel, 1979, p. 16).

At first sight, Hegel's position on the issue of positive legislation seems quite straightforward. He says in the *Philosophy of Right* that 'the principle of rightness becomes the law' when 'it is posited'. In acquiring this 'determinate character' the right 'becomes positive law in general' (Hegel, 1979, pp. 134-5). This gives the impression that it is Hegel's opinion that the task of applying the formal principles of natural law to the historical circumstances confronted by a particular society is delegated to the principles of statute law. This task is associated with positive laws which are 'made' (Hegel, 1979, p. 135). Support for such an interpretation appears to be provided by some comments which Hegel makes in his *Lectures on the Philosophy of History*. There he suggests that 'the state involves a body of abstract principles and a practical application of them. This application must be the work of a subjective will, a will which resolves and decides' (Hegel, 1955, p. 448).

If this were Hegel's view, pure and simple, then this would bring his position very close to that of Hobbes, and to that of the doctrine of absolutism. M. B. Foster seems, at times, to be suggesting that this is indeed the case. According to Foster's interpretation of Hegel 'the universal of law must become particularised'. This means, however, that it must step 'into the realm of the accidental, which cannot be determined by the concept'. Thus, 'for the particular details of application', individual subjects 'can demand no reason'. They 'must submit' therein 'to the fiat of a will' (Foster, 1935, p. 119). It may be noted, in passing, that this account of Hegel's approach to positive legislation tends to support the overall assessment of Hegel's political thought which is offered by Manfred Riedel and Bruce Haddock which, as we have seen, emphasises the influence on Hegel of Kant rather than Aristotle, and which rejects a natural law interpretation of Hegel's later political thought.

There is, however, an ambiguity in relation to Hegel's use of the term 'positive law' which, once it has been revealed, casts some doubt on the adequacy of this particular interpretation of his views on legislation. For although Hegel certainly does at times use the term 'positive law' to refer to statute law, as distinct from customary law, nevertheless he also has a tendency to use it to refer to customary law as well (Hegel, 1979, pp. 134-5).

It could be argued, as we have already observed, that in Hegel's view it is, in the first instance anyway, the task of customary law, and not statute law, to apply the formal principles of natural law to the particular circumstances that are to be found within a given historical community or nation. The task of statute law and positive legislation is, for Hegel, merely a secondary or subordinate one. It is simply to assist in this process of 'determination'. In so far as Hegel is concerned, the principle task of legislation is not to interpret the formal principles of natural law directly, but rather to 'codify' those existing customary laws which are already carrying out this important task (Hegel, 1979, pp. 16, 134-5; Kainz, 1974, pp. 36-7; Suter, 1971, p. 71).

The notion of 'codification' is extremely important for an understanding of Hegel's views on legislation generally, and hence for his political thought as a whole. Hegel is a firm advocate of legal reform and of the idea that, in the modern age, positive law needs to be 'codified' or made more 'rational' (Hegel, 1971, p. 260; Hegel, 1979, pp. 134-6, 138-9, 159, 271-3; Avineri, 1972, pp. 71-4, 183, 214, 220; Mehta, 1968, p. 76; Pelczynski, 1969, pp. 27-39, 40-3, 55, 116; Smith, 1991, p. 148; Suter, 1971, p. 67, 71; Wood, 1991, pp. 103-4). He considers the process of codification to be important, even necessary. For in his view all law 'must be a system'. Only as such 'can it be recognised in a civilised country' (Hegel, 1979, pp. 271-2). Hegel's attitude towards this process is that, once again, it is one in which it is the task of art, or rather will, to complement nature.

This is, indeed, something which Foster himself seems to appreciate. For at one point he acknowledges that the act of 'positing' is for Hegel 'an act rather of codifying' rather than 'of laying down the law'. It is the act by which 'the right', which has 'hitherto been valid for a people in the form of customary law', is formulated 'as a public system of intelligible rules' (Foster, 1935, p. 119). In Foster's more considered view, then, the point of legislation or codification for Hegel is not, as Pelczynski would have it, to 'replace' customary laws with laws of quite a different type (Pelczynski, 1969, p. 54). It is, rather, to make it possible for obedience to positive law to be based, 'no longer upon unreflective custom', but on a 'recognition' of these rules 'as right' (Foster, 1935, p. 119). In this way those principles which before were 'natural' are placed on a new foundation. They become 'rational' and are stamped with the authority of a sovereign, legislative will. For Hegel 'the highest point of a people's development is the rational consciousness of its life and conditions, the scientific understanding of its laws, its system of justice, its morality' (Hegel, 1953, p. 92). This cannot be achieved without a codification of its laws.

This is something which is also recognised by Bruce Haddock who, despite his claim that it is the notion of 'will' that is central to Hegel's views on legislation and indeed his political thought as a whole, nevertheless at the same time acknowledges that Hegel remains a 'traditionalist' in 'certain respects'. According to Haddock, Hegel 'opposed unthinking adherence to customary practice'. Hence he did not 'share the misgivings of Savigny and the historical school of jusrisprudence about the formulation of a systematic legal code'. This is so because he took the view that the 'codification of a system of law' was not necessarily a 'distortion' of tradition. On the contrary, the point of codification, for Hegel, is to provide 'the ideals which inform a tradition' with 'the status of coherent legal principles' (Haddock, 1993, p. 132).

Considered from this standpoint, Hegel's view of the process by which laws come to be 'posited' is a complex one. It is not to be carried out, as Foster at first suggests, *ex nihilo* by a simple act of will. For in the first instance this process involves a reliance on (and an appeal to) the principles of customary law. At this stage the act of 'positing' is, as again Foster later acknowledges, 'an act not of will but of thought'. It is 'the task of the lawyer rather than the lawgiver' (Foster, 1935, p. 119). It is only after this first stage has been gone through that the final decision to 'posit' the abstract principles of right in one way rather than another might be said to be morally arbitrary, and hence to require a specific act of 'will'. One might say, then, that in so far as matters of legislation are concerned Hegel is once again of the opinion that nature and art, or alternatively reason and will, have different though complementary functions to perform.

This interpretation of Hegel's views on legislation takes him away from Hobbes, and the doctrine of absolutism, and much closer to the historically based, constitutionalist position of figures like Montesquieu and Burke. Moreover, it does so in a manner which grants due importance to both the concept of 'nature' and to that of 'will', not only for Hegel's views on legislation, but also for his political thought as a whole.

It is evident that Hegel's views on legislation have definite implications for his views on constitutional reform. We have already noted that in Hegel's view the task of legislation is not to create new laws out of nothing, by an act of legislative will. It is rather to apply, interpret and codify pre-existing customary law. It seems clear that someone with this general attitude towards the nature and purpose of positive legislation will have little time for the liberal Enlightenment idea of constitution building. As Foster has put it, for Hegel 'the act of legislation' must not issue in the 'constitution' of law, 'but only in the more detailed specification of a law' which is 'in its general outlines pre-constituted', a prior law which may itself be seen as in some sense 'determining the legislative act' (Foster, 1935, p. 193).

In connection with Hegel's views on legislation and codification, Pelczynski has argued that Hegel 'is obviously committed to advocating the ultimate replacement of all custom, precedent, charter and agreement by statutory, public and private law' (Pelczynski, 1969, p. 54). It is not at all clear, however, that when Hegel advocates the codification of existing customary laws what he means is that these laws should be replaced, or done away with altogether. For, as Pelczynski acknowledges elsewhere, it is Hegel's view that 'the valid laws of a nation do not cease to be its customs by being written and codified' (Hegel, 1979, p. 135; Pelczynski, 1969, p. 116). The process of codification, as Hegel understands it, does not pose a threat to those existing customs which have retained their historical validity. For the purpose of codification, as Hegel himself indicates, is not to construct 'a legal system with a novel content'. Rather, it is to apprehend, or grasp in thought, 'the content of existing laws' in their 'determinate universality' (Hegel, 1979, p. 136).

Hegel's views on history

What is the relevance of Hegel's philosophy of history for our attempt to establish whether Hegel is a liberal or a conservative? It is evident that Hegel does have a philosophy of history. He is of the opinion that there is a definite pattern, or meaning and purpose, which underpins all historical events. This is certainly something which he has in common with the philosophers of the Enlightenment. It is also clear that Hegel does indeed subscribe to some sort of doctrine of 'progress'. He suggests that 'historical change' has 'long been understood as involving a progress towards the better, the more perfect'. There is therefore a 'principle of development' in history, which is based on an 'inner principle', that is to say 'a presupposed potentiality' which 'brings itself into existence' or actualises itself (Hegel, 1953, pp. 68-9).

It might be thought that the very fact that Hegel subscribes to a philosophy of history at all, together with a view of historical progress, is enough to show that his views are at one with those of Enlightenment figures like Condorcet. More than one commentator has taken this view. For example, V. R. Mehta has suggested that Hegel's philosophy of history expresses 'the characteristic belief of the Enlightenment'. The Enlightenment idea of progress 'reached its culmination in the philosophy of Hegel' (Mehta, 1968, pp. 92-3; but see Houlgate, 1991, pp. 28-9).

At first sight, then, the significance of Hegel's philosophy of history appears to be that it demonstrates the affinities which exist between Hegel's philosophy and the ideology of classical liberalism. This view, however, is really quite superficial. For, as we have seen, it is a mistake to assume that all philosophies of history are liberal philosophies of history, or that all ideas of progress are liberal ideas of progress. A philosophy of history is something which Hegel has in common, not only with the philosophers of the Enlightenment, but also with a number of thinkers in pre-modern times, especially Saint Augustine. And a commitment to the idea of progress is something which Hegel has in common with critics of liberalism like Burke. It is evident that in the writings of Augustine and Burke the philosophy of history and the idea of progress have quite a different political significance from that which they have for the ideology of liberalism. G. D. O'Brien has observed that it is 'easily assumed that' Hegel's philosophy of history really comes 'to the same conclusion' as that of Condorcet. In fact, however, 'nothing could be further from the truth'. There is in fact an enormous difference between 'Hegel's and the Enlightenment's search for an end for history' (O'Brien, 1975, p. 108).

More than one of Hegel's interpreters has drawn attention to the affinity between Hegel's philosophy of history and the Christian apologetics of pre-modern thinkers like Augustine. Harry Meyerhoff, for example, has claimed that Hegel's philosophy of history represents 'the self realisation of the historical consciousness that Saint Augustine had bequeathed to the western world'. According to Meyerhoff, there are 'distinct formal analogies between philosophical and religious historiographies' which suggest that both 'express the same type of historical consciousness'. This is particularly true in the case of Hegel, in which 'the parallels are striking and in detail'. Hegel's philosophy of history throughout 'reflects the Augustinian model'. The only difference is that it 'eliminates the dimension of faith and translates the religious concepts into a rationalist vocabulary' (Meyerhoff, 1959, pp. 5-6; also Lowith, 1949, pp. 57-9; Nisbet, 1969, p. 77, 222; O'Brien, 1975, p. 53; Walsh, 1967, pp. 118-19). Moreover, this is something which Hegel himself freely admits. In the Introduction to his *Lectures on the Philosophy of History* he acknowledges that one of his principal tasks in this work is to 'translate the language of religion into that of philosophy' (Hegel, 1953, p. 25).

Hegel's philosophy of history has much more in common with those of pre-modern times than it does with the philosophies of history of the French Enlightenment. Indeed, Hegel explicitly draws a parallel between his own beliefs and those of earlier Christian thinkers. For them, he says, it is a 'religious truth' that 'the world is not abandoned to chance and external accident but controlled by Providence'. This truth that 'a divine Providence presides over the events of the world corresponds to our principle' (Hegel, 1953, pp. 14-15; Wilkins, 1974, pp. 48-51; but see also Collingwood, 1976, pp. 116-17).

In effect, for Hegel, just as for the Christian thought of pre-modern times, the purpose of a philosophy of history is to justify the ways of God to man (Hardimon, 1994, p. 20; Lowith, 1949, pp. 54-5; Taylor, 1979, p. 96; Taylor, 1989, p. 389). In Hegel's view, the philosophy of history is at the same time 'a theodicy'(Hegel, 1953, p.18). The principal purpose of the philosophy of history is thus to 'reconcile' men to 'the evil in the world' (Hegel, 1953, p. 18). According to Hegel, to 'recognise reason as the rose in the cross of the present' is 'the rational insight' which is brought to us by philosophy and which thereby 'reconciles us to the actual' (Hegel, 1979, p. 12). This attitude towards the general purpose of a philosophy of history is admirably summarised in the closing paragraph of Hegel's *Lectures On The Philosophy of History*. There Hegel says that the recognition that 'the history of the world' is the process of development and the realisation of spirit' is 'the true *Theodicaea*, the justification of God in history. Only this insight can reconcile spirit with the history of the world - viz., that what has happened, and is happening every day, is not only not "without God", but is essentially His work' (Hegel, 1955, p. 457).

The idea of 'reconciliation' is therefore, as Michael Hardimon quite rightly points out, 'the central aim of Hegel's social philosophy' It is the aim of Hegel's philosophy of history and 'of his philosophy as a whole' (Hardimon, 1994, pp. 4-5; also pp. 1-3, 6-7, 19-21, 22-25, 84-123; Cullen, 1979, p. 16; Dallmayr, 1993, pp. 4, 68, 95-96. Plant, 1973, pp. 71-72, 79, 125-26, 130).

It might be thought that this demonstrates, without any shadow of a doubt, that Hegel is a conservative thinker. His philosophy of history is, it would seem, clearly a conservative philosophy of history, and his notion of progress is clearly a conservative notion of progress, if only because Hegel evidently puts it to a conservative use, namely to defend the *status quo* (Houlgate, 1991, p. 78; also Bury, 1920, pp. 255-56; Collingwood, 1979, p. 120; Stanley, 1969, p. xxxiii).

Whether or not we accept this claim depends, crucially, on what we mean when we refer to the *status quo* (Brod, 1992, p. 19). On the one hand, this term might be used in a strictly local sense to refer to the conditions which currently prevail in a particular society at a particular time. On the other hand, however, it might be used much more widely to refer to those conditions which might be said to currently exist at the global level, when considered from the standpoint of world history.

It is Hegel's view that world history is a series of progressive stages, and that 'each stage, being different from the other, has its definite, peculiar principle'. Such a principle 'is a particular national spirit' (Hegel, 1953, pp. 78-9). It is the decline of one such national spirit which leads to the development of 'another epoch of world history' associated with a different national spirit, and hence a different 'world historical people'. From this point of view, world history itself is nothing more than the 'transition and connection' of different national spirits, which leads us to 'the connection of the whole' (Hegel, 1953, p. 87). The historical *status quo*, understood in global sense, is defined at the level of world history by those conditions which currently prevail in that nation which is the most historically advanced so far (Beiser, 1993, p. 293; Hardimon, 1994, pp. 75-6; Mehta, 1968, p. 10; Wood, 1990, p. 205).

It is evident that the *status quo* when considered from the global point of view may well not be the *status quo* when considered from the local point of view. Those conditions which prevail in the most advanced nation in a given epoch of world history might not yet prevail in those nations which are less advanced, despite the fact that history has shown that the world (and hence each particular nation within it) is actually ready for them.

The relevance of this for the assessment of Hegel's philosophy of history, and its relationship to conservatism, should be readily apparent. Generally speaking, Hegel is not a defender of the *status quo* in any simple or local sense. His attitude is that when considered from the standpoint of world history the constitutions of a number of nations are evidently ripe for reform. They are quite simply out of date. It is his view, as we have seen, that the guidelines for political reform are (at least in part) provided by the political experience and conditions of that which in world historical terms is the most advanced nation so far. In the conditions of the early nineteenth century this nation is post-revolutionary France. As Frederick Beiser has put it, Hegel made the ideals of liberty and equality of the French Revolution into the very end of history itself'. The French Revolution has shown that it is 'impossible in the post revolutionary era to return to the old *status quo ante* of the *ancien regime*. This would be to fail to recognise the fate of the modern world, the fundamental spirit of modern life since the French Revolution' (Beiser, 1993, p. 295; also Taylor, 1989, p.418).

It is, therefore, quite wrong to claim that Hegel's philosophy of history is a conservative philosophy of history, if the grounds for making this claim are that this philosophy of history is associated with an attempt to defend the *status quo* in the purely local sense. Hegel's philosophy of history certainly is a conservative philosophy of history, but it is not so for this particular reason. As Mehta has put it, it seems obvious that Hegel is a conservative of some sort. However, 'Hegel's conservatism is not the conservatism that is often identified with rigidity'. Nor is it an 'unqualified defence of the *status quo*' (Mehta, 1958, p. 130).

The real reason why Hegel's philosophy of history is a conservative philosophy of history is because, like Burke and Coleridge, Hegel attitude towards historical change is balanced between an acceptance of the two principles of 'permanence', on the one hand and 'progress' on the other. What this means in practice is that at the local level Hegel's philosophy of history combines a positive acceptance of the need for change, or for historical progress in the direction of liberty, with an equally positive acceptance of the value of existing customs and traditions, and hence of the existing social order. In practical terms, Hegel's conservative philosophy of history is associated, not with a commitment to radical social change, or with any attempt to rigidly defend the local *status quo*, but with an acceptance of the need for social and political reforms. The purpose of these reforms is to recreate locally what world history has shown to be necessary globally.

G. D. O'Brien has quite rightly claimed that Hegel's philosophy of history is 'the basis for his "conservative" political bias'. This is so in the sense that 'the conservative does not believe that history proceeds by leaps'. For the conservative, 'progress does not come about when finally an exasperated humanity lets some moral or philosophical genius rearrange society in the proper rational fashion'. Rather, for the conservative, 'progress truly is the work of history' (O'Brien, 1975, p. 158). This is an accurate assessment of Hegel's attitude. And it is this attitude which, as O'Brien points out, differentiates Hegel's philosophy of history from the liberal philosophies of history of Enlightnment thinkers like Condorcet (O'Brien, 1975, pp. 157-8).

Hegel's acceptance of historical change, and of the need for social and political reform, stands in an interesting relationship to his idea of philosophical 'reconciliation'. Michael Hardimon maintains quite rightly that, despite his emphasis on the idea of reconciliation, 'Hegel does not endorse the *status quo* as such'. There is in fact a tension in Hegel's thinking between the two principles of reconciliation and reform. According to Hardimon, Hegel appears to be confronted with a stark choice here. Either he must take the view that 'since the social world is worthy of reconciliation it does not need to be reformed'. Or alternatively he must take the view that 'since the social world needs to be reformed it is not worthy of reconciliation' (Hardimon, 1994, p. 27). In fact though, Hardimon insists, the position which Hegel actually maintains is neither of these two. It is, rather, a synthesis of them both. Hegel's considered position is that 'the social world, though imperfect' is indeed 'worthy of reconciliation'. This is a synthesis which, in Hardimon's opinion, 'would make it possible to unite basic acceptance of the social world with liberalising reform'. Thus Hegel's attitude towards the relationship between reconciliation and reform places him 'squarely in the camp of the moderate liberal progressives of his age' (Hardimon, 1994, p. 27).

As an account of Hegel's attitude towards the *status quo*, and towards the relationship between the notions of reconciliation and reform, there can be no quarrel with this. Hardimon goes astray, however, when he concludes on the basis of this analysis that Hegel must evidently be considered to be some sort of 'liberal progressive' thinker. This does not follow at all. The attitude of mind which Hardimon describes is not that of a liberal. It is entirely typical of the standpoint of traditional conservatism. Moreover, when Hardimon claim's that Hegel is a 'progressive liberal' he clearly contradicts his earlier view that Hegel's position is neither 'conservative nor 'progressive', but specifically and uniquely 'Hegelian' (Hardimon, 1994, p. 4).

Some of those commentators who claim that Hegel is a conservative thinker are nevertheless embarrassed by Hegel's philosophy of history. This is so because they wrongly associate the idea of progress exclusively with the ideology of liberalism. They are embarrassed because Hegel's 'progressive' views appear to be inconsistent, not only with what Hegel himself has to say elsewhere in his writings, but also with their own claim that Hegel is best considered as a conservative thinker.

This is the opinion of Robert Nisbet, whose views regarding Hegel, conservatism and history are actually quite contradictory. Nisbet subscribes to three beliefs in relation to this issue. First, he believes that Hegel is most certainly a conservative thinker (Nisbet, 1986, pp. 2, 19-20, 35, 37-8, 49, 79, 89, 111). Second, he believes that conservatism is quite opposed to the idea of progress. He associates conservatism with the late eighteenth century 'assault on the idea of progress' (Nisbet, 1986, p. 91). Third, he believes that Hegel nevertheless does have a philosophy of history which is based on the idea of progress (Nisbet, 1986, p. 88).

Not surprisingly, Nisbet is quite unable to resolve the contradiction which exists between these three beliefs. Thus he insists that Hegel should be considered to be a conservative thinker despite his philosophy of history and not because of it. In effect Nisbet considers a commitment to the idea of progress to be an alien intrusion within Hegel's philosophy. It is something which does not sit at all well with the conservative tenor of the rest of Hegel's thinking. Nisbet's explanation for this is that the force of 'progressivist' thinking in the early nineteenth century was so great that 'a great many conservatives' were 'caught up' in it despite themselves, and despite the fact that embracing such views clearly contradicted their own conservative principles (Nisbet, 1986, p. 91; also p. 87; Bury, 1920, pp. 257-8).

This explanation of Hegel's commitment to a belief in progress is really rather lame. A much better explanation would be simply to deny that the idea of progress *per se* is alien to conservatism. As we have seen, there is a conservative conception of progress, just as there is a liberal conception of progress. There is, therefore, no need for us to take the view that Hegel's philosophy of history is inconsistent with the conservative tenor of his philosophy as a whole.

Conclusion

Given the general principles of Hegel's philosophy, it is not at all surprising to find that some commentators have recognised that Hegel's political thought is indeed best seen as an attempt to reconcile two opposing theoretical approaches. For these commentators, the ideas to be found in the *Philosophy of Right* constitute a classic example of an Hegelian synthesis (Beiser, 1993, pp. 293-7; Brod, 1992, pp. 5-6; Colletti, 1975, pp. 31-4; Dallmayr, 1993, pp. 4-5, 7-8, 74, 173; Gamble, 1983, pp. 97-8; Gooch, 1965, pp. 297-8; Hardimon, 1994, pp. 4, 27, 35-6, 40; O'Sullivan, 1976, pp. 26, 58; de Ruggiero, 1981, pp. 228-9, 240; Schoolman, 1993, p. xii; Smith, 1991, pp. 6, 243). There is also broad agreement regarding the general nature of this synthesis. On the other hand, however, there is considerable disagreement regarding its specific details. In particular there is disagreement over the issue of how Hegel's political thought as a whole might best be characterised.

In so far as the general nature of this synthesis is concerned, most commentators are in agreement that the essence of the Hegelian project is to reconcile the insights into politics that are provided by pre-modern political thought and experience, on the one hand, and the political thought and experience of the modern era on the other. A good illustration of this is provided by Lucio Colletti. In his view, what lies at the heart of Hegel's approach to politics is the belief that it is the task of the modern state 'to restore the ethic and the organic wholeness of the antique *polis*', where 'the individual was profoundly 'integrated' into the community', and to do this 'without sacrificing the principle of subjective freedom'. Thus, according to Colletti, Hegel's main ambition is 'to find a new mode of unity which will recompose the fragments of modern society', and especially the 'division' between 'civil society' and 'the state' (Colletti, 1975, p. 31).There is, of course, a considerable measure of truth in these remarks. It should be noted, however, that for Colletti the pre-modern thought and experience which had a decisive influence upon Hegel's thinking was that of the ancient Greeks. Colletti's account of the Hegelian project ignores altogether the influence upon Hegel of the political thought and experience of the medieval period. To that extent, therefore, it might be said to be deficient.

Another example of a commentator who appreciates the general character of the Hegelian synthesis is S. B. Smith. Like Colletti, Smith takes the view that 'the chief conflict that Hegel set himself to resolve was that between the "substantial" culture of the Greek world and the principle of subjective freedom' which reached 'its culmination in the liberal commercial order of modernity' (Smith, 1991, p. 243). The task that Hegel set for himself 'was to combine the liberal or enlightened belief in life, liberty and the pursuit of happiness with the ancient Aristotelian conception of politics as a collective pursuit aimed at some idea of a public good' (Smith, 1991, p. 6). Once again, there is certainly a measure of truth in these remarks. It should be noted though that, like Colletti, Smith appears to attach relatively little importance to the medieval influences which acted upon Hegel. It is also worth noting that, in Smith's view, the final product of this Hegelian synthesis is best described as a form of liberalism. According to Smith, the implication to be drawn from this general assessment of the character of the Hegelian project is that 'Hegel was a liberal', a 'corporate liberal' (Smith, 1991, p. 236; also pp. x, 4, 6).

Of particular interest in this connection are the views of those commentators who, like Michael Hardimon and Frederick Beiser, are prepared to acknowledge that there is, undeniably, a conservative dimension to Hegel's thinking. As in the case of Ernst Cassirer, however, Hardimon and Beiser consider conservatism to be just one aspect of Hegel's political thought as a whole (Beiser, 1993, pp. 293-7; Hardimon, 1994, p. 4).

According to Hardimon, for example, we really ought to 'avoid' trying to locate Hegel in 'one or the other of two established' categories 'progressive or conservative'. For Hegel's thought incorporates both of these mutually opposing tendencies at the same time. It is both 'progressive *and* conservative' (Hardimon, 1994, p. 4). Thus Hegel's political thought as a whole is quite unique an not susceptible of classification in conventional terms. As with Colletti and Smith, this assessment of the general character of the Hegelian project does contain a certain element of truth. It might, however, be criticised for its inadequate characterisation of the ideology of conservatism. Hardimon suggests, quite wrongly, that to be conservative is simply either to 'endorse the *status quo* merely because it is place', or to 'exclude reform', or to 'require abandonment of criticism and opposition' (Hardimon, 1994, p. 24).

A similar view is taken by Beiser. Beiser points out that there are two traditional interpretations of Hegel. The first (advanced by liberals from Haym onwards) claims that Hegel's aims were 'fundamentally conservative, indeed reactionary'. Hegel was 'the spokesman for the restoration in Prussia'. He defended 'established institutions and traditions against those radicals who would model all of society according to abstract principles'. The second sees Hegel's philosophy of history 'as the inspiration for their own radical doctrines. The Hegelian dialectic 'allegedly passed the death sentence on any *status quo*' (Beiser, 1993, p. 292).

In Beiser's opinion neither of these two interpretations of Hegel is correct. 'The truth lies somewhere between'. As a matter of fact, Hegel 'appealed to history to justify the middle path of reform, to criticise both radicals and reactionaries alike'. For radicals 'could not see that their ideals have to be adapted to the history of a nation, while the reactionaries were blind to the fact that history undergoes ceaseless change'. Thus, 'in the spectrum of political belief in Germany after the French Revolution, Hegel reveals himself to be a progressive moderate'.

According to Beiser, this amounts to saying that 'unlike the reactionaries' of the day Hegel actually 'approved of the fundamental ideals of the French Revolution'. On the other hand, however, unlike the radicals, 'Hegel did not believe that these ideals could be achieved through popular agitation, still less by sweeping away all of the historical traditions and institutions of Germany'. Thus, 'the ideals of the Revolution would have to be established through piecemeal reform from above, through gradually adapting them to the historical conditions prevalent in Germany' (Beiser, 1993, p. 293). In Beiser's view, Hegel's political thought might for this reason be said to constitute a synthesis of 'progressive' and 'conservative' ideas (Beiser, 1993, p. 296).

Beiser's account of Hegel's views on history, and their significance for practical politics, is in some respects quite excellent. Beiser does succeed in capturing the essence of Hegel's attitude towards constitutional reform. On the other hand, however, like that of Hardimon, Beiser's interpretation of Hegel is based on an inadequate understanding of the nature of conservatism. This view is inadequate because it makes no distinction between the ideas of a conservative and those of a reactionary. It could certainly be argued against both Hardimon and Beiser that it is wrong to identify conservative and reactionary political thought. Mainstream conservatism, the conservatism of Edmund Burke, does not simply 'endorse the *status quo*'. It does not 'exclude reform'. And it does not require 'the abandonment of criticism and opposition'. Conservatism itself, properly understood, is best seen as a synthesis of progressive and traditionalist ideas of precisely the sort that Hardimon and Beiser associate with Hegel.

What is especially significant about the views of Hardimon and Beiser is the fact for both of them the part that conservatism has to play in the Hegelian project is that of thesis or antithesis. It does not occur to either of these commentators to associate the ideology of conservatism with the final synthesis, that is to say with Hegel's political thought as a whole.

A line of reasoning similar to that of Beiser and Hardimon is also adopted by Noel O'Sullivan. O'Sullivan associates German conservatism with the adoption of a 'dialectical' approach to political questions. He suggests that a significant disadvantage of such an approach is that it leads to the pursuit of 'an ambiguous and recondite synthesis of ideas' which must inevitably fail 'to present a distinctively conservative alternative to the new radicalism' associated with the ideology of classical liberalism at the end of the eighteenth century. The most significant consequence of adopting such an approach, therefore, is that of 'blurring the line between conservatism and liberalism'. According to O'Sullivan, 'such was the fate' of Hegel's political thought (O'Sullivan, 1976, p. 82). From O'Sullivan's point of view then, and precisely because of its synthetic character, Hegel's political thought as a whole should not be considered to be a form of conservatism

It is interesting to compare O'Sullivan's attitude towards Hegel with his quite different assessment of the political thought of Coleridge. A dialectical synthesis of the two principles of 'permanence' and 'progression' is an integral aspect of Coleridge's political thought. It is central to Coleridge's conservatism. When commenting on Coleridge's ideas, O'Sullivan is quite happy to accept that, here at least, conservatism is not simply a commitment to 'permanence' at the expense of 'progression'. It is, rather, a commitment to the principles of 'permanence' *and* 'progression' together. In the case of Coleridge, then, if not in that of Hegel, O'Sullivan is prepared to acknowledge that the ideology of conservatism is neither the thesis nor the antithesis, but the synthesis, of a dialectical process of development. O'Sullivan freely admits that Coleridge is undeniably a conservative thinker, despite the synthetic nature of his political thought as a whole. Like John Stuart Mill before him, O'Sullivan recognises that Coleridge seeks 'to base a new conservative synthesis upon a balance between the opposing forces of order and progress at work in modern society' (O'Sullivan, 1976, p. 85; Mill, 1967, pp. 167-8).

In this particular respect, however, the political thought of Hegel is much the same as that of Coleridge. An attempt to construct a synthesis of the ideals of traditionalism with those of liberalism, or of the ideals of 'permanence' and 'progression', lies at the heart of the Hegelian project also. There is therefore no good reason for O'Sullivan to treat the case of Hegel any differently from the way in which he treats the case of Coleridge. The appropriate conclusion to be drawn here is the reverse of that which O'Sullivan actually draws. It is that, like Coleridge, Hegel most certainly is a conservative thinker.

This synthetic character of the ideology of conservatism has been noted by Klaus Epstein. As Epstein puts it, 'the conservative affirmation of plurality of values calls for an equilibrium' between 'liberty and order', 'equality and hierarchy', 'individualism and collectivism', 'cosmopolitanism and nationalism', 'reason and emotion' and 'dynamism and stability' (Epstein, 1966, p. 17). This is true of the ideology of conservatism in general. It is especially true, however, of the political thought of Hegel.

Hegel's political thought, then, might be said to represent the theoretical highpoint of the development of conservatism as an ideology. David Kettler has claimed that the 'dialectical thinking' of Hegel successfully managed to 'rationalise' what earlier conservatism had achieved, 'thereby integrating it into a single comprehensive theory' constructed 'under conservative auspices' (Kettler, 1986, p. 18). As Karl Mannheim has said, 'Germany achieved for the ideology of conservatism what France did for progressive enlightenment'. She 'worked it out most fully to its logical conclusions'. Thus conservatism 'originated in England' and 'achieved its most consistent exposition on German soil' (Mannheim, 1986, p. 47). Of no-one is this remark more true than Hegel.

Like Coleridge, Hegel follows and expands upon the ideas of Edmund Burke by offering his readers, quite explicitly and in a theoretically sophisticated manner, a creative synthesis of pre-modern and modern political thought. In so doing, he brings to fruition and provides a theoretical justification for a tendency which is actually central to the ideology of traditional conservatism from its inception. Hegel's political thought is thus most emphatically not a rejection of conservatism. Nor is it an attempt to move beyond conservatism by developing a system of political thought which transcends its inherent limitations. Nor, finally, is it unique and hence resistant to classification in conventional terms. Once we have seen that conservatism itself, properly understood, has a synthetic character it becomes apparent that Hegel is quite clearly a conservative thinker. On this one point at least, therefore, we find ourselves in agreement with Roger Scruton. As Scruton has quite rightly maintained, Hegel is *the* principal theoretician within the conservative political tradition. He is 'the most substantial and authoritative of modern conservatives'(Scruton, 1988, pp. 135-36).

Conclusion

We have, throughout, tried to show that a consideration of the ideas that are associated with the conservative and natural law traditions of political thought helps us to understand the political thought of Hegel, and *vice versa*. There are, however, some commentators who would object to this enterprise on methodological grounds. These commentators deny that it is actually possible to talk about such a thing as *the* natural law tradition, or *the* conservative tradition of political thought. We have already noted that in the case of natural law theory, for example, this position is adopted by Paul Foriers and Chaim Perelman (Foriers and Perelman, 1973, p. 14). And in the case of the ideology of conservatism, the same view is taken by Walter Kaufmann (Kaufmann, 1970, pp. 8-9). In the study of political thought or the history of ideas generally, however, this is a view which is associated pre-eminently with the methodological standpoint that is adopted by Quentin Skinner (Skinner, 1969, pp. 37, 39).

It is Skinner's opinion that to attempt to discuss any concept from the point of view of its embodiment in the writings of different theorists, writing at different times and in different cultures, is to adopt the position, not of a serious historian of ideas, but of a manufacturer of 'mythologies' and 'historical absurdities' (Skinner, 1969, pp. 3, 7, 10-12). According to Skinner, as is well known, the meaning and significance of the major *texts* in the history of political thought can only be properly understood when those texts are set against the historical and specifically the intellectual *context* in which they were written (Skinner, 1969, p. 34). Thus, for example, if we take the case of natural law, although it is true that Aquinas and Hobbes both employ the term 'natural law', it is Skinner's view that they could not have meant the same thing by it. When these two theorists talk about natural law they are in effect talking about two different things. Hence it is quite impossible for a commentator today to make generalisations about *the* concept of natural law (or about natural law theory) on the basis of an analysis of the writings of these two thinkers. For, as the same concept is not in fact to be found in both the writings of Aquinas and those of Hobbes, there is evidently no basis for any valid generalisation. In Skinner's opinion, the assumption that 'any

163

fixed "idea" has persisted' here is entirely 'spurious'. And to think that it has is clearly to make 'the mistake of taking the word for the thing' (Skinner, 1969, p. 35; also p. 38). The views of Aquinas and of Hobbes on natural law simply do not have enough in common to justify the making of *any* generalisations which might meaningfully and usefully be regarded as applying to both of them. Skinner would sympathise with d'Entreves's claim that 'except for the name, the medieval and the modern notions of natural law have little in common' (d'Entreves, 1970, p. 15). Indeed, he would almost certainly argue that d'Entreves's judgement does not go far enough. At times he appears to take the view that the *only* thing which Hobbes's natural law theory could possibly have in common with that of Aquinas is the name.

Another way of putting this point would be to say that, according to Skinner, the concepts of natural law or natural law theory cannot be precisely defined, and hence does not possess a definite meaning. For any definition of the meaning of this concept in the traditional Aristotelian manner must attempt to isolate precisely those characteristic features which are held in common by all of the particular individuals to which this general concept is applicable. This is one of Skinner's reasons for thinking that there are no perennial problems, timeless truths or permanent values in the history of political thought (Skinner, 1969, pp. 4-5, 7, 10, 32, 35, 50; Bevir, 1994). In his view, it is evident that 'the literal meanings of key terms sometimes change over time', so that authors at one time might employ a term or make a statement which has (for them) quite a different meaning from that which it has for those who read their works at a later time (Skinner, 1969, p. 31).

From Skinner's point of view, then, there is no strict rule which rigidly delimits the employment of, or encapsulates the essential meaning of, general terms such as 'natural law', 'natural law theory', 'conservatism', and so on. As Skinner has pointed out, the 'great mistake' which is frequently made by historians of ideas generally, is that of 'essentialism'. It 'lies not merely in looking for 'the essential meaning' of an 'idea' as something which must necessarily 'remain the same', but even in thinking of any 'essential' meaning (to which individual writers contribute) at all' (Skinner, 1969, p. 37; also 39; Berki and Parekh, 1973, p. 165).

An important implication of this view, in so far as Skinner is concerned, is that it is in some sense illegitimate, from a methodological standpoint, for anyone to even talk about (let alone attempt to write the history of) a general political idea or concept such as, for example, the concept of 'progress, equality, sovereignty, justice' or 'natural law' (Skinner, 1969, p. 39). This is so for the obvious reason that there just '*is* no determinate idea to which various writers contributed'. Hence 'there *is* no history of the idea to be written' (Skinner, 1969, p. 38). The entire project of 'studying histories of "ideas" *tout court*' rests on 'a fundamental philosophical mistake' (Skinner, 1969, p. 37). As Skinner has put it much more recently, these terms are employed in 'such divergent ways', by different people at different times, 'that it seems an obvious confusion to suppose that any stable concepts are being picked out' (Skinner, 1988, p. 283).

One of the things that is interesting about the arguments which Skinner employs in defence of this claim is the appeal which he makes to the philosophy of the later Wittgenstein, and to the theory of meaning which Wittgenstein develops in the *Blue and Brown Books* and in the *Philosophical Investigations* (Skinner, 1969, pp. 6, 37; Wittgenstein, 1969; Wittgenstein, 1972). Skinner accepts Wittgenstein's idea that 'the meaning of a word is its use in the language' (Wittgenstein, 1972, p. 20; Skinner, 1969, p. 37; Berki and Parekh, 1973, pp. 165, 175; Schochet, 1973, p. 267). In his view, however, different people, living in different societies at different times, will almost certainly use the same word or concept in different ways to do different things. It is not the case, therefore, that this concept has just one 'fixed' meaning. On the contrary, it has as many different meanings as it has different uses. Once again, therefore, to talk about *the* meaning of a word or concept is entirely inappropriate from the methodological point of view.

As a matter of fact Skinner is quite right to suggest that general concepts like the concept of natural law, or of natural law theory, or of conservatism, cannot be precisely defined in the traditional Aristotelian usual manner, by reference to a closed list of necessary and sufficient conditions which must be satisfied before we are to be justified in using these general concepts to refer to some particular case. In the case of natural law theory, for example, contrary to what some commentators might think, there just is no hard core of ideas which all of the different types of natural law theory possess in common. Nor is there any 'closed' list of specific features which a particular doctrine must necessarily possess in order for us to be justified in describing it as an example of natural law theory. The assumption that it is possible to define these concepts precisely, and indeed that this must be possible, for otherwise these concepts would be meaningless, is an example of what Wittgenstein has described (and deplored) as 'a craving for generality' which has 'shackled philosophical investigation' from the time of Aristotle onwards (Wittgenstein, 1969, pp.18-9). In this particular sense at least, then, it is certainly true that there is no such thing as *the* natural law tradition.

The problem with Skinner's methodological approach however is that, despite his advocacy of Wittgenstein's theory of meaning in use, Skinner himself appears at times to suffer from precisely that 'craving for generality' of which Wittgenstein is so critical. Skinner frequently gives the impression that, in his view, if a word or concept (like that of natural law theory or conservatism) has a multiplicity of different meanings, in different contexts, then it evidently does not possess any *one* meaning, and hence could not be said to have *any* meaning at all. Skinner comes very close to suggesting that if such a concept cannot be precisely defined, and thus has no 'fixed' meaning, then it must be completely meaningless. Thus he seems at times to be adopting a position which Wittgenstein explicitly rejects, namely the view that 'a word has no meaning' if there is nothing (in this case some precisely defined "idea") which 'corresponds to it' (Wittgenstein, 1972, p. 20). It is of course for precisely this reason that, from the standpoint of Skinner's methodology, it is not legitimate for us to attempt to write an intellectual history of the word or concept in question.

However, it certainly does not follow from the fact that a general concept (like that of natural law theory or conservatism) cannot be precisely defined that the concept in question must be meaningless. The main thrust of Wittgenstein's theory of meaning in use is certainly not to establish such a conclusion. According to Wittgenstein, if some general concept is to be meaningful then there must be some rule at least which governs its use. That is to say, there must be an 'open' list of criteria which regulate the legitimate application of the concept, and which enable us to differentiate between correct and incorrect instances of its employment. Concepts of this sort have what Frederick Waismann has referred to as an 'open texture' (Waismann, 1978, pp. 38).

In the case of the concept which we have of natural law theory, for example, if such a rule is to exist it is not necessary that there should be certain essential features which all natural law theories possess (and must possess) in common. All that is necessary is that some natural law theories should possess at least some characteristic features in common with one another. All that is required is that the various different types of natural law theory should have what Wittgenstein calls a 'family resemblance' to one another (Wittgenstein, 1972, pp. 31-7; 1969, pp. 1, 17-20, 25-7; Albritton, 1970; Bambrough, 1970; Hospers, 1973, pp.67-76; Khatchadourian, 1970; Wellman, 1962).

The appropriate conclusion to be drawn from an acceptance of Wittgenstein's theory of meaning in use, therefore, is not that general concepts, like that of natural law theory or conservatism, are actually meaningless. It is simply that these concepts have a meaning which cannot be precisely defined and which is therefore vague (Greenleaf, 1973b, pp. 178-9; Greenleaf, 1983b, pp. 189-346; Boucher, 1985, p. 111). As Wittgenstein puts it, concepts which have an open texture are concepts with 'blurred edges' (Wittgenstein, 1972, p. 34). It follows from this, of course, that a concept of this sort does in fact have a meaning that might be clarified after all, and hence that it is perfectly legitimate for us to seek to clarify it.

It seems evident that both the use and the meaning of a general concept, like that of natural law theory or conservatism, is one which shifts, changes and alters over time (Haddock, 1974, p. 426). It is for precisely this reason that the meaning of such concepts is vague and indefinite. However, the fact that this is so is not necessarily an obstacle to the clarification of the meaning of these concepts. It is, rather, precisely this fact which provides us with the solution to the problem of how to elucidate their meaning. For what this implies is that in order to clarify the meaning of a concept it is necessary, in effect, to write the intellectual history of that concept. This however, as we have already noted, is something which Skinner rules out of court on general methodological grounds. As Andrew Lockyer has quite rightly pointed out, in so doing Skinner neglects completely 'the *continuity* of language and concepts through time' (Lockyer, 1979, p.206).

It is not at all obvious, then , that the methodological position which Skinner adopts is one which necessarily follows from his commitment to Wittgenstein's theory of meaning in use. It could certainly be argued, against Skinner, that a commitment to Wittgenstein's theory of meaning does not at all rule out the possibility of writing the intellectual history of an idea or concept. On the contrary, it might even be said to necessitate the writing of such a history.

In contrast to the methodology advocated by Skinner, an alternative approach to the history of ideas would be firmly committed (in one sense at least) to a belief in the existence of 'perennial problems' and 'universal truths'. Such an approach would involve an appreciation of the different ways in which the *same* term or expression has been used by individual theorists writing at different times. And it would be committed to clarifying the meaning of political concepts by demonstrating an awareness of how that meaning has changed and developed over time. The effort to trace the historical development of the meaning of a concept in this way would be, as R. N. Berki and B. Parekh have quite rightly pointed out, a search for 'abiding truths and general categories' amidst the historical multiplicity of political ideals and values (Berki and Parekh, 1973, pp. 178, 182-3).

Such an alternative approach to the study of political thought need not reject completely Skinner's basic insight that the meanings of political words and concepts are determined by the context in which they are used. For all that is being claimed here is that, as Mark Bevir has suggested, the different 'linguistic contexts' which give the same word or concept a different meaning at different times can actually 'overlap' (Bevir, 1994, p. 668). It makes perfect sense, therefore, for us to refer to the existence of 'stable concepts' in the history of political thought, even if at the same time we also acknowledge that the specific meaning of these concepts, at a particular moment in time, depends on the particular 'linguistic context' in which they are used.

From the standpoint of such an alternative approach to political thought it is, therefore, entirely legitimate for us to speak of such a thing as *the* natural law tradition or *the* conservative tradition of political thought, provided that when we do so we make it plain that we are using the term 'tradition' very loosely, and are not committing ourselves to the 'essentialist' notion that the concepts in question can be strictly defined in the Aristotelian manner. It makes perfectly good sense to say that two different theorists writing at different times might nevertheless be said to belong to the same tradition of political thought, even though when they use the relevant terminology it is evident that they do not mean exactly the same thing by it. All that is necessary for us to be justified in speaking in this way is that there should indeed be a 'family resemblance' between their respective systems of political thought. In other words, all that is necessary is that we should be able to trace at least some historical line of connection between the ideas of the two theorists in question.

The existence and importance of theoretical traditions, understood in this sense, is something which has been emphasised by a number of commentators (Boucher, 1985, pp. 99-150; Greenleaf, 1964; Haddock, 1974, p. 427; Lockyer, 1979). According to Andrew Lockyer, for example, the range of problems which a particular group of political theorists writing at different times have attempted to answer, together with the answers that they give to these problems, may be said to 'constitute a tradition of discourse'. These problems and answers, and hence that tradition of discourse, 'have a history'. They have a history precisely because the concepts which are employed by the theorists in question in their effort to formulate and to solve these problems 'have different meanings in different contexts', meanings which change over time as a consequence of 'changing political and social arrangements' (Lockyer, 1979, p.217). From this point of view, as David Boucher has pointed out, theoretical traditions in politics are 'fluid'. They undergo change whilst at the same time retaining their identity, because all of their features 'do not change at once' (Boucher, 1985, pp. 113-4).

The intellectual roots of this alternative methodological approach to the study of the history of ideas is (as again a number of commentators have indicated) provided by the philosophy of Hegel. Such an approach would involve the exploration of what Hegel would refer to as 'identity in difference', or of 'diversity in uniformity'. The ideas and concepts which are associated with the various traditions of political thought are, in effect, what Hegel would refer to as 'concrete universals' (Berki and Parekh, 1973, pp.178, 182-3; Boucher, 1985, pp. 108, 113-14; Lockyer, 1979, pp. 215-6).

We may conclude, then, that Hegel's ideas certainly do provide us with an insight into the character of both the conservative and the natural law traditions of political thought. Indeed we may go further than this and maintain, in contradiction to the claims of Quentin Skinner, that Hegel's ideas also help us to construct an alternative methodology which makes it possible for us to establish the very existence of these two traditions of political thought as legitimate objects of study.

Bibliography

Aaron, R. I. (1965), *John Locke,* Oxford University Press.

Aaron, R. I. (1967), *The Theory of Universals,* London.

Acton, H. B. (1975), 'Introduction' to Hegel, G. W. F., *On the Scientific Ways of Treating Natural Law.*

Albritton, R. (1970), 'On Wittgenstein's Use of the Term "Criterion",' in Pitcher, G. (ed), *Wittgenstein: The Philosophical Investigations.*

Allan, D. J. (1970), *The Philosophy of Aristotle,* Oxford University Press.

Allison, L. (1984), *Right Principles: A Conservative Philosophy of Politics,* Basil Blackwell.

Aquinas, T. (1964), *Commentary on the Ethics of Aristotle,* Litzinger, G. I. (ed), Chicago.

Aquinas, Saint Thomas (1966), *Summa Theologica,* 28, *On Law,* Eyre and Spottiswoode.

Aquinas, T. (1969), *Summa Theologica,* 29, Eyre and Spottiswoode, London.

Arblaster, A. (1984), *The Rise and Decline of Western Liberalism,* Blackwell, Oxford.

Armstrong, R. A. (1966), *Primary and Secondary Precepts in Thomistic Natural Law Teaching,* Martinus Nijhoff, The Hague.

Aris, R. (1965), *History of Political Thought in Germany: From 1789 to 1815,* Frank Cass.

Aristotle, (1925), *Ethica Nichomachea,* trans. Ross, W. D., Oxford.

Aristotle, (1926), *Categories,* trans. Edgehill, E. M., Oxford.

Aristotle (1947), *The Politics of Aristotle,* trans. Barker, E., Oxford.

Arthur, C.(1987, Spring), 'Review of Fine, B., *Democracy and the Rule of Law',* *Radical Philosophy,* 45.

Augustine, Saint (1945), *De Civitate Dei,* trans. Tasker, R. V. G., Dent and Sons.

Augustine, Saint (1972), *Concerning the City of God Against the Pagans,* trans. Bettenson, H., Penguin Books.

Austin, J. (1995), *The Province of Jurisprudence Determined,* Trumble, W. (ed), Cambridge University Press.

Avineri, S. (1970), 'Hegel and Nationalism', in Kaufmann, W. (ed), *Hegel's Political Philosophy.*

Avineri, S. (1972), *Hegel's Theory of the Modern State*, Cambridge University Press.

Baillie, J. (1953), *The Belief in Progress: A Re-evaluation,* London.

Baker, K. M. (1975), *Condorcet: From Natural Philosophy to Social Mathematics,* Chicago.

Baker. K. M. (1976), 'Introduction' to *Condorcet: Selected Writings.*

Bambrough, R. (1970), 'Universals and Family Resemblances', in Pitcher, G. (ed), *Wittgenstein: The Philosophical Investigations,* Macmillan.

Barker, E. (ed) (1948), *Social Contract: Essays by Locke, Hume and Rousseau,* Oxford.

Barker, E. (1951), 'Saint Augustine's Theory of Society', in Barker, E., *Essays on Government,* London.

Barker, E. (1959), *The Political Thought of Plato and Aristotle,* New York.

Barker, E. (1960), 'Introduction' to Gierke, O., *Natural Law and the Theory of Society,* Beacon Press.

Barnes, H. E. (1969), 'Ancient and Medieval Social Philosophy', in Barnes, H. E., *An Introduction to the History of Sociology,* Chicago University Press.

Battaglia, A. (1981), *Towards a Reformulation of Natural Law,* New York.

Boucher, D. (1984), 'The Denial of Perennial Problems: The Negative Side of Quentin Skinner's Theory', *Interpretation,* 12.

Boucher, D. (1985), *Texts in Context: Revisionist Methods For Studying the History of Ideas,* Martinus Nijhoff, The Hague.

Brailsford, H. N. (1954), *Shelley, Godwin and Their Circle,* Oxford University Press.

Barrow, R. H. (1950), *Introduction to Saint Augustine: The City of God,* London.

Battaglia, A. (1981), *Towards a Reformulation of Natural Law,* New York.

Baum, G. (1961), 'Protestants and Natural Law', *The Commonweal,* 73.

Baumrin, B. (1976), 'Autonomy in Rawls and Kant', *Mid West Studies in Philosophy,* 1.

Becker, C. (1979), *The Heavenly City of the Eighteenth Century Philosophers,* Yale University Press.

Begin, R. F. (1959), *Natural Law and Positive Law,* Canon Law Studies, 393, Catholic University of America, Washington, D.C.

Beiser, F. C. (1992), *Enlightenment, Revolution and Romanticism: The Genesis of Modern German Political Thought: 1790-1800,* Harvard University Press, Cambridge, Mass.

Beiser, F. C. (ed) (1993), *The Cambridge Companion to Hegel,* Cambridge University Press.

Beiser, F. C. (1993), 'Hegel's Historicism', in Beiser, F. C. (ed), *The Cambridge Companion to Hegel.*

Bellamy, R. (1993), 'Liberalism', in Eatwell, R. and Wright, A. (eds), *Contemporary Political Ideologies.*

Benhabib, S. (1984), 'Obligation, Contract and Exchange: On the Significance of Hegel's Abstract Right', in Pelczynski, Z. A. (ed), *The State and Civil Society.*

Bentham, J. (1977), *A Comment on the Commentaries,* Burns, J. H. and Hart, H. L. A. (eds), London.

Berki, R. N. and Parekh, B. (1973, March-April), 'The History of Political Ideas: A Critique of Quentin Skinner's Methodology', *Journal of the History of Ideas,* pp. 163-84.

Berki, R. N. (1984), *The History of Political Thought: A Short Introduction,* Dent.

Berlin, I. (1954), *Historical Inevitability,* Oxford University Press.

Berlin, I. (1964), 'Hobbes, Locke and Professor MacPherson', *Political Quarterly,* 35.

Berlin, I. (1969), *Four Essays on Liberty,* Oxford University Press, Oxford.

Berlin, I. (1973), 'Two Concepts of Liberty', in Quinton, A. (ed), *Political Philosophy.*

Berlin, I. (1978), 'Historical Inevitability', in Gardiner, P. (ed), *The Philosophy of History.*

Bevir, M. (1994), 'Are There Perennial Problems in Political Theory?', *Political Studies,* 42, pp. 662-75.

Bindoff, S. T. (1953), *Tudor England,* Penguin Books.

Blackstone, W. (1966), *Commentaries on the Laws of England,* in four volumes, New York.

Blackstone, W. T. (1965), 'The Golden Rule: A Defence', *Southern Journal of Philosophy,* 3.

Bock, K. (1978), 'Theories of Progress, Development, Evolution', in Bottomore, T. and Nisbet, R. (eds), *A History of Sociological Analysis,* Heinemann.

Boorstin, P. J. (1973), *The Mysterious Science of Law: An Essay on Blackstone's Commentaries,* Gloucester, Massachusetts.

Bosworth, S. (1991), *Hegel's Political Philosophy: The Test Case of Constitutional Monarchy,* Garland Press.

Bowle, J. (1961), *Western Political Thought: From the Origins to Rousseau,* Methuen.

Bradley, A. C. (1989, March), 'Aristotle as a Conservative Thinker', *Salisbury Review.*

Bramstead, E. K. and Melhuish, K. J. (eds) (1978), *Western Liberalism: A History in Documents From Locke to Croce,* Longman, London.

Briefs, G. A. (1941), 'The Economic Philosophy of Romanticism', *Journal of the History of Ideas,* 2.

Brod, H. (1992), *Hegel's Philosophy of Politics: Idealism, Identity and Modernity,* Westview Press.

Bronough, R. N. (1968), 'Formal Criteria For Moral Rules', *Mind.*

Bronowski, J. and Mazlish, B. (1963), *The Western Intellectual Tradition*, Penguin Books.

Brudner, A. (1981), 'Constitutional Monarchy As The Divine Regime: Hegel's Theory of The Just State', *History of Political Thought*, 2, 1, pp. 120-40.

Brumfitt, J. H. (1972), *The French Enlightenment*, Macmillan.

Buck, P. W. (1975a), 'Introduction' to Buck, P. W. (ed), *How Conservatives Think*.

Buck, P. W. (ed) (1975), *How Conservatives Think*, Penguin Books.

Bullock, A. and Shock, M. (eds) (1967), *The Liberal Tradition From Fox to Keynes*, Oxford.

Burger, T. (1987), *Max Weber's Theory of Concept Formation: History, Laws and Ideal Types*, second edition, Duke University Press.

Burke, E. (1815-1827), *The Works of Edmund Burke*, Rivington, J. (ed), in sixteen volumes, London.

Burke, E. (1874-78), *Select Works*, ed. Payne, E. J., in three volumes, Oxford.

Burke, E. (1874-78a), 'First Letter On A Regicide Peace', in Burke, E., *Select Works*, Payne, E. J. (ed), 3.

Burke, E. (1874-78b), 'Second Letter On A Regicide Peace', in Burke, E., *Select Works*, Payne, E. J. (ed), 3.

Burke, E. (1874-78c), 'Fourth Letter On A Regicide Peace', in Burke, E., *Select Works*, Payne, E. J. (ed), 3.

Burke, E. (1969), *Reflections on the Revolution in France*, O'Brien, C. C. (ed), Penguin Books.

Burke, E. (1968), *Edmund Burke on Revolution*, Smith, R. A. (ed), Harper Torchbooks.

Burke, E. (1968b), *An Appeal From the New to the Old Whigs*, in Burke, E., *Edmund Burke on Revolution*.

Burke, E. (1975), *Edmund Burke On Government, Politics and Society*, Hill, B. W. (ed), Fontana.

Burke, E. (1975a), 'A Letter to the Sheriffs of Bristol', in Hill, B. W. (ed), *Edmund Burke on Government, Politics and Society*.

Burke, E. (1975b), 'Speech on Conciliation With the Colonies', in Hill, B. W. (ed), *Edmund Burke on Government, Politics and Society*.

Burlamaqui, J. J. (1748), *Principes du droit naturel*, Geneva.

Burns, A. (1984), 'The Source of the *Encyclopedie* Article 'Loi naturelle morale', *The British Journal For Eighteenth Century Studies*, 7, 1, pp. 39-48.

Burns, A. (1986), 'The Sources of the *Encyclopedia* Article on Justice: A Reply to Professor Thielemann', *Diderot Studies*, 22, pp. 27-40.

Burns, A. (1994), Review of Bosworth, S. *Hegel's Political Philosophy: The Test Case Of Constitutional Monarchy*, *Bulletin of the Hegel Society of Great Britain*, 30, pp. 64-71.

Burns, A. (1995), 'The Ideological Location of Hegel's Political Thought', in Lovenduski, J. and Stanyer, J. (eds), *Contemporary Political Studies, 3*, pp. 1301-1308, Political Studies Association.

Burns, A. (1995), 'Hegel and Natural Law Theory', *Politics, 15*, 1, pp. 27-32.

Burns, J. H. (ed) (1988), *The Cambridge History of Medieval Political Thought*, Cambridge University Press.

Burns, J. H. (1994), *The Cambridge History of Political Thought: 1450-1700*, Cambridge University Press.

Bury, J. B. (1920), *The Idea of Progress*, Macmillan.

Buttle, N. (1984), 'Negative and Positive Liberty Revisited', *Politics, 4*, 1.

Cairns, H. (1949), *Legal Philosophy From Plato to Hegel*, John Hopkins University Press.

Callahan, T. G. (1975), *William Ockham and Natural Law*, Michigan State University, Ph.D. Thesis.

Calleo, D. P. (1966), *Coleridge and the Modern State*, Harvard University Press.

Cameron, D. (1973), *The Social Thought of Rousseau and Burke: A Comparative Study*, Weidenfield and Nicolson.

Canavan, F. (1960), *The Political Reason of Edmund Burke*, Duke University Press.

Carlyle, R. W. and Carlyle, J. (1903-36), *Medieval Political Theory in the West*, in six volumes, London.

Carritt, E. F. (1935), *Morals and Politics*, Oxford University Press.

Cassirer, E. (1961), *The Philosophy of the Enlightenment*, Beacon Press.

Cassirer, E. (1967), *The Myth of the State*, Yale University Press.

Cecil, H. (1937), *Conservatism.*, Thornton Butterworth, London.

Chloros, A. G. (1958), 'What is Natural Law?', *Modern Law Review*, 21, 6.

Church, W. F. (1964), *The Influence of the Enlightenment on the French Revolution*, D. C. Heath.

Cicero, (1928a), *De Republica*, trans. Keyes, C. W., Loeb Classical Library, London.

Cicero, (1928b), *De Legibus*, trans. Keyes, C. W., Loeb Classical Library, London.

Cicero, (1929), *On the Commonwealth*, trans. Sabine, G. H. and Barney Smith, S., Bobbs Merrill.

Cicero, (1960), *De Officiis*, Warrington, J. (ed), Dent and Sons.

Clark, F. (1971), 'Voluntarism and Rationalism in the Ethics of Ockham', *Franciscan Studies*, 31.

Clarke, D. (1975), 'The Conservative Faith in the Modern Age', in Buck, P. W. (ed), *How Conservatives Think*.

Cobban, A. B. C. (1960), *In Search of Humanity: The Role of the Enlightenment in Modern History*, Cape.

Cobban, A. B. C. (1962), *Edmund Burke and the Revolt Against the Eighteenth Century*, Allen and Unwin.

Cochrane, A. (1966), 'Natural Law in the Teachings of John Calvin', in Smith, E. A. (ed), *Church and State Relations in Ecumenical Perspective.*

Coleman, J.(1990), 'Saint Augustine: Christian Political Thought at the End of the Roman Empire', in Redhead, B. (ed), *Plato to Nato: Studies in Political Thought,* BBC Books.

Coleridge, S. T. (1913), *Aids to Reflection.,* Bell and Sons, London.

Coleridge, S. T. (1972), *On the Constitution of the Church and State.* Dent.

Colletti, L. (1975), 'Editor's Introduction' to Marx, K., *Early Writings,* Penguin Books.

Collins, I. (1957), *Liberalism in Nineteenth Century Europe,* Historical Association, London.

Collingwood, R. G. (1976), *The Idea of History,* Oxford University Press.

Condorcet, (1955), *Sketch For A Historical Picture of the Progress of the Human Mind,* London.

Condorcet, (1976), *Condorcet: Selected Writings,* Baker, K. M. (ed), Bobbs Merrill.

Copleston, F. C. (1955), *Aquinas,* Penguin, Harmondsworth

Copleston, F. C. (1962), *A History of Philosophy,* 1, *Greece and Rome,* 2, Doubleday.

Cornforth, M. (1968), *Open Society and the Open Philosophy,* Lawrence and Wishart.

Cottingham, J. (1984), *Rationalism,* Paladin Books.

Courtney, C. P. (1963), *Montesquieu and Burke.,* Oxford.

Cowling, M. (ed) (1978), *Conservative Essays,* Cassell.

Cowling, M. (1978a), 'Introduction' to Cowling, M. (ed), *Conservative Essays.*

Cristi, F. R. (1983), 'The *Hegelische Mitte* and Hegel's Monarch', *Political Theory,* 11, 4, pp. 601-22.

Crocker, L. G. (1959), *An Age of Crisis: Man and World in Eighteenth Century French Thought,* Baltimore.

Crocker, L. G. (1962), 'The Priority of Justice or Law', *Yale French Studies,* 28, pp. 34-42.

Crocker, L. G. (1963), *Nature and Culture: Ethical Thought in the French Enlightenment,* Baltimore.

Crocker, L. (1980), *Positive Liberty,* Martinus Nijhoff, The Hague.

de Ruggiero, G. (1927), *The History of European Liberalism,* Oxford University Press.

Copleston, F. (1955), *Aquinas,* Penguin Books.

Crowe, M. B. (1977), *The Changing Profile of Natural Law,* Martinus Nijhoff, The Hague.

Curtler, H. M. (1971), 'What Kant Might Say to Hare', *Mind,* 80.

Dallmayr, F. (1993), *G. W. F. Hegel: Modernity and Politics,* Sage.

Darwall, S. (1976), 'A Defence of the Kantian Interpretation', *Ethics,* 86.

Deane, H. A. (1966), *The Political and Social Ideas of Saint Augustine,* London.

De Crespigny, A. and Cronin, J. (eds) (1980), *Ideologies of Politics,* Oxford.

Del Vecchio, G. (1952), *Justice,* trans. Campbell, A. H., Edinburgh.

D'Entreves, A. P. (1959), *The Medieval Contribution to Political Thought,* New York.

D'Entreves, A. P. (1970), *Natural Law,* Hutchinson.

Derathe, R. (1970), *Jean Jacques Rousseau et la science politique de son temps,* Presses Universitaires de France, Paris.

De Ruggiero, G. (1981), *The History of European Liberalism,* R. G. Smith, Gloucester, Mass.

Dickinson, H. T. (1977), *Liberty and Property: Political Ideology in Eighteenth Century England,* Methuen.

Diderot, D. and d'Alembert, J. (eds) (1966), *Encyclopedie ou dictionnaire raisonne des sciences, des arts, et des metiers: nouvelle impression en facsimile de la premiere edition de 1751-1780,* in seventeen volumes, Friedrich Fromann Verlag, Stuttgart Bad Canstatt.

Donagan, A. (1964-65), 'Mr. Hare and the Conscientious Nazi', *Philosophical Studies.*

Doyle, P. (1966), *A History of Political Thought,* Cape.

Drury, S. B. (1981), 'H. L. A. Hart's Minimum Content Theory of Natural Law', *Political Theory,* 9, 4.

Dunn, J. (1969), *The Political Thought of John Locke: An Historical Account of the Argument of the 'Two Treatises of Government',* Cambridge University Press.

Dunn, J. (1971), 'Consent in the Political Theory of John Locke', in Schochet, G. J. (ed), *Life, Liberty and Property: Essays on Locke's Political Ideas.*

Eatwell, R. and Wright, A. (eds) (1993), *Contemporary Political Ideologies,* Pinter.

Eccleshall, R. et. al. (1986), *Political Ideologies: An Introduction,* Hutchinson.

Eccleshall, R. (1986), 'Liberalism', in Eccleshall, R. et. al. (eds), *Political Ideologies: An Introduction.*

Eccleshall, R. (1978), *Order and Reason in Politics: Theories of Absolute and Limited Monarchy in Early Modern England,* Oxford University Press.

Eccleshall, R. (ed) (1986), *British Liberalism: Liberal Thought From the 1690s to the 1980s,* Longman, London.

Eccleshall, R. (1990), *English Conservatism Since the Restoration: An Introduction and Anthology,* Unwin Hyman.

Edelstein, L. (1968), *The Idea of Progress in Classical Antiquity,* John Hopkins University Press.

Emmett, D. (1963), 'Universality and Moral Judgement', *Philosophical Quarterly.*

Epstein, K. (1966), *The Genesis of German Conservatism,* Princeton University Press.

Erikson, E.(1964), 'The Golden Rule in the Light of New Insight', in Erikson, E., *Insight and Responsibility.*

Evans, G. R. (1982), *Augustine on Evil,* Cambridge.

Fay, S. B. (1946-47), 'The Idea of Progress', *American Historical Review,* 52.

Figgis, J. N. (1921), *The Political Aspects of Saint Augustine's 'City of God',* London.

Figgis, J. N. (1914), *The Divine Right of Kings,* Cambridge.

Fine, R. (1984), *Democracy and the Rule of Law,* Pluto Press, London

Finnis, J. (1980), *Natural Law and Natural Rights.* Clarendon, Oxford.

Finnis, J. (1980), *Natural Law and Natural Rights,* Clarendon.

Fletcher, A. (1976), *Tudor Rebellions,* Longman.

Flew, A. (ed) *A Dictionary of Philosophy,* Macmillan.

Foriers, P. and Perelman, Ch. (1973), 'Natural Law and Natural Rights', *Dictionary of the History of Ideas,* 3, New York.

Foster, M. (1935), *The Political Philosophies of Plato and Hegel,* Oxford.

Frankel, C. (1969), *The Faith of Reason: The Idea of Progress in the French Enlightenment,* New York.

Frazer, J. (1933), *Condorcet on the Progress of the Human Mind,* Oxford.

Freeman, M. (1980), *Edmund Burke and the Critique of Political Radicalism,* Blackwell.

Friedman, M. (1979), *Free To Choose,* Penguin Books.

Friedmann, W. (1967), *Legal Theory,* Stevens, London

Friedrich, C. J. (1963), *The Philosophy of Law in Historical Perspective,* Chicago University Press.

Friedrich, C. J. (1972), *Tradition and Authority,* Macmillan.

Gamble, A. (1983), *An Introduction to Modern Social and Political Thought,* Macmillan.

Gardiner, P. (ed) (1959), *Theories of History,* Collier Macmillan, New York.

Gardiner, P. (ed) (1978), *The Philosophy of History,* Oxford University Press.

Gauthier, D. P. (1977), 'The Social Contract as Ideology', *Philosophy and Public Affairs,* 6, 2.

Gawlick, G. (1963), 'Cicero and the Enlightenment', *Studies on Voltaire and the Eighteenth Century,* 25, pp. 657-82.

Gay, P. (1964), *The Party of Humanity,* Weidenfield.

Gay, P. (1966), *The Enlightenment: An Interpretation,* 1, *The Rise of Modern Paganism,* Wildwood House, London.

Gay, P. (1970), *The Enlightenment: An Interpretation,* 2, *The Science of Freedom,* Wildwood House, London.

Gay, P. (1954), 'The Enlightenment in the History of Political Theory', *Political Science Quarterly,* 69, pp. 371-89.

Germino, D. (1969), 'Hegel as a Political Theorist', *Journal of Politics,* 31

Germino, D. (1970), 'Hegel's Theory of the State: Humanist or Totalitarian?', *Statsvetenskaplig Tidskrift,* 19

Gewirth, A. (1978a), *Reason and Morality*, Chicago University Press.

Gewirth, A. (1978b), 'The Golden Rule Rationalised', *Mid West Studies in Philosophy*, 3.

Gierke, O. (1958), *Political Theories of the Middle Age*, Beacon Press, Boston.

Gilby, T. (1958), *Principality and Polity: The Political Thought of Saint Thomas Aquinas*, Chicago.

Gilmour, I. (1978), *Inside Right: Conservatism, Policies and the People*, Quartet Books.

Ginsburg, M. (1963), 'The Concept of Justice', *Philosophy*, 38, pp. 99-116; also in Ginsberg, M., *On Justice in Society*, Penguin Books.

Gooch, G. P. (1965), *Germany and the French Revolution*, Frank Cass.

Goodwin, B. (1987), *Using Political Ideas*, John Wiley and Sons.

Gough, J. W. (1955), *Fundamental Law in English Constitutional History*, Oxford.

Gough, J. W. (1957), *The Social Contract*, Clarendon.

Gough, J. W. (1973), *John Locke's Political Philosophy: Eight Studies.* Clarendon, Oxford.

Gould, J. A. (1963), 'The Not-So-Golden Rule', *Southern Journal of Philosophy*, 1.

Gould, J. A. (1980), 'Blackstone's Meta-Not-So-Golden Rule', *Southern Journal of Philosophy*, 18.

Gould, J. A. (1983a), 'Kant's Critique of the Golden Rule', *New Scholasticism*, 57.

Gould, J. A. (1983b), 'The Golden Rule', *American Journal of Theology and Philosophy*, 4.

Grabowski, S. J. (1957), *The Church: An Introduction to the Theology of Saint Augustine*, Saint Louis, Miss.

Gray, J. and Pelczynski, Z. A.(eds) (1984), *Conceptions of Liberty in Political Philosophy*, London.

Gray, J. (1986), *Liberalism*, Open University Press, Milton Keynes.

Green, R. W. (1973), *Protestantism and Capitalism: The Weber Thesis and Its Critics*, D. C. Heath, Boston.

Greenleaf, W. H. (1964), *Order, Empiricism and Politics: Two Traditions of English Political Thought: 1500-1700*, Oxford University Press.

Greenleaf, W. H. (1968), 'Idealism, Modern Philosophy and Politics', in King, P. and Parekh, B. (eds), *Politics and Experience: Essays Presented to Professor Michael Oakeshotton the Occasion of His Retirement*, Cambridge University Press.

Greenleaf, W.H. (1973a), 'Theory and the Study of Politics', *The British Journal of Political Science*, 2, pp. 467-77.

Greenleaf, W. H. (1973b), 'The Character of Modern British Conservatism', in Benewick, R., Berki, R. N. and Parekh, B. (eds), *Knowledge and Belief in Politics: The Problem of Ideology*, Allen and Unwin.

Greenleaf, W. H. (1975), 'The Character of Modern British Politics', *Parliamentary Affairs*, 28.

Greenleaf, W. H. (1983), *The British Political Tradition, 1, The Rise of Collectivism*, Methuen.

Greenleaf, W. H. (1983), *The British Political Tradition, 2, The Ideological Heritage*, Methuen.

Grimsley, R. A. (ed) (1979), *The Age of the Enlightenment: 1715-1789*, Penguin Books.

Grotius, H. (1925), *De Jure Belli et Pacis*, trans. Kelsey, F. W., Oxford.

Guthrie, W. K. C. (1967), *The Greek Philosophers: From Thales to Aristotle*, Methuen.

Haddock, B. (1974), 'The History of Ideas and the Study of Politics', *Political Theory*, 2, 4, pp. 420-31.

Haddock, B. (1989), 'Saint Augustine: The City of God', in Forsyth, M. and Keens Soper, M. (eds), *A Guide to the Political Classics*, Oxford.

Haddock, B. (1993), 'Georg Wilhelm Friedrich Hegel: *Philosophy of Right*', in Forsyth, M. and Keens Soper, M. and Hoffmann, J. (eds), *The Political Classics: Hamilton to Mill*.

Haines, C. G. (1965), *The Revival of Natural Law Concepts*, Russell and Russell, New York.

Halevy, E. (1972), *The Growth of Philosophic Radicalism*, Faber.

Hall, J. A. (1988), *Liberalism: Politics, Ideology and the Market*, Paladin, London.

Hampsher Monk, I. (1987), 'Introduction', to Hampsher Monk, I. (ed), *The Political Philosophy of Edmund Burke*.

Hampshire, S. (1955), 'Introduction' to Condorcet, *Sketch For A Historical Picture of the Progress of the Human Mind*.

Hampson, N. (1968), *The Enlightenment*, Penguin Books.

Hardimon, M. O. (1994), *Hegel's Social Philosophy: The Project of Reconciliation.*, Cambridge University Press.

Hare, R. M. (1972), *Freedom and Reason*, Oxford University Press.

Hare, R. M. (1981), *Moral Thinking: Its Levels, Method and Point*, Clarendon Press.

Harris, N. (1971), *Beliefs in Society: The Problem of Ideology*, Penguin Books.

Harris, R. W. (1968), *Reason and Nature in Eighteenth Century Thought*, Batsford.

Harris, R. W. (1969), *Romanticism and the Social Order: 1780-1830*, Batsford.

Hart, H. L. A. (1958), 'Positivism and the Separation of Law and Morals', *Harvard Law Review*, 71.

Hart, H. L. A. (1961), *The Concept of Law*, Clarendon Press, Oxford.

Hart, H. L. A. (1983), *Essays in Jurisprudence and Philosophy*, Oxford.

Hartman, R. S. (1953), 'Introduction' to Hegel, G. W. F., *Reason in History: A General Introduction To The Philosophy of History*.

Hayek, F. (1976), 'Why I Am Not A Conservative', in Hayek, F., *The Constitution of Liberty.*

Hayek, F. (1980), 'The Principles Of A Liberal Social Order', in de Crespigny, A. de and Cronin, J. (eds), *Ideologies of Politics.*

Hayek, F. (1973), *Economic Freedom and Representative Government,* I.E.A.

Hayek, F. (1976), *The Constitution of Liberty,* Routledge.

Hazard, P. (1963), *European Thought in the Eighteenth Century: From Montesquieu to Lessing,* Meridian Books.

Hazard, P. (1964), *The European Mind: 1680-1715,* Penguin Books.

Hearnshaw, F. J. C. (ed) (1923), *The Social and Political Ideas of the Middle Ages,* Harrap.

Hearnshaw, F. J. C. (ed) (1930), *The Social and Political Ideas of Some Great French Thinkers of the Age of Reason,* London.

Hearnshaw, F. J. C. and Carlyle, A. J. (1923), 'Saint Augustine and the City of God', in Hearnshaw, F. J. C. (ed), *Social and Political Ideas of the Middle Ages.*

Hegel, G. W. F. (1892-96), *Lectures on the History of Philosophy,* in three volumes, trans. Haldane, E. S. and Simon, F. H., London.

Hegel, G. W. F. (1953), *Reason In History: A General Introduction To The Philosophy of History.* Ed. Hartman, R. S. Bobbs Merrill.

Hegel, G. W. F. (1955), *Grundlinien der Philosophie des Rechts,* Hoffmeister, J. (ed), Hamburg.

Hegel, G. W. F. (1956), *The Philosophy of History,* trans. Sibree, J., Dover, New York.

Hegel, G. W. F. (1964), *Grundlinien der Philosophie des Rechts,* Glockner, H. (ed), Stuttgart Bad Cannstatt.

Hegel, G. W. F. (1966), *Texts and Commentary,* Kaufmann, W. (ed), Doubleday.

Hegel, G. W. F. (1969), *Political Writings,* Pelczynski, Z. A. (ed), Oxford, Clarendon Press.

Hegel, G. W. F. (1969a), 'Proceedings of the Estates Assembly in the Kingdom of Wurtemburg: 1815-1816', in Hegel, G. W. F., *Political Writings.*

Hegel, G. W. F. (1969b), 'The German Constitution', in Hegel, G. W. F., *Political Writings.*

Hegel, G. W. F. (1971), *Hegel's Philosophy of Mind: Being Part Three of the Encyclopaedia of the Philosophical Sciences,* trans. Wallace, W. and Miller, A. V., Oxford University Press.

Hegel, G. W. F. (1975a), *The Scientific Ways of Treating Natural Law,* University of Pennsylvania Press, Philadelphia

Hegel, G. W. F. (1975b), *Logic: Being Part One of the Encyclopaedia of the Philosophical Sciences,* trans. Wallace, W., Oxford University Press.

Hegel, G. W. F. (1977), *Phenomenology of Spirit,* trans. Miller, A. V., Oxford University Press.

Hegel, G. W. F. (1979), *The Philosophy of Right*, Knox, T. M. (ed), Oxford University Press.

Hegel, G. W. F. (1991), *Elements of the Philosophy of Right*, Wood, A. (ed), Cambridge University Press.

Held, D. (1983), 'Central Perspectives on the Modern State', in Held, D. et. al. (eds), *States and Societies*, Martin Robertson.

Heywood, A. (1992), *Political Ideologies: An Introduction*, Macmillan.

Hinchman, L. (1984), *Hegel's Critique of the Enlightenment*, University of Florida Press, Gainesville.

Hirst, E. W. (1934), 'The Categorical Imperative and the Golden Rule', *Philosophy*, 9.

Hobbes, T. (1839-45), *The English Works of Thomas Hobbes*, in eleven volumes, Molesworth, W. (ed), London.

Hobbes, T. (1839-45a), *Philosophical Rudiments Concerning Government and Society*, in Hobbes, T., *English Works*.

Hobbes, T. (1838-45b), *A Dialogue Between a Philosopher and a Student of the Common Laws of England*, in Hobbes, T., *English Works*.

Hobbes, T. (1992), *Leviathan*, Tuck, R. (ed), Cambridge University Press.

Hobhouse, L. T. (1911), *Liberalism*, Thornton Butterworth, London.

Holdsworth, W. (1923-32), *A History of English Law*, third edition, in nine volumes, Methuen.

Honderich, T. (1990), *Conservatism*, Penguin Books.

Hook, S. (1970a), 'Hegel Rehabilitated?', in Kaufmann, W. (ed), *Hegel's Political Philosophy*.

Hook, S. (1970b), 'Hegel and His Apologists', in Kaufmann, W. (ed), *Hegel's Political Philosophy*.

Hooker, R. (1836), *Of The Laws of Ecclesiastical Polity*, Keble, J. (ed), Oxford.

Hospers, J. (1973), *An Introduction to Philosophical Analysis*, Routledge.

Huntington, S. (1957, June), 'Conservatism as an Ideology', *American Political Science Review*, 51.

Hyppolite, J.(1969), *Studies on Marx and Hegel*, Harper Torchbooks.

Hyppolite, J. (1969), 'The Significance of the French Revolution in Hegel's *Phenomenology*', in Hyppolite, J., *Studies on Marx and Hegel*.

Ilting, K. H. (1971), 'The Structure of Hegel's Philosophy of Right', in Pelczynski, Z. A. (ed), *Hegel's Political Philosophy*.

Inge, W. R. (1920), *The Idea of Progress*, Oxford.

Inwood, M. (1992), *A Hegel Dictionary*, Blackwell, Oxford.

Jay, R. (1986), 'Democracy', in Eccleshall, R. et. al., *Political Ideologies: An Introduction*.

Johnson, O. A. (1974-75), 'The Kantian Interpretation', *Ethics*, 85.

Johnson, O. A. (1976-77), 'Autonomy in Kant and Rawls: A Reply', *Ethics*, 87.

Kainz, H. P. (1974), *Hegel's Philosophy of Right: With Marx's Commentary: A Handbook For Students.*, Martinus Nijhoff, The Hague.

Kant, I. (1965), *The Metaphysical Elements of Justice*, Bobbs Merrill, New York

Kant, I. (1972), *The Moral Law: Kant's Groundwork of a Metaphysic of Morals*, Hutchinson.

Kant, I. (1991), *Political Writings*, Reiss, H. (ed), Cambridge University Press.

Kant, I.(1991), 'An Answer to the Question "What is Enlightenment",' in Kant, I., *Political Writings*.

Kaufmann, W. (1965), *Hegel: Reinterpretation, Texts and Commentary*, London.

Kaufmann, W. (ed) (1970), *Hegel's Political Philosophy*, Athlone Press, New York.

Kaufmann, W. (1970a), 'The Hegel Myth and its Method', in Kaufmann, W. (ed), *Hegel's Political Philosophy*.

Kelly, G. A. (1978), *Hegel's Retreat From Eleusis: Studies in Political Thought*, Princeton University Press.

Kelsen, H. (1957), *What is Justice? Justice, Law and Politics in the Mirror of Science: Collected Essays by Hans Kelsen*, Berkeley and Los Angeles.

Kelsen, H. (1961), *A General Theory of Law and the State*, New York.

Kelsen, H. (1973), *Essays in Legal and Moral Philosophy*, Reidel, Dordrecht

Kettler, D. et. al. (1986), 'Editors' Introduction' to Mannheim, K., *Conservatism*.

Keyes, G. L. (1966), *Christian Faith and the Interpretation of History: A Study of Saint Augustine's Philosophy of History*, Lincoln, Nebraska.

Khatchadourian, H. (1970), 'Common Names and "Family Resemblances",' in Pitcher, G. (ed), *Wittgenstein: The Philosophical Investigations*.

Kirk, R. (1951), 'Burke and Natural Rights', *The Review of Politics*, 13.

Kirk, R. (1964), *The Conservative Mind: From Burke to Santayana*, Chicago.

Kitch, M. J. (ed) (1969), *Capitalism and the Reformation*, Longman.

Klosko, G.(1980), 'Montesquieu's Science of Politics: Absolute Values and Ethical Relativism', *Studies on Voltaire and the Eighteenth Century*, 189, pp. 153-78.

Knox, T. M. (1957-58), 'Hegel's Attitude to Kant's Ethics', *Kant Studien*, 49.

Knox, T. M. (1970), 'Hegel and Prussianism', in Kaufmann, W. (ed), *Hegel's Political Philosophy*.

Knox, T. M. (1979a), 'Translator's Foreword' to Hegel, G.W.F., *Philosophy of Right*.

Knox, T. M. (1979b), 'Translators Notes' to Hegel, G. W. F., *Philosophy of Right*.

Krieger, L. (1957), *The German Idea of Freedom: History of a Political Tradition*, Chicago University Press.

Kumar, K. (1986), *Prophecy and Progress: The Sociology of Industrial and Post-Industrial Society*, Penguin Books.

Lactantius, (1998), *The Divine Institutes*, trans. Fletcher, W., Edinburgh.

Lang, A. (1909), 'The Reformation and Natural Law', *Princeton Theological Review*, 7.

Laski, H. J. (1961), *Political Thought in England: From Locke to Bentham*, Oxford.

Laski, H. J. (1962), *The Rise of European Liberalism*, Unwin Books.

Lefebvre, G. (1947), *The Coming of the French Revolution*, Vintage Books.

Lessnoff, M. (1986), *Social Contract,* Macmillan.

Levin, M. and Williams, H. (1983), 'Inherited Power and Popular Representation: A Tension in Hegel's Political Theory', *Political Studies,* 35, pp. 105-15.

Levine, A. (1974), 'Rawls' Kantianism', *Social Theory and Practice',* 3.

Levinson, R. B. (1953), *In Defence of Plato,* Cambridge, Mass.

Lewis, E. K. (1946), 'Natural Law and Expediency in Medieval Political Theory', *Ethics,* 50.

Lewis, E. K. (1954), *Medieval Political Ideas,* New York.

Lindsay, A. D. (1932), 'Hegel the German Idealist', in Hearnshaw, F. J. C. (ed), *The Social and Political Ideas of Some Representative Thinkers of the Age of and Reconstruction,* London.

Lloyd, D. (1959), *Introduction to Jurisprudence,* London.

Lloyd, D. (1972), *The Idea of Law,* Penguin Books.

Locke, J. (1958), *Essays on the Law of Nature,* Von Leyden, W. (ed), Clarendon Press, Oxford.

Locke, J. (1969), *An Essay Concerning Human Understanding,* Woozley, A. D. (ed), Fontana.

Locke, J. (1988), *Two Treatises of Government,* Laslett, P. (ed), Cambridge University Press.

Locke, J. (1988a), *The Second Treatise Of Government: An Essay Concerning the True Original, Extent and End of Government.* In Locke, J., *Two Treatises of Government.*

Lockyer, A. (1979), '"Traditions" as Context in the History of Political Theory', *Political Studies,* 27, 2, pp. 201-18.

Lovejoy, A. O. (1948), *Essays in the History of Ideas,* Baltimore.

Lovejoy, A. O. (1960), *The Great Chain of Being: A Study of the History of an Idea,* New York.

Lowith, K. (1949), *Meaning in History,* Chicago.

MacCallum jnr., G. C. (1967), 'Negative and Positive Freedom', *Philosophical Review,* 76.

Mason, H. (1976), 'On the Kantian Interpretation of Rawls' Theory', *Mid West Studies in Philosophy,* 1.

McNeill, J. T. (1941), 'Natural Law in the Thought of Luther', *Church History,* 10.

McNeill, J. T. (1946), 'Natural Law in the Teachings of the Reformers', *Journal of Religion,* 26.

MacPherson, C. B. (1971), 'The Social Bearing of Locke's Political Theory', in Schochet, G. J. (ed), *Life, Liberty and Property: Essays on Locke's Political Ideas.*

MacPherson, C. B. (1975), *The Political Theory of Possessive Individualism,* Oxford University Press.

Mannheim, K. (1986), *Conservatism: A Contribution to the Sociology of Knowledge,* Kettler, D., Meja, V. and Stehr, N. (eds), Routledge.

MacPherson, C. B. (1965), 'Hobbes's Bourgeois Man', in Brown, K. C. (ed), *Hobbes Studies,* Oxford.

MacPherson, C. B. (1975), *The Political Theory of Possessive Individualism,* Oxford.

MacPherson, C. B. (1980), *Burke,* Oxford University Press.

Manning, D. J. (1976), *Liberalism,* Dent, London.

Manuel, F. E. (1965), *Shapes of Philosophical History,* Allen and Unwin.

Maritain, J. (1958), *Man and the State,* Chicago.

Marshall, G. (1982), *In Search of the Spirit of Capitalism: An Essay on Max Weber's Protestant Ethic Thesis,* Hutchinson.

Martin, K. (1962), *French Liberal Thought in the Eighteenth Century,* Phoenix Books.

Marx, K. (1977), *Early Writings,* Colletti, L. (ed), Penguin Books.

Mason, S. M. (1975), *Montesquieu's Idea of Justice,* Martinus Nijhoff, The Hague.

Mayerhoff, H. (ed) (1959), *The Philosophy of History in Our Time,* Doubleday, New York.

Mazzeo, J. A. (1969), 'The Idea of Progress', in Mazzeo, J. A., *Renaissance and Revolution: The Remaking of European Thought,* Methuen.

McDonnell, K. (1974), 'Does William of Ockham Have a Theory of Natural Law?, *Franciscan Studies,* 34.

McIlwain, C. H. (1910), *The High Court of Parliament and Its Supremacy,* London.

McIlwain, C. H. (1932), *The Growth of Political Thought in the West From the Greeks to the Middle Ages,* New York.

Mehta, V. R. (1968), *Hegel and the Modern State,* New Delhi.

Meyer, P. (1967), 'Politics and Morals in the Thought of Montesquieu', *Studies on Voltaire and the Eighteenth Century,* 56, pp. 845-91.

Mill, J. S. (1967), *Mill on Bentham and Coleridge.*Leavis, F. R. (ed), Chatto and Windus.

Mill, J. S. (1967), 'Coleridge', in Mill, J. S., *Mill On Bentham And Coleridge.*

Mill, J. S. (1972), *Utilitarianism, On Liberty and Representative Government,* Acton, H. B. (ed), Dent.

Miller, D. (1984), 'On the Connection Between Negative and Positive Liberty', *Politics,* 4, 2.

Mommsen, T. E. (1951), 'Saint Augustine and the Christian Idea of Progress', *Journal of the History of Ideas.* 12.

Montesquieu, (1952), *The Spirit of the Laws,* trans. Nugent, T. and Prichard, J. V., London.

Montrose, J. L. (1961), 'Edmund Burke and the Natural Law', *Natural Law Forum,* 6.

Morrall, J. B. (1962), *Political Thought in Medieval Times,* Harper Torchbooks.

Morrow, G. R. (1948), 'Plato and the Law of Nature', in Konvitz, M. R. and Murphy, A. E. (eds), *Essays in Political Theory,* New York.

Morley, J. (1880), *Burke,* Macmillan.

Neumann, F. (1957), 'Types of Natural Law', in Neumann, F., *The Democratic and the Authoritarian State.*

Murphy, J. G. (1970), *Kant: The Philosophy of Right,* Macmillan.

Nisbet, R. (1978), 'Conservatism', in Bottomore, T. and Nisbet, R. (eds), *A History of Sociological Analysis.*

Nisbet, R. (1970), *Social Change and History: Aspects of the Western Theory of Development,* Oxford University Press.

Nisbet, R. (1973), *The Sociological Tradition,* Heinemann.

Nisbet, R. (1976), *The Social Philosophers,* Paladin Books.

Nisbet, R. (1978), 'Conservatism', in Bottomore, T. B. and Nisbet, R. (eds), *A History of Sociological Analysis,* Heinemann.

Nisbet, R. (1980), *History of the Idea of Progress,* Heinemann.

Nisbet, R. (1986), *Conservatism,* Open University Press.

Norton, P. and Aughey, A. (1981), *Conservatives and Conservatism,* Temple Smith, London.

Oakley, F. (1963), 'Medieval Theories of Natural Law: William of Ockham and the Significance of the Voluntarist Tradition', *Natural Law Forum,* 6.

Oakley, F. (1964), *The Political Thought of Pierre d'Ailly: The Voluntarist Tradition,* London.

O'Brien, G. D. (1975), *Hegel on Reason and History: A Contemporary Interpretation,* Chicago University Press.

O'Connor, D. J. (1967), *John Locke,* Dover, New York.

O'Gorman, F. (1973), *Edmund Burke: His Political Philosophy,* Unwin Books.

O'Gorman, F. (ed) (1986), *British Conservatism: Conservative Thought From Burke to Thatcher,* Longman.

O'Hagan, T. (1987), 'On Hegel's Critique of Kant's Moral and Political Philosophy', in Priest, S. (ed), *Hegel's Critique of Kant.*

Olafson, F. A. (1966), 'Thomas Hobbes and the Modern Theory of Natural Law', *Journal of the History of Philosophy,* 4.

O'Sullivan, N. (1976), *Conservatism,* Dent.

O'Sullivan, N. (1993), 'Conservatism', in Eatwell, R. and Wright, A. (eds), *Contemporary Political Ideologies.*

O'Sullivan, R. (1945), 'Natural Law and Common Law', *Grotius Society Transactions,* 31.

Paine, T. (1976a), *Common Sense,* Penguin Books.

Paine, T. (1976b), *Rights of Man,* Penguin Books.

Parkin, C. W. (1990), 'Burke and the Conservative Tradition', in Thompson, D. (ed), *Political Ideas.*

Parkin, C. (1956), *The Moral Basis of Burke's Political Thought,* Cambridge University Press.

Parkinson, G. H. R. (1983), 'Hegel's Conception of Freedom', in Inwood, M. J. (ed), *Hegel.*

Pascal, B. (1972), *Pensees,* Penguin Books.

Parry, G. (1978), *John Locke,* Allen and Unwin.

Pearson, R. and Williams, G. (1984), *Political Thought and Public Policy in the Nineteenth Century,* Longman.

Pelczynski, Z. A. (1969a), 'Introduction' to Hegel, G. W. F., *Political Writings.*

Pelczynski, Z. A. (1970), 'Hegel Again', in Kaufmann, W. (ed), *Hegel's Political Philosophy.*

Pelczynski, Z. A. (1971), *Hegel's Political Philosophy: Problems and Perspectives,* Cambridge University Press.

Pelczynski, Z. A. (1971a), 'The Hegelian Doctrine of the State', in Pelczynski, Z. A. (ed), *Hegel's Political Philosophy: Problems and Perspectives.*

Pelczynski, Z. A. (1984), *The State and Civil Society: Studies in Hegel's Political Philosophy,* Cambridge University Press, Cambridge.

Pelczynski, Z. A. (1984), 'Political Community and Individual Freedom in Hegel's Philosophy of the State', in Pelcyzynski, Z. A. (ed), *State and Civil Society.*

Perelman, Ch. (1963), *The Idea of Justice and the Problem of Argument,* London.

Peters, R. S. (1990), 'Hegel and the Nation State', in Thompson, D. (ed), *Political Ideas.*

Pickles, D. (1971), *Democracy,* Unwin Books.

Pitcher, G. (ed) (1970), *Wittgenstein: The Philosophical Investigations,* Macmillan.

Plamenatz, J. (1958), *The English Utilitarians,* Oxford.

Plamenatz, J. (1963), *Man and Society: A Critical Examination of Some Important Social and Political Theories From Machiavelli to Marx,* 2, Longman.

Plamenatz, J. (1971), 'History as the Realisation of Freedom', in Pelczynski, Z. A. (ed), *Hegel's Political Philosophy.*

Plamenatz, J. (1976), 'The Belief in Progress', in Plamenatz, J., *Man and Society,* 2.

Plant, R. (1973), *Hegel,* Unwin.

Plato (1968), *The Republic,* trans. Lee, H. D. P., Penguin Books.

Plato, (1975), *Gorgias,* trans. Hamilton, W. , Penguin Books.

Plato, (1972), *Laws,* trans. Saunders, T. J., Penguin Books.

Pocock, J. G. A. (1957), *The Ancient Constitution and the Feudal Law,* Cambridge.

Pocock, J. G. A. (1973), 'Burke and the Ancient Constitution: A Problem in the History of Ideas', in Pocock, J. G. A., *Politics, Language and Time: Essays on Political Thought and History,* Athenaeum, New York.

Poggi, G. (1978), *The Development of the Modern State: A Sociological Introduction*, Hutchinson.

Poggi, G. (1983), *Calvinism and the Capitalist Spirit: Max Weber's 'Protestant Ethic'*, Macmillan.

Pollard, S. (1968), *The Idea of Progress: History and Society*, Penguin Books.

Pollock, F. (1961), *Jurisprudence and Legal Essays*, Goodhart, A. L. (ed), Macmillan.

Pollock, F. (1961), 'The History of the Law of Nature', in Pollock, F., *Jurisprudence and Legal Essays*.

Popper, K. (1969), *The Open Society and Its Enemies*, 2, Routledge, London.

Price, E. H. (1947), 'Montesquieu's Historical Conception of the Fundamental Law', *Romanic Review*, 38, pp. 234-42.

Priest, S. (ed) (1987), *Hegel's Critique of Kant*, Clarendon Press, Oxford.

Pufemdorf, S. (1931), *Elementorum Jurisprudentiae Universalis*, trans. Oldfather, W., Clarendon Press, Oxford.

Pufendorf, S. (1934), *De Jure Naturae et Gentium*, trans. Oldfather, W., Clarendon Press, Oxford.

Quinton, A. (ed) (1973), *Political Philosophy*, Oxford University Press.

Rawls, J. (1978), *A Theory of Justice*, Oxford University Press.

Reiss, H. (ed) (1955), *The Political Thought of the German Romantics*, Blackwell, Oxford

Reyburn, H. A. (1967), *The Ethical Theory of Hegel: A Study of the Philosophy of Right*, Oxford University Press.

Riedel, M. (1971), 'Nature and Freedom in Hegel's Philosophy of Right', in Pelczynski, Z. A. (ed), *Hegel's Political Philosophy*.

Riedel, M. (1984), *Between Tradition and Revolution: The Hegelian Transformation of Political Philosophy*, Cambridge University Press.

Rieff, P. (1912), *Friedrich Gentz: An Opponent Of The French Revolution and Napoleon*, University of Illinois Press, Urbana Champagne, Illinois.

Ritchie, D. G. (1903), *Natural Rights*, Macmillan.

Ritter, J. (1982), *Hegel and the French Revolution: Essays on the Philosophy of Right*, Cambridge, Mass.

Robins, M. H. (1974), 'Hare's Golden Rule Argument: A Reply to Silverstein', *Mind*, 83.

Rommen, H. (1979), *The Natural Law*, New York.

Ross, A. (1958), *On Law and Justice*, London.

Ross, D. (1964), *Aristotle*, Methuen.

Rousseau, J. J. (1975), *The Social Contract and Discourses*, Cole, G. D. H. (ed), Everyman.

Ryan, A. (1965), 'Locke and the Dictatorship of the Bourgeoisie', *Political Studies*, pp. 219-30.

Ryan, A. (ed) (1979), *The Idea of Freedom*, Clarendon, Oxford.

Sabine, J. H. and Barney-Smith, S. (1929), 'Introduction' to Cicero, *On the Commonwealth.*

Sabine, J. H. (1973), *A History of Political Theory,* Holt Saunders.

Salmond, J. W. (1895), 'The Law of Nature', *Law Quarterly Review,* 42.

Saloman, A. (1955), *The Tyranny of Progress,* New York.

Sampson, R. V. (1956), *Progress in the Age of Reason.*, Cambridge, Mass.

Schacht, R. L. (1972), 'Hegel on Freedom', in MacIntyre, A. (ed), *Hegel: A Collection of Critical Essays.*

Scott, K. J. (1956), 'Liberty, License and Not Being Free', *Political Studies,* 4.

Schapiro, J. S. (1978), *Condorcet and the Rise of Liberalism,* Octagon Books, New York.

Schuettinger, R. L. (1970), *The Conservative Tradition in European Thought,* Putnam, New York.

Schochet, G. (1973), 'Quentin Skinner's Method', *Political Theory,* 2, 3, pp. 261-76.

Scruton, R. (1988), 'G. W. F. Hegel', in Scruton, R. (ed), *Conservative Thinkers: Essays From the Salisbury Review,* Claridge.

Scruton, R. (1989), *The Meaning of Conservatism,* second edition, Macmillan.

Selznick, P. (1961), 'Sociology and Natural Law', *Natural Law Forum,* 6.

Siedentop, L. (1979), 'Two Liberal Traditions', in Ryan, A. (ed), *The Idea of Freedom.*

Seidman, S. (1983), *Liberalism and the Origins of European Social Theory,* Blackwell, Oxford.

Sheehan, J. (1978), *German Liberalism in the Nineteenth Century,* Methuen, London.

Shepherd, M. A, (1932), 'William of Ockham and the Higher Law', *American Political Science Review,* 26.

Shepherd, M. A. (1933), 'William of Ockham and the Higher Law', *American Political Science Review,* 27.

Sieyes, l'abbe de (1963), *What Is The Third Estate?* trans. Blondel, M., Pall Mall Press.

Sigmund, P. E. (1971), *Natural Law in Political Thought,* Winthrop, Cambridge, Mass.

Sigmund, P. (1988), *Aquinas on Politics and Ethics,* Norton.

Silverstein, H. S. (1972), 'A Note on Hare on Imagining Oneself in the Place of Others', *Mind,* 81.

Singer, M. (1963), 'The Golden Rule', *Philosophy,* 38.

Skinner, Q. (1969), 'Meaning and Understanding in the History of Ideas', *History and Theory,* 8, pp. 3-53.

Skinner, Q. (1974), 'Some Problems in the Analysis of Political Thought and Action', *Political Theory,* 2, 3, pp. 277-303.

Skinner, Q. (1984), 'The Idea of Negative Liberty: Philosophical and Historical Perspectives', in Rorty, R., Schneewind, B. and Skinner, Q. (eds), *Philosophy in History.*

Skinner, Q. (1988), 'A Reply to My Critics', in Tully, J. (ed), *Meaning and Context: Quentin Skinner and his Critics.*

Smith, A. (1905), *An Inquiry into the Nature and Causes of the Wealth of Nations,* Routledge.

Smith, R. A. (1968), 'Introduction' to Burke, E., *Edmund Burke on Revolution.*

Smith, S. B. (1989), 'What is "Right" in Hegel's *Philosophy of Right*?', *American Political Science Review,* 83, 1.

Smith, S. B. (1991), *Hegel's Critique of Liberalism: Rights in Context,* Chicago University Press.

Soles, D. E. (1988), 'Intellectualism and Natural Law in Locke's Second Treatise', *History of Political Thought,* 8.

Sommerville, J. P. (1986), *Politics and Ideology in England: 1603-1640,* Longman.

Sorel, A. (1969), *Europe and the French Revolution: The Political Traditions of the Old Regime,* Cobban, A. B. C. and Hunt, J. W. trans. (eds), Collins, London.

Sorel, G. (1969), *The Illusions of Progress,* Stanley, J. (ed), University of California Press.

Stanley, J. (1973), 'Introduction' to Sorel, G., *The Illusions of Progress.*

Staniland, H. (1972), *Universals,* Macmillan.

Stanlis, P. (1958), *Edmund Burke and the Natural Law,* Ann Arbor, Michigan.

Stephen, L. (1962), *History of English Thought in the Eighteenth Century,* in two volumes, Harbinger Press.

Stern, F. (1974), *The Politics of Cultural Despair: A Study in the Rise of Germanic Ideology,* University of California Press.

Sternhell, Z. (1979), 'Fascist Ideology', in Lacqueur, W. (ed), *Fascism: A Reader's Guide,* Penguin Books.

Stone, L. (1971), *The Crisis of the Aristocracy: 1558-1641,* Oxford.

Strauss, L. (1965), *Natural Right and History,* Chicago University Press.

Strauss, L. (1968), 'Natural Law', *International Encyclopedia of the Social Sciences,* 11. New York.

Suarez, F. (1944), *De Legibus ac Deo Legislatore,* trans. Scott, J. B., Clarendon Press, Oxford.

Suter, J. F. (1971), 'Burke, Hegel and the French Revolution', in Pelczynski, Z. A. (ed), *Hegel's Political Philosophy*

Tawney, R. H. (1938), *Religion and the Rise of Capitalism,* Penguin Books.

Taylor, A. J. P. (1976), *The Course of German History: A Survey of the Development of German History Since 1815,* Methuen.

Taylor, C. (1979), *Hegel and Modern Society,* Cambridge University Press.

Taylor, C. (1989), *Hegel,* Cambridge University Press.

Teggert, F. J. (ed) (1949), *The Idea of Progress: A Collection of Readings*, Berkeley, California.

Thielemann, L. (1963), 'Diderot's Encyclopaedic Article on Justice: Its Sources and Significance', *Diderot Studies*, 4, pp. 261-83.

Thompson, D. (ed) (1990), *Political Ideas*, Penguin Books.

Tillyard, E. M. W. (1978), *The Elizabethan World Picture*, Penguin Books.

Tonnies, F. (1955), *Community and Association*, Routledge.

Tully, J. (ed) (1988), *Meaning and Context: Quentin Skinner and His Critics*, Polity Press.

Ullmann, W. (1961), *Principles of Government and Politics in the Middle Ages*, London.

Ullmann, W. (1965), *A History of Political Thought: The Middle Ages*, Penguin Books..

Van Doren, C. (1967), *The Idea of Progress*, New York.

Viereck, P. (1950), *Conservatism Revisited: The Revolt Against Revolt: 1815-1949*, John Lehmann, London.

Viereck, P. (ed) (1956), *Conservatism: From John Adams to Churchill*, Anvil Books, New York.

Vincent, A. (1992), *Modern Political Ideologies*, Blackwell.

Vincent, A. (1994), 'British Conservatism and the Problem of Ideology', *Political Studies*, 42.

Viner, J. (1963), 'Possessive Individualism as Original Sin', *Canadian Journal of Economics and Political Science*, 29.

Von Leyden, W. (1958), 'Introduction' to Locke, J., *Essays on the Law of Nature*.

Waddicor, M. H. (1970), *Montesquieu and the Philosophy of Natural Law*, Martinus Nijhoff, The Hague.

Waismann, F. (1978), 'On Verifiability', in Parkinson, G. H. R. (ed), *The Theory of Meaning*, Oxford University Press.

Walsh, W. H. (1967), *An Introduction to Philosophy of History*, Hutchinson.

Walsh, W. H. (1969), *Hegelian Ethics.*, Macmillan, London

Walzel, O. (1932), *German Romanticism*, New York.

Warnock, G. J. (1967), *Contemporary Moral Philosophy*, Macmillan.

Warrender, H. (1957), *The Political Philosophy of Hobbes*, Oxford University Press.

Warrender, H. (1962a), 'Obligations and Rights in Hobbes', *Philosophy*, 37.

Warrender, H. (1962b), 'Hobbes's Conception of Morality', *Rivista critica di Storia della Filosofia*, 17.

Warrender, H. (1979), 'Political Theory and Historiography: A Reply to Mr. Skinner on Hobbes', *The Historical Journal*, 4.

Watson, G. (1971), 'The Natural Law and Stoicism', in Long, A. A. (ed), *Problems in Stoicism*, London.

Weber, M. (1964), *The Theory of Social and Economic Organization*, Talcott Parsons (ed), Collier Macmillan, New York.

Weber, M. (1967), *The Protestant Ethic and the Spirit of Capitalism*, trans. Talcott Parsons, Unwin Books.

Weber, M. (1969), *The Methodology of the Social Sciences*, Shils, A. and Finch, H. A. (eds), The Free Press, New York.

Webster, C. (ed) (1974), *The Intellectual Revolution of the Seventeenth Century*, Routledge.

Weiss, J. (1977), *Conservatism in Europe: 1770-1945: Traditionalism, Reaction and Counter- Revolution*, Thames and Hudson.

Wellman, C. (1962), 'Wittgenstein's Concept of a Criterion', *Philosophical Review*, 71, pp. 433-47.

Weston, J. (1961), 'Edmund Burke's View of History', *Review of Politics*, 23.

Westphal, K. (1993), 'The Basic Context and Structure of Hegel's Philosophy of Right', in Beiser, F. C. (ed), *The Cambridge Companion to Hegel*.

White, R.J. (1964), *The Conservative Tradition*, London.

White, D. M. (1970), 'Negative Liberty', *Ethics*, 81.

Wild, J. (1953), *Plato's Modern Enemies and the Theory of Natural Law*, Chicago University Press, Chicago.

Wilford, R. (1986), 'Fascism', in Eccleshall, R. et. al., *Political Ideologies and Introduction*.

Wilkins, B. T. (1967), *The Problem of Burke's Political Philosophy*, Oxford University Press.

Wilkins, B. T. (1974), *Hegel's Philosophy of History*, Chicago University Press.

Willey, B. (1962), *The Eighteenth Century Background*, Penguin Books.

Willetts, D. (1992), *Modern Conservatism*, Penguin, Harmondsworth.

Williams, T. C. (1968), *The Concept of the Categorical Imperative: A Study of the Place of the Categorical Imperative in Kant's Ethical Theory*, Oxford University Press.

Wilson, I. M. (1973), *The Influence of Hobbes and Locke in the Shaping of the Concept of Sovereignty in Eighteenth Century France*, Studies on Voltaire and the Eighteenth Century, Banbury.

Wittgenstein, L. (1969), *The Blue and Brown Books: Preliminary Studies for the 'Philosophical Investigations'*, Blackwell.

Wittgenstein, L. (1972), *Philosophical Investigations*, Blackwell.

Wolff, C. (1758), *Principes du droit de la nature et des gens*, Formey, M. (ed), Amsterdam.

Wolff, C. (1772), *Institutions du droit de la nature et des gens*, Leyden.

Wolff, R. P. (1969), *The Poverty of Liberalism*, Beacon Press, New York.

Wolff, R. P. (1973), *The Autonomy of Reason: A Commentary on Kant's Groundwork of the Metaphysics of Morals*, Harper Torchbooks.

Wolff, R. P. (1977), *Understanding Rawls: A Reconstruction and Critique of 'A Theory of Justice'*, Princeton University Press.

Wollheim, R. (1967), 'Natural Law', *The Encyclopaedia of Philosophy*, 5, Collier Macmillan, New York.

Wood, A. (1990), *Hegel's Ethical Thought,* Cambridge University Press, Cambridge.

Wood, A. (1991), 'Editor's Introduction', to Hegel, G. W. F., *Elements of the Philosophy of Right.*

Wootton, D. (ed) (1986), *Divine Right and Democracy: An Anthology of Political Writing in Stuart England,* Penguin Books.

Woozley, A. D. (1969), 'Universals', in Woozley, A. D., *Theory of Knowledge,* Hutchinson.

Worsthorne, P. (1978), 'Too Much Freedom', in Cowling, M. (ed), *Conservative Essays.*

Yolton, J. W. (1958), 'Locke on the Law of Nature', *Philosophical Review,* 67.

Zagorin, P. (1954), *A History of Political Thought in the English Revolution,* London.

Index

absolutism, 91-2, 95-7, 107, 109-11, 117, 119, 134, 140, 150, 152
abstract right, 42-3, 45, 59, 61, 63, 74, 138, 171
abstraction, 47, 70-1
abstractions, 53, 70, 128
actuality, 69, 72, 74, 123, 141, 144
adultery, 31, 34-5, 37
Age of Reason, 179, 187
American Revolution, 95
ancien regime, 155
ancient constitution, 109-11, 112-14, 121, 145, 185
appearance, 70-4
Aquinas, 38-40, 60-1, 68, 76-8, 84, 88, 163, 169, 174, 177, 187
Aristotle, 5, 7, 16-7, 39-40, 53, 56-7, 59-63, 65, 67-72, 74, 77-8, 87, 122-3, 125-6, 150, 165, 169-71, 178, 186
Aristotelian, 39, 53-4, 56-7, 59-63, 65-7, 69-71, 77, 84, 103, 120, 122-5, 126, 159, 164-5, 167
Aristotelian natural law theory, 53, 56, 66
articulated, 95, 129-30, 132, 136
articulation, 130, 132
Augustine, 27, 76-9, 82-5, 88, 153, 169-70, 174, 176-79, 181, 183

authority, 77, 86-7, 110, 115, 118, 131, 134-5, 140, 146, 151, 176

Bentham, 28, 36-7, 171, 181, 183
Blackstone, W., 171
Brandes, 134, 145
bureaucratic, 127
Burke, 2, 5, 53, 63, 100-15, 119-22, 133-4, 136-40, 142, 145-6, 148, 152-3, 156, 160-1, 172-4, 176, 178, 181, 183-5, 188, 190
Burlamaqui, 50, 172

capitalism, 75, 80
Carneades, 27-8
Categorical Imperative, 50-1, 61, 180, 190
Christian, 49, 76, 79, 84-5, 88, 98, 103, 112, 153-4, 174, 181, 183
Christianity, 76, 82, 98
Cicero, 15-23, 27-30, 35, 38, 173, 176, 187
civil law, 16, 21, 37, 90-1, 92
civil society, 28, 44-5, 48, 102, 127, 130-2, 135-6, 149, 158, 171, 185
classical, 18, 86-9, 173, 175
codification, 151, 152
Coleridge, 103, 113-4, 145, 156, 161, 173-4, 183
collectivism, 178

common good, 78-9, 82, 85, 94, 96

community, 35, 37, 52, 54, 59-60, 62-7, 79-82, 85, 88, 99, 103-7, , 110-11, 115, 118, 121, 123, 127-32, 136, 139-43, 147-8, 150, 158, 185, 189

concrete, 60, 62, 67, 70, 74, 130, 139, 168

concrete universal, 168

Condorcet, 18, 97, 98, 99, 153, 156, 170, 174, 176, 178, 187

consent, 96, 175

conservatism, 1, 2, 7, 9-11, 75, 100-12, 114-5, 117-20, 129, 133-38, 140, 145, 155-7, 159-66, 173, 175, 177, 180-1, 183-4, 187, 189-90

conservative, 2, 5, 7, 9-11, 65-6, 100-11, 112, 114-5, 117-9, 133-4, 137-9, 145-6, 152, 154-63, 167-9, 171, 173-4, 179, 181, 184, 187, 190-1

conservative tradition, 138, 163, 167

constitution, 62-3, 93, 102, 107, 109-12, 121, 122, 128, 132, 134, 137, 139-42, 145, 147-9, 152, 174, 179, 185

constitutional, 7, 122, 171, 172, 177

constitutional monarchy, 119, 134, 149, 171-2

constitutional reform, 122, 142-6, 152, 160

contract, 170-1, 176-7, 182, 186

conventional, 4, 10-11, 24-9, 42, 67, 70, 72-4, 91, 92, 95, 103, 117, 159, 162

conventional justice, 67, 70

corporate, 104, 106-7, 129, 132-3, 136, 147, 159

corporatism, 78, 104, 132-3

cosmopolitanism, 53, 161

custom, 17, 81-2, 85, 92, 115, 118-20, 151-2

customary law, 14, 62, 80-1, 91, 107, 109, 139-40, 150-1, 152

customs, 52-3, 60, 63, 81, 107, 111, 120-1, 128, 139-40, 142-4, 152, 156

d'Ailly, 32, 34, 184

d'Alembert, 12, 16, 175

Decalogue, 61

democracy, 96-7, 111-2, 119, 127, 147-9, 169, 176, 180, 185, 191

democratic, 112, 149, 184

dialectic, 101, 159

dialectical, 160-1

Diderot, 12, 16, 172, 175, 189

Divine Right of Kings, 176

Droits de l'homme et du citoyen, 62

duty, 44, 79, 82, 85, 91-2, 99, 103, 105, 115, 126, 132, 135, 139

economic, 79-80, 89-90, 104-6, 134-6

economics, 79, 90, 105-6, 134-6, 189

egotism, 79, 99, 123

egotistical, 77

elite, 147

empirical, 47, 49, 52, 56, 70, 72, 74, 93

empirical conception of natural law, 47, 49, 56

empiricism, 68-9, 72, 73, 177

empiricist, 68-9, 108

Encyclopedia, 172, 188

Encyclopedie, 12, 15-6, 25, 33, 172, 175

English Revolution, 86, 93, 191

Enlightenment, 12, 28, 86-8, 97-99, 101, 103, 113-4, 141, 152-4, 170-4, 176, 178, 180-1

equality, 62, 77, 81, 87, 89, 92, 96, 99, 102-3, 107, 109, 115, 119, 126, 147, 149, 155, 161, 164

equality before the law, 81, 92, 107, 115, 119, 127
equity, 49, 60-1, 63
essence, 26, 33-4, 38, 45, 47, 70-1, 73-4, 144, 158, 160
essentialism, 164
essentialist, 167
Estates, 61, 78, 128-9, 135, 147-8, 179
ethical, 3-4, 32, 38, 44, 48, 52-4, 57, 59-60, 62-5, 118, 121, 123, 125, 127-31, 136, 139-41, 143, 147, 174, 181, 186, 190-1
ethical life, 44, 52-3, 57, 59, 121, 123, 125, 127-31, 136, 141, 147
ethics, 25, 50-1, 67-8, 72, 169, 173-4, 180-2, 187, 189-90

family resemblance, 166-7
fascism, 6, 96, 132-3, 188, 190
fascist, 6-7, 133, 188
feudal, 78, 80, 100
feudalism, 75
formal conceptions of natural law, 35-9, 47, 52, 56, 59
formalism, 50-1, 138
freedom, 44, 56, 60, 93-5, 97, 99, 109-10, 118, 124-6, 131-40, 144, 147-9, 158, 176, 178-9, 181-2, 185-7, 191
French Revolution, 86, 92, 97, 100-1, 119, 128, 143, 145-7, 149, 155, 160, 173, 177, 180-1, 186, 188
French revolutionaries, 73, 93, 95, 97, 110

gemeinschaft, 79, 89
general interest, 82, 94, 96
Gentz, 137, 186
German conservatism, 119, 133-4, 137-8, 145, 160
Germany, 8, 97, 117, 119, 129, 133, 137-8, 160-1, 169, 177

gesellschaft, 79, 88
Glockner, 58, 179
God, 31-4, 76, 77-8, 81-5, 102, 112, 154, 169-70, 176, 178-9
Golden Rule, 49-51, 171, 176-7, 180, 186-7
Government, 33, 37, 96, 110-11, 112, 127, 133-5, 140, 147, 170, 172, 175, 179-80, 182-3, 189
Great Chain of Being, 76, 79, 82, 85, 102, 182
Greece, 122, 174
Greek, 27, 52, 125, 158, 178
Grotius, 16, 28, 31, 33, 178, 184

Hanoverian School, 133-4, 145
Hardenberg, 145-6
Hare, 51, 174-5, 178, 186-7
Hegelian metaphysics, 66-7
hierarchy, 60-2, 78-9, 85, 99, 104, 115, 161
history, 3-4, 15-18, 23, 27, 30, 37, 41, 47, 66, 83-4, 87, 91, 94, 97-9, 112-4, 117, 119, 121-2, 141-5, 149, 152-60, 163-4, 166-8
Hobbes, 4, 29, 35, 37-40, 47-9, 62-4, 87-8, 91, 92, 150, 152, 163, 171, 180, 183-4, 189-90
Hobbesian, 38
Hoffmeister, 179
Hooker, 18, 180
human nature, 77, 87-8, 90, 93, 98, 102, 112, 123-6
humanity, 22, 156, 176

ideal types, 75
idealism, 68-9, 71
Ideological, 5-11, 117, 173, 178
ideologies, 1, 2, 5, 8, 10-11, 75, 101, 109, 111, 115, 171, 175, 179-80, 184, 189, 190
ideology, 2, 6-11, 85-6, 88, 90, 93, 95, 99-102, 105-7, 109-11, 114-

15, 133-5, 137, 139, 153, 157, 159-61, 162-3, 175-8, 180, 188-9

imperfect, 18, 76-7, 103, 156

individual, 4, 20, 24, 26-9, 35-7, 42-4, 46, 48, 50, 53, 55-6, 60, 62, 64-5, 70, 72-6, 79, 86-7, 89-97, 99, 101-7, 109-11, 126, 128-9, 131-3, 137, 139-42, 149-50, 158, 164, 167, 185

individualism, 48, 53, 59, 62, 89-90, 104-5, 115, 131, 161, 182-3, 189

individualist, 92

inequality, 48, 77-8, 81, 82, 85, 89, 99, 102, 104, 111, 115, 126, 135, 147

intellectualism, 76, 188

justice, 12-18, 20-2, 24-28, 31, 33-4, 39, 41, 52, 59-60, 62, 64-5, 67-8, 70, 74, 78, 91, 109, 118, 122, 151, 164, 172, 174-5, 177, 181, 183, 185-6, 189-90

Kant, 18, 47, 51, 56, 59-61, 63, 87, 123-4, 126, 138-9, 150, 170, 174, 177, 180-1, 184, 186, 190

Lactantius, 27, 181

laissez faire, 94, 105

law, 1-7, 11-68, 70, 72-4, 77, 80-2, 90-4, 96, 98, 102, 106-7, 109-10, 112, 115, 118-27, 134, 139-40, 143-4, 149-52, 163-71, 173-191

law of nature, 16, 18, 21, 37, 39, 49, 54, 60

laws, 13-15, 18, 21-2, 24, 27-8, 30, 48-9, 53, 60, 62, 67, 72-4, 94, 96, 98, 111, 121, 125, 133, 139-40, 142-3, 149-52, 171-2, 180, 183, 185

legal equality, 107

legal justice, 13-4, 24, 67-8

legal positivism, 3-6, 12-14, 24-40, 58, 64-5, 74

legislation, 13, 50, 62, 81, 149-52

legislature, 112, 147-8

legitimacy, 92, 149

liberal, 2, 6-7, 9-11, 44, 47, 59, 65-6, 73, 86-90, 92-102, 104-8, 114-15, 117-19, 128, 133, 135, 137-9, 141, 143, 145-6, 152-3, 156-8, 172, 175, 179, 183, 187

liberalism, 169, 171, 174-5, 177-8, 180-1, 183, 187-8, 190

liberty, 55, 60, 81, 93-5, 99, 108-10, 112, 115, 132, 136-40, 145, 155-6, 159, 161, 171, 173-5, 177, 179, 182-3, 187-8, 190

Locke, 28, 33-4, 43, 47, 49, 91-6, 122, 139, 169-71, 175, 177, 181-2, 184-6, 188-91

Luther, 32, 182

Marx, 3, 4, 48, 174, 180, 183, 185

materialism, 68

medieval, 15, 19, 27, 31-4, 37-8, 60-2, 65, 75-7, 79-86, 88, 90, 92, 97-101, 103, 105-6, 115, 132, 158-9, 164, 170, 173, 175, 182, 184

medieval conception of kingship, 82

medieval political thought, 80, 100, 173

metaphysics, 66-7, 69-72

Middle Ages, 76, 84, 97, 129, 179, 183, 189

Mill, 94-5, 161, 178, 183

monarch, 82, 147-8, 174

monarchy, 82, 91, 119, 134, 149, 171-2, 175

Montesquieu, 48, 53, 60, 62, 119, 121-2, 128, 139-41 143, 152, 174, 179, 181, 183, 186, 189

moral, 12-14, 16-17, 20-1, 24-8, 30, 33, 35-7, 39, 43, 50-1, 56, 59-61, 62-4, 68, 74, 76, 79, 87, 89, 92-5, 98, 103-5, 107-8, 111, 120, 123,

131, 136, 138-40, 144, 156, 171, 175, 178, 181, 184-5, 189

moral justice, 13-14, 24, 26

morality, 14, 22, 24, 25, 49-2, 57, 59-61, 64, 77-8, 90-1, 101, 102, 108, 126, 130, 144, 146, 151, 177, 189

morals, 51, 53, 76, 86, 99, 101, 173, 178, 181, 183, 190

Mosaic law, 62

murder, 31, 34-7, 50, 61, 95, 139

nation, 52, 121, 128, 141-2, 150, 152, 155, 159, 185

nationalism, 161, 170

natural equality, 89, 92, 102, 147

natural inequality, 78, 81, 82, 102, 104, 111, 126, 147

natural justice, 14, 26-7, 67-8, 70

natural law, 1-7, 11-74, 77, 80-2, 91, 106-7, 120, 121-5, 139-40, 143-4, 150, 163-70, 173-6, 178-9, 181-90

natural law theorist, 1, 3-5, 12-19, 22, 24-5, 27-8, 30, 32-4, 37-40, 42-5, 48-9, 57-9, 65

natural law theory, 1-6, 11-62, 64-6, 106, 140, 163-6

natural law tradition, 19, 21, 24, 29-31, 34, 36, 38, 40-1, 43, 54, 56-7, 63, 106, 120, 163, 165, 167-8

natural right, 58, 124, 176, 181, 186, 188

natural rights, 2, 6, 43-4, 46, 53-5, 59, 62-4, 66, 92, 95, 97, 106-7, 111, 176, 181, 186

nature, 2, 11, 15, 16, 18, 21, 25, 28, 33, 37, 39, 43-4, 47-9, 53-5, 59-60, 64-6, 68, 76-80, 82-5, 86-91, 93, 98, 100-3, 109, 112, 123-7, 129, 140, 144-8, 151-2, 158, 160, 161, 174, 178, 182-4, 186-91

Nazi, 175

negative freedom, 138

negative liberty, 188, 190

Nichomachean Ethics, 67

Nisbet, 7, 78, 83, 97, 100-5, 110-14, 117, 128-9, 131, 145, 154, 157, 171, 184

nominalism, 33, 68

nominalist, 68

Ockham, 31, 32, 34, 173, 183-4, 187

On the Scientific Ways of Treating Natural Law, 46, 58, 169

open texture, 166

optimism, 99

order, 3, 12-13, 21, 26-7, 30, 34-5, 38, 47, 50, 56, 61, 71, 76-7, 79, 81, 83, 84-5, 87, 91-2, 98-100, 102-4, 109-10, 113-15, 118, 128-33, 135-40, 143, 145-6, 149, 156, 158, 161, 165-6, 175, 177-9

organic, 61-2, 79, 89, 104, 128-9, 158

organic theory of society, 79, 89, 104

organism, 89, 128, 130, 141

Paine, 96, 97, 184

paradigm, 19, 21, 40

particular, 1, 3-4, 6-7, 9-10, 12-16, 18-20, 23-4, 26-7, 29-32, 35-37, 39, 41, 43-4, 47, 49, 51-3, 56, 58-60, 62-3, 65-8, 70-2, 74-5, 78, 79-85, 89, 92-7, 99, 101, 106-8, 110-11, 118-19, 121-3, 125-9, 132-3, 135, 139-44, 146-8, 150, 155, 158-9, 161, 164-5, 167-8

particulars, 69

Pascal, 27, 185

paternalism, 82, 96, 111, 115, 147

paternalistic, 82

Pelczynski, 4, 6, 11, 43, 62, 66, 73-4, 93, 120, 122, 127-30, 133-5,

138-9, 143-4, 148, 151-2, 171, 177, 179-80, 185-6, 188
perfectibility, 86, 98, 103, 113
perfection, 98
person, 13, 25, 36, 38, 63, 94, 127
personality, 65, 123, 125
persons, 43, 87, 95, 127
pessimism, 84
pessimistic, 77, 84-5, 99, 113
philosophy of history, 83-4, 97-9, 112-14, 143-4, 152-9
Philosophy of Right, 4-6, 10, 42-6, 48, 51, 55, 56-60, 62, 64, 66, 73-4, 121-4, 126-7, 129, 131, 135-7, 141-3, 147, 150, 158, 178, 180-1, 184, 186, 188, 190-1
Plato, 3, 27, 68-71, 77-8, 81, 87, 170, 173-4, 176, 182, 184-5, 190
Platonic, 102
pluralism, 104, 132
pluralist, 129, 133
polis, 52-3, 125, 158
political equality, 89, 147, 149
political justice, 67-8, 70, 74
political science, 52, 66, 123, 125, 176, 180, 187-9
Popper, 3, 6, 7, 130, 186
positive freedom, 138, 182
positive law, 13-14, 16-29, 31-2, 34-40, 43, 45, 54, 59-68, 70, 72-74, 91, 106-7, 121, 143-4, 150-1, 170
positive liberty, 173-4, 183
positivism, 3-6, 12-14, 24-28, 32-33, 40, 58, 64-5, 72-4, 120, 178
positivist, 3-6, 12-14, 22, 24-28, 32, 34, 39-40, 42, 44-5, 54, 59, 65, 73-4, 120
prejudice, 69
privacy, 94, 110, 115
private, 48, 77, 79, 82, 89, 94-5, 97, 105, 110-11, 115, 118, 130-34, 136, 152
progress, 84, 86, 97-9, 113-15, 120,

143, 153-4, 156-7, 161, 164, 170-1, 173-6, 178, 180-9
progressive, 113, 155, 157, 159-61
property, 38, 43-4, 50, 55, 62-3, 79, 89, 91, 92-5, 97, 104, 107, 112, 115
property rights, 43, 50, 55, 63, 91-2, 107, 115
Providence, 112, 154
Prussia, 159, 181
Prussian, 117, 140, 145-6
Prussian reforms, 145-6
public, 94-5, 110-11, 115, 118, 130-6, 147-9, 151-2, 159, 176, 185
public and private spheres, 131
Pufendorf, 16, 33-4, 50, 186

rational, 30, 43, 49-50, 52, 54, 61-2, 73-4, 88, 93, 109, 128, 141-5, 151, 154, 156
rationalism, 31, 68-9, 71, 73, 76, 93, 120, 173-4
rationalist, 33, 65, 68-9, 101, 120, 154
Rawls, 51, 170, 180, 182, 186, 190
reaction, 89, 146, 190
reactionary, 7, 117, 145, 159-60
real interests, 82
realism, 68-9, 71
reality, 70-4, 80, 120
reason, 1-2, 8-10, 15-18, 20, 22-4, 26-8, 31-3, 35, 39-41, 54, 58, 63-4, 69, 71-3, 76-8, 81, 83, 85-7, 90, 93-6, 99, 101-2, 111, 112, 118, 120-1, 122-4, 138, 143-4, 147-8, 150, 152, 154-6, 160-1, 164, 166, 173, 175-9, 184, 187, 190
reciprocal, 2, 82
reciprocity, 49, 60-1, 63
reconciliation, 154, 156-7
Rehberg, 134, 145, 146
relativism, 140, 181

relativist, 25
religion, 76, 102-3, 115, 146, 154, 182, 188
religious, 76, 78, 99, 101-3, 112, 153-4
Renaissance, 183
right, 4-7, 10, 14-17, 22, 26, 28-9, 31, 38, 42-6, 48-51, 55-64, 66, 68, 73-4, 82, 87, 89, 91, 95-6, 108, 118, 121-9, 131, 135-8, 141-4, 146-7, 149-52, 158, 165, 169, 171, 176-8, 180-1, 184, 186, 188, 190-1
rights, 2, 43-4, 46-7, 49, 50, 52-5, 59, 62-4, 66, 79, 82, 87, 89, 91-3, 95, 97, 104, 106-7, 109-11, 115, 121, 132, 136, 140, 142, 184, 188-9
Rights of Man, 93, 95, 106, 184
Roman law, 43, 80
romantic, 105, 133-4
romanticism, 133, 170-1, 178, 189
Rousseau, 21, 47-8, 97, 124, 138, 170-1, 173, 175, 186
rule of law, 93, 107, 109, 115, 118-19, 134, 139-40, 169, 176

Savigny, 151
sceptical, 77, 101
scepticism, 76, 86
scholastic natural law theory, 35, 60-2, 66
science, 52, 58, 66, 86, 99, 108, 123, 125, 171, 175-7, 180-1, 187, 188-9
science of politics, 181
scientific, 46, 58, 86, 98, 151, 169, 179
Scruton, 7, 102-4, 109, 111, 113, 117, 130-1, 133, 162, 187
secondary precepts of natural law, 61
secular, 86, 88, 98, 102, 112

self, 16, 48, 69, 71, 78-9, 82, 88-90, 96, 99, 103-5, 111, 123, 136, 138, 141, 147, 153
self interest, 79, 82, 88, 90, 104-5, 147
selfish, 77, 82, 103, 109
selfishness, 88
Sieyes, 92, 96-7, 187
sin, 15, 77, 84, 86, 88, 98, 103, 189
sinful, 79, 82
Sittlichkeit, 121
Skinner, 94, 163-5, 167-8, 170-1, 187-9
Smith, Adam, 87, 90, 94, 135, 184, 187
social contract, 47, 52-3, 59, 89, 93, 108, 121, 170, 176-7, 182, 186
Spirit of the Laws, 48, 53, 121, 142, 183
spiritual equality, 103
state, 4, 6, 14, 16, 18, 22, 37, 40, 43-8, 53-5, 58-60, 64-6, 75, 81, 86, 90-1, 93-6, 106-7, 109-10, 112, 115, 121-3, 125, 127-36, 140-2, 147-50, 158, 170-4, 176, 180-6
state intervention, 135-6
state of nature, 37, 43, 47-8, 53, 54, 59, 91, 93
station, 78, 82, 104, 129-30, 132
status quo, 117-19, 146, 149, 154-7, 159-60
statute law, 14, 62, 81, 91, 107, 127, 140, 150
Steuart, 134, 136
stoic, 15-25, 28-30, 32, 34-41, 43, 45, 54-5, 59, 62-4, 77, 143
stoicism, 77, 189
Suarez, 16, 188
subjective freedom, 56, 125, 149, 158

theft, 20, 31, 34-5, 37-8, 50, 61, 63, 95

theological, 181

theology, 76, 79, 82, 84, 93, 177

Tonnies, 79, 88, 189

tory, 107

totalitarian, 6-7, 9, 95, 97, 130, 132, 139, 176

totalitarianism, 6-7, 11, 96, 110-11, 117, 134

tradition, 6, 19, 21, 24, 29-31, 34, 36, 38, 40-1, 43, 54, 56-7, 63, 81-2, 85, 92, 100, 106-7, 113, 115, 117-22, 124, 126, 138, 146, 151, 162-3, 165, 167-8

traditional, 1-2, 19, 22-3, 28, 38, 53, 73, 75, 84, 86, 103, 115, 118, 124, 128, 131, 133, 136, 140, 157, 159, 162, 164-5

traditionalism, 73, 115, 120, 145, 161

traditionalist, 73, 117-21, 151, 160

traditions, 19, 29, 52-3, 60, 63, 75-6, 81, 107, 111, 115, 120-1, 126, 128-9, 140, 142-4, 156, 159-60, 168, 177, 182, 187-8

understanding, 71-3, 87, 182, 187, 190

universal, 15, 17, 21, 24, 26, 50, 52, 65, 68, 70, 72, 74, 84, 112, 120, 144, 147-8, 150, 167-8

universal interest, 147-8

universalisability, 51

universals, 66, 68-71

Voltaire, 83, 176, 181, 183, 190

voluntarism, 31-2, 173

voluntarist, 31-4, 41, 184

Weber, 75, 80, 172, 177, 183, 186, 189-90

Whig, 6, 94, 107, 109, 122

Whigs, 172

will, 2, 7-11, 15-17, 19, 20, 26-7, 30, 32-5, 41, 42, 50, 59-60, 63, 65, 68, 74, 77, 84, 95, 97, 99, 103, 109-10, 112, 121, 123-5, 132, 138-9, 147, 149-52, 158, 165

Wittgenstein, 165-7, 169-70, 181, 185, 190

Wolff, C., 190

world history, 143-4, 149, 155-6

Wurtemberg, 128-9, 135